ADVANCE

Raising a Sc

"A great resource for parents who are looking for reliable, common-sense information about online threats posed to their kids so they can evaluate risks without letting fear drive parental decision-making."
—John F. Clark, president and CEO of
the National Center for Missing and Exploited Children

"Julianna Miner describes the state of the science around kids and technology accurately. It is messy. The digital landscape is changing faster than the speed of scientific research. Miner's approach of using the best evidence, common sense, and a lot of calm is perfect."
—W. Keith Campbell, PhD, coauthor of *The Narcissism Epidemic*
and professor of psychology at the University of Georgia

"What I love about *Raising a Screen-Smart Kid* is Julianna Miner's clear eyed understanding that our hope, as parents, should not be to scare, threaten, or push our kids into a certain relationship with tech and screens, but to teach them to use these tools in a way that furthers their goals and increases their happiness. This is a book that will calm your fears and help you help your kids learn to live in this world."
—KJ Dell'Antonia, author of *How to Be a Happier Parent*

"The internet can be a dangerous place for children—one in which seemingly innocuous websites can in fact lead to treacherous and heart-breaking consequences. *Raising a Screen-Smart Kid* is filled with expert advice, as well as accounts from kids and their mentors, and provides a critical understanding of how parents and coaches can best support the youth in their lives in navigating our increasingly complicated digital world."   —Steve Salem, president and CEO, Cal Ripken, Sr. Foundation

"The manual every parent needs right now! Parenting tweens and teens in the digital age can be terrifying, so it's nice to know Julianna Miner is on our side."

—Jen Mann, bestselling author of *People I Want to Punch in the Throat*

"Believe me, kids know more about the internet than a parent ever will. If you want to make your kids safer and be on the same page with them, read this book."

—John Walsh,
cofounder of the National Center for Missing and Exploited Children
and host of *America's Most Wanted*

"*Raising a Screen-Smart Kid* will help parents connect with and find empathy for young people growing up in the digital age. . . . Julianna Miner's insights on the nuances of friendship, dating, and self-esteem help parents identify the most crucial points for understanding and supporting kids without succumbing to anxiety and despair."

—Devorah Heitner, PhD, author of *Screenwise*

"Full of humor and empathy, Julianna Miner shows anxious parents that navigating the digital age with their kids isn't as daunting as they might think."

—Jill Smokler,
New York Times–bestselling author of *Confessions of a Scary Mommy*

Raising a Screen-Smart Kid

Embrace the Good
and Avoid the Bad
in the
Digital Age

Julianna Miner

A TARCHERPERIGEE BOOK

tarcherperigee

An imprint of Penguin Random House LLC
penguinrandomhouse.com

TarcherPerigee with tp colophon is a registered trademark of
Penguin Random House LLC.

Most TarcherPerigee books are available at special quantity discounts for bulk purchase for sales promotions, premiums, fund-raising, and educational needs. Special books or book excerpts also can be created to fit specific needs. For details, write: SpecialMarkets@penguinrandomhouse.com.

Library of Congress Cataloging-in-Publication Data

Names: Miner, Julianna, author.
Title: Raising a screen-smart kid : embrace the good and avoid the bad in the digital age / Julianna Miner.
Description: New York : TarcherPerigee, 2019. | Includes bibliographical references and index.
Identifiers: LCCN 2019005256 | ISBN 9780143132073 (paperback) | ISBN 9780525503811 (ebook)
Subjects: LCSH: Parenting—Psychological aspects. | Internet and children—Safety measures. | Smartphones—Social aspects. | BISAC: FAMILY & RELATIONSHIPS / Life Stages / School Age. | COMPUTERS / Web / Social Networking. | PSYCHOLOGY / Developmental / Adolescent.
Classification: LCC BF723.P25 M564 2019 | DDC 155.6/46—dc23
LC record available at https://lccn.loc.gov/2019005256
p.   cm.

Printed in the United States of America
10 9 8 7 6 5 4 3 2 1

Book design by Kristin del Rosario

This book is dedicated to my husband,
Matt,
without whom I would be lost.

And to our children.
This book exists for one reason: because I love you.

CONTENTS

1 | The Last Analog Dinosaurs Raising
the First True Digital Generation   1

2 | Social Media and the Imaginary Audience   26

3 | Well-Being, Self-Esteem, and Social Comparison
in the Selfie Generation   49

4 | Teen Friendships in the Age of the Internet   72

5 | Digital Dating and Teen Relationships Online   97

6 | The Social Culture of Video Games   123

7 | Digital Addiction and Risky Behavior Online   147

8 | Growing Up Online with Anxiety, Depression,
ADHD, or Autism   170

9 | Safety, Predators, Harassment,
and Bullying Online   193

10 | Hoping for the Best and Avoiding the Worst   218

APPENDIX 1:
CELL PHONE CONTRACT OR AGREEMENT   245
APPENDIX 2:
SEXUALITY AND SEX ED ONLINE RESOURCES FOR TEENS   251
ACKNOWLEDGMENTS   253
NOTES   255
INDEX   265

Raising a Screen-Smart Kid

1 | The Last Analog Dinosaurs Raising the First True Digital Generation

MY STORY (AGE THIRTEEN, 1986)

I vividly remember being thirteen years old and the new girl in eighth grade. It was 1986 in Princeton, New Jersey. I was an only child and I had just transferred back to public school after several years as a student in a fancy private school. My mother had remarried the year before, and the additional income my new stepfather brought to the table put us somewhere between losing my need-based scholarship and being able to afford the full tuition. I spent most of my time alone. I didn't really belong with my more affluent peers but seemed to have little in common with the kids in my neighborhood, many of whom I didn't even know.

That meant a fresh start for eighth grade in a public school near my dad and stepmother's house. While that prospect was scary, I was ready for it. Switching schools was going to open doors and allow me to reinvent myself. I was awkward and wore the wrong clothes. I was (or had been) the scholarship kid, and everyone knew it. And if that wasn't enough, I was a blurter.

I may have been an ADHD kid, but back then teachers just told my mother that I was a daydreamer who couldn't seem to work to her potential. I was easily distracted and would allow myself to wander into dreamy wormholes during class or at the lunch table, achieving Walter Mitty–like trances, where I would become almost completely unaware of my surroundings. And then I would blurt out something that reflected the reality in my head.

I think we can all agree that is not a prescription for being cool in middle school.

I did not let my social awkwardness stop me, however. I had a picture of who I wanted to be at my new school, someone cool. Someone—dare I say it?—popular. Most of this mental picture was formed by the seventies-era sitcoms I watched over and over again after school. I could be cool, right? It was possible.

Well, no, the actual cool kids let me know that wasn't going to happen after about a week. The good news was, I met a friend who helped break that fall. She was the other new girl, and she was nice enough to overlook the fact that I was kind of a mess. Things were awkward for me at home, with a new stepfather at one house and my stepmother newly pregnant at the other. Things were equally awkward at school because I had no idea how to get out of my own head and just be a person. Eventually I made a couple of nice friends, and it seemed as if I might survive the year and make it to high school.

Now back in 1986 in my hometown, by the time you made it to middle school (fifth grade), you were basically feral by current parenting standards. We rode around town on our bikes, buying slices of pizza with change we scrounged up. We loitered in the town square. We went to the shopping center and walked around for hours. No adults really knew where we were or what we were doing. Many, many things happened that parents seemed to know nothing about.

By midyear, there was a contagious outbreak of falling in love. First one person would select another and let it be known that they liked them. The other person would often reciprocate the liking publicly, which was the start of being known as boyfriend and girlfriend. Within a couple of days, there was generally French-kissing, followed by proclamations of love. This all seemed to be the norm, at least from my perspective.

When it was my turn to participate in this ritual, I was a little shocked by how horrible it felt. I don't recall even liking the boy very much; I just remember being grateful that someone wanted to date me. After a couple of weeks, though, I couldn't take it. I wrote my friend a note about how I didn't like him anymore and wished I could be done with it. I went on to describe how I would very much prefer to be dating a cooler, older, more popular boy, but sadly, he had a much-cooler-than-me girlfriend. I may have said something unkind about her, even though I recall her being a very nice person.

My friend read the note in class, folded it up, and accidentally dropped it on the floor. It was picked up by another girl (whom I became friends with several years later), who saw her chance to do something dramatic and took it. She made lots of photocopies of that note, but first asked me to pay her ten dollars to delay passing them out around school. I suspected everyone already knew the contents of what I had written (they did) and also knew I couldn't get my hands on ten dollars even if I sold my right kidney on the black market.

The next few weeks were a whirlwind of humiliation, near constant stomach-aches, and cruel notes from classmates (some signed, some anonymous) telling me what an asshole I was and how much they wished I had never come to their school. I remember some of the notes told me I was a bitch and a slut. Some of them told me to go back to my old school—and then made fun of my family for being too poor to send me there. My clothes were mocked. My face and body were mocked. One person drew a very creative cartoon that depicted my death.

My friend who dropped the note felt bad and did an admirable job of both standing by me and distancing herself from the nonsense. The boy I wanted to break up with was deeply embarrassed by the whole thing and never spoke to me again, which I deserved. I lived in fear that his older sister would kick my ass, but she displayed remarkable restraint and just glared at me whenever I crossed her path.

I went to school each day with my head down, feeling sick with anticipation at what people would say to me or what they were thinking as they stared at me. I went home each night knowing everyone hated me but never, ever disclosing a single thing to my parents. I watched too much TV, took a lot of naps, ate a lot of string cheese, and read ridiculous books that were easy to get lost in. I would try to recharge at home, hoping no one would ride their bike past my house or prank-call me. The calls would be a tip-off to my parents that something was going on.

I was miserable, and I was not myself. I knew I had brought this on myself as a result of my poor judgment and unkind words, and that knowledge increased my shame and self-loathing. I escaped into my head, imagining alternate endings to the story where I was cool and had friends, where things worked out okay.

After a couple of very long weeks, it passed. By the time the eighth grade dance came around in June, there was plenty of other drama to supplant my pathetic note-writing. I got a dress and a date and felt immensely relieved to be out of the spotlight. While everyone remembered what had happened, no one seemed to care anymore. It had never felt so good to have nobody care about me.

I had survived eighth grade.

And Now that Awkward Eighth Grader Is a Mother

The great irony of being a parent is that you get to relive the best and worst moments of growing up through your kids. I recall so clearly how hard it was to be in middle school and high school, and now my kids are the same age. One of my personal challenges as a parent is to consciously stop projecting all my own bad decisions, experiences, and baggage onto my kids. They are not me. They will make all their own choices and all their own mistakes.

And of course they live in a totally different world. Kids don't write notes anymore—they text each other and send Snaps. As parents, we keep an eye on their Instagram feeds, lurking to see who is liking what and who is liking whom. We're careful about what they watch, eat, and listen to. We track our kids' locations now, and always know where they are. We organize their social time and drive them to practice. Things are so different from when I grew up in the eighties that I started to question my own parenting choices and looked to books and the Internet for guidance. What I found was that no matter what choice you make about raising your kids, someone is going to have an opinion about it.

Mommy Blogging and Parenting Norms

My reaction to the unspoken rules and hard truths of modern parenting was to write about them. I'm one of the horrible mommy bloggers you've heard about. You would think I'd learned in eighth grade not to write down things that I might later regret, but apparently not. I've been writing about raising kids since 2009.

I've tried to be mindful of my children's privacy along the way. I wrote about my kids through their baby, toddler, and preschool years, feeling comfortable that the universal joys and frustrations of early childhood were things that could be shared without hurting them later. As they got older, I began to struggle with the impact of writing about them at all. This mirrored their growing independence from me. Though it pained me to see them becoming big kids, and now tweens and teens, I knew it was the natural order of things—that I had to slowly start letting go of the small people who had once literally been a part of me. I began to focus more on my experiences dealing with the current culture of parenting. Sometimes the feedback was good, and sometimes I couldn't bear to read the comments.

At about the same time, I began working as an adjunct professor at a university nearby, teaching undergrads an overview course on public health. That job was a game changer for me. It made me think in new ways, allowing concepts and ideas to click. I had to make complex information relatable, challenge my students when they didn't want to be pushed, and support them in the classroom when things were going wrong.

In short, it was a lot like parenting. Being a mother forces me to be a much better person than I'm naturally inclined to be. Being a teacher forces me to be a better thinker and to put myself in the shoes of the young adults I'm working with. It has given me an appreciation for the intelligence, mental toughness, and work ethic required to make it in today's brave new world.

Expert, Cautionary Tale, or Both?

Taking all this into account, I should have been uniquely qualified to help my kids negotiate social media and the online world. But the truth is, I was terrified about how to effectively parent them in the age of the Internet. I live so much of my professional and social life through my laptop and my phone. When my kids were old enough to want to be Internet people themselves, I struggled with how to make that work without being a hypocrite.

The fear that was driving me wasn't even really based in reality. Half of it had to do with the all-too-vivid memories of my own adolescence—

filled with poor choices, ridiculous shenanigans, and (thank you, baby Jesus) no cell phones. The other half had to do with the worst-case scenarios that I feared could befall my kids online, fueled by tragic news stories that seem to be everywhere, intent on giving me stomachaches.

So what happens when a mommy blogger's kids are finally old enough to get iPhones and Instagram accounts and do their own thing online? This is the situation in which I found myself.

I took a deep breath and decided to start from the most logical place—the beginning. My experiences as both a professional Internet person and an adjunct professor of public health gave me the tools I needed to start understanding how social media influences our behavioral decision-making. I wanted to figure out what the risk factors were that led to the scary outcomes that permeate our consciousness as parents. More important, I wanted to learn about the protective factors that help position young people to become responsible digital citizens. I also wanted to get a better sense of how teenagers work so I could wrap my head around how and why they make the choices they do.

RISK FACTORS AND PROTECTIVE FACTORS

Risk factors are those things that predispose us toward harm or a bad health outcome (for example, smoking is a risk factor for lung cancer). Protective factors can both decrease the potential harmful effect of a risk factor[1] and contribute to a positive outcome (for example, being physically active can both reduce the risk of developing heart disease and help maintain a healthy weight). These interact in many ways, on an individual or family basis, or among peer groups and within communities.

We're All Figuring This Out As We Go Along

Parents right now are in the unenviable position of raising the first generation of true digital natives *and* being the standard-bearers for all the families who come after us. So no pressure or anything. We can't look back to our youth for comparison or ask our parents and grandparents how they dealt with gaming addiction or online bullying. There is no precedent to draw from.

We're the last generation of truly pre-Internet parents. We can't fully understand or relate to what it means to grow up with the kind of connectedness our kids take for granted. Our kids can't really conceive of what it was like for us in the days before wireless technology made constant contact the norm. When the next generation of parents begins handing out iPhones to their teenagers, they will have had the benefit of growing up online themselves.

I've come to realize that the people I'm raising are growing up and into a newly made digital society, one that I'm obligated to teach them how to live in. The world I knew as a kid is gone. One of the things that public health has taught me is that you have to solve problems in the world as it is, not as you'd like it to be. That means accepting that things are messy and complicated, filled with unknown factors that seem to be working in ways you can't always understand. This is the world we've got, no matter how we may feel about it. The choices we make (and that our kids will make) in this environment are influenced by technology, culture, social determinants, biology, politics, that pesky free will that we humans always want to exert, and a million other things we can't predict. We may not love that this tech has permeated our lives, and the lives of our kids, to the degree that it has. But it's not going anywhere, so we need to figure out how to make it work the best we can.

Everything Is Different Now, and Why

Many of us look back at how different childhood was for us (and for our parents) and compare it to how things are now. In the 1970s and 1980s, teenagers stayed connected with their friends by spending too much time on the phone (mine was a Princess phone with an extra-long cord) and by exercising the freedom to run around with their friends. This was usually done without the adults in their lives knowing exactly where they were or what they were doing (at least in the same way parents do now). This is a critical point in understanding how parenting culture intersects with kids and tech. I would argue that today, neither in childhood nor in adolescence, do most kids in America have the freedom or the privacy that their parents had at the same age. There are a million reasons why this is the case, and technology, of course, tops the list. It's simply easier to be in touch than it was twenty years ago. If my daughter is late, I don't have to pace the floor and worry that she's dead in a ditch somewhere (though honestly I still do, because I have issues). I can text her. I can check the location of her phone. I can see if she's posted an update on one of her social media feeds. We're connected, and it makes me feel better as a mom.

My mother also worried if I came home after the streetlights came on in the evening, as hers did before her. The salient point, however, is that my mother allowed me to play out of her sight and earshot at a fairly young age, *and this was considered totally normal.* Many of us would now consider sending a ten-year-old off to the park with some friends as not just neglectful but downright dangerous (and in some places, unlawful). There is certainly no shortage of examples of people calling the police when they see children in these situations. Allowing your ten-year-old to have an iPhone and an Instagram account, however, is relatively acceptable.

This is a weird time to raise small humans. Were we all better off as free-range/feral kids, learning how to problem-solve and be independent? Or are we all just incredibly lucky to have survived to adulthood? Are our kids that much better off? Or is the real danger lurking in their cell phones? I honestly don't have an answer. We had more freedom and were a lot more resourceful. We also made a lot of mistakes. While teens today have less free time and independence, they drink less, do fewer drugs, and have fewer pregnancies. Sadly, they also struggle in much higher numbers with things like anxiety and depression.

PERCENTAGE OF TENTH GRADERS WHO BINGE DRINK AND USE DRUGS

	1996	2015
Binge Drinking	23%	11%
Drug Use*	18.4%	9.8%

*illicit drugs except marijuana

Source: Johnston, L. D., Miech, R. A., O'Malley, P. M., Bachman, J. G., Schulenberg, J. E., & Patrick, M. E. (2018). Monitoring the Future national survey results on drug use, 1975–2017: Overview, key findings on adolescent drug use.

RATE PER 1,000 OF TEEN PREGNANCY, ABORTION, AND BIRTH

	1996	2011
Teen Pregnancy	96.1	43.4
Teen Abortion	29.0	10.6
Teen Birth	53.5	26.4

Source: Kost, K., Maddow-Zimet, I., & Arpaia, A. (2017). Pregnancies, births and abortions among adolescents and young women in the United States, 2013: national and state trends by age, race and ethnicity.

A Brief Historical Overview to Figure Out
How We Got Here

While most conversations about the drastic changes in parenting and childhood are currently focused on technology, the changes actually started with major social and economic shifts that predate cell phones and the wireless revolution, most of which can be traced back to the early 1980s. Let's start with what it was like to raise a family forty years ago.

As a backdrop, consider the serious economic recession of the early 1980s, which drove changes in labor and market forces that drastically altered how families lived. Industrial and manufacturing jobs were disappearing, and American factories were closing. As U.S. economic growth began to decline for the first time since World War II, other countries (notably Japan) began to take a greater share in world trade.

Women's labor force participation increased more than 58 percent from 1950 to 1990.[2] More mothers were working full time, and the impact of this on our understanding of parenting norms really can't be underestimated. The fact that families had two working parents meant that someone other than mom or dad was watching the kids all day. It meant extended family, babysitters, and childcare workers were joining the ranks of primary caregivers.

Also consider that between 1960 and 1980, the rate of divorce more than doubled nationally, from 9.2 divorces per 1,000 married women to 22.6 divorces per 1,000 married women.[3] This resulted in an unprecedented growth of single-parent households. The reasons for the drastic change in divorce rates are varied, ranging from the economic changes described above, to the widespread passage of no-fault divorce laws state by state starting in 1969, to cultural changes like the social revolution of the late 1960s and early 1970s.

These shifts led not only to parental guilt about not being there or not providing a more traditional upbringing but also to drastic changes in the culture of childhood itself simply due to the logistics of raising kids in a new economic and social reality. The rosy-hued childhood where every kid could play outside with their friends until the streetlights came on was quickly diminishing. In its place came structured play.

Julie Lythcott-Haims describes this shift in her outstanding *New York Times* bestselling book *How to Raise an Adult*. She writes that in 1984 "the playdate emerged as a practical scheduling tool at a time when mothers were entering the workforce in record numbers. . . . Once parents started scheduling play, they began observing play, which led to involving themselves in play."[4]

The perception of the nation's once golden educational system also began to change. Several important books and reports were published around this time (including *A Nation at Risk* in 1983) that described how America's educational outcomes and its students were falling behind in comparison to other countries', particularly in the areas of math and science. This created a sense of urgency that parents needed to be doing more to help kids be successful.

The self-esteem movement was also gaining popularity in the United States at the same time. This movement preached the benefits of children feeling good about themselves—self-esteem appeared to be correlated with lots of positive outcomes like good health, academic achievement, and happiness. As this message spread, parents began working to protect and foster their children's self-esteem and, as a result, became more involved in their schoolwork and their sports teams, as well as their friendships and social lives.

Another important factor was the drastic shift in our collective awareness of the risk of danger, particularly child abduction, due to several tragic high-profile cases, including the 1979 disappearance of Etan Patz and the death of Adam Walsh in 1981. A TV movie about the Walsh case was broadcast in 1983 and received high ratings and four Emmy Awards; it was rebroadcast annually for several years. The creation of the National Center for Missing and Exploited Children (NC-MEC) followed in 1984.

Consider all these things converging on the consciousness of parents and society as a whole at about the same time. It set the stage for researchers to coin the term *helicopter parent* in 1990. So that's where we found ourselves in terms of parenting culture by the start of that decade. We were working more than ever, were more likely to be divorced or single parents, and had less time to spend with our kids. Kids, meanwhile, had less free time to play and more scheduled activities, almost always with adult supervision. We were worried about our children's safety in ways we never were before. We were concerned about their ability to compete in terms of education on a global stage. Could they even make a living wage with just a high school diploma if all the manufacturing jobs were drying up? And what if our fears trickled down to them and impacted their self-esteem? Parents worked harder to build them up so that wouldn't happen.

In addition to these changes, or perhaps as a result of them, our understanding of what it meant to be a teenager also began to shift. Adolescence began to elongate. Dr. Laurence Steinberg, the author of *Age of Opportunity* and a professor of psychology at Temple University, stated in an interview with *Psychology Today* that "it's often said that adolescence begins in biology and ends in culture—it starts with puberty and ends when people establish their own households and become financially independent. If you look at the statistics on both of these markers, you see how adolescence has grown over time. The age of puberty keeps dropping, but it has been taking longer and longer for young people to become adults."[5]

Now Add the Internet to the Equation

In the early 1990s came the Internet, which exploded between 1995 and 2000, changing the way we live and access information. In the ten years that followed, wireless innovation put the entirety of the World Wide Web into our back pockets. The rapid adoption of technology swept across the United States, completely changing how we live, work, and communicate. Trying to put that in historical perspective is difficult. Sociologists and scholars struggle to understand the impact.

All this has made being a parent (and being a kid) infinitely more complicated. So here we are, analog dinosaurs raising digital natives, in a culture where many of the rules that defined our own upbringing no longer apply.

ADOPTING NEW TECHNOLOGY

In his book *Me, MySpace, and I: Parenting the Net Generation*, author and psychology professor emeritus at California State University Dr. Larry Rosen explains that the current generation of young people have seen more change and rapid adoption of technology than any other in history. He uses a consumer research measure called the penetration rate to show how many years it takes for a new technology to be adopted by an audience of 50 million people. Here are some examples:

Radio—38 years

Telephone—20 years

Television—13 years

Cable TV—7 years

Cell phones—12 years

Internet—4 years

iPods—4 years

Blogs—3 years

MySpace—125 million users in 2.5 years

Facebook—2 years

YouTube—1 year

Angry Birds—35 days

Pokémon Go—19 days[6]

He also notes that historically, adoption of new technology was largely driven by adults (wage earners), while more recent technological advances have been driven by young people.

The first iPhone was released in 2007, with sales around 1.4 million in the first year. In 2016, about 201 million units were sold.[7] In 2008, the first Android smartphone was released in the United States. In 2016, it was estimated that more than 107 million Americans owned an Android smartphone.[8] U.S. market saturation for smartphones was estimated to have taken place in late 2011 or early 2012.[9] That means that as a nation, we went from zero to the majority of the population using this technology in fewer than five years.

No wonder it's hard to have any true perspective on this—we're still in the middle of it. We have some general understanding of what the far-reaching implications are, but there is no long-term data yet.

What Happened to Me When My Kid Got an iPhone

When my oldest daughter was twelve and just starting middle school, she got her first cell phone. It quickly became clear to our family that her school's administration and most of her teachers assumed that every seventh grader already had one. Our family was really busy, and at twelve, my daughter was becoming more independent and used the phone as a tool to coordinate logistics.

She didn't really care about logistics, though. She was excited about texting her friends and finally getting to jump into social media. Imagine, if you will, how delighted she was when I told her she had to wait until she was thirteen to get Instagram. I was paranoid about what might happen, as a first pass at research about teens and social media (i.e., a Google search) yielded frightening accounts of my own worst nightmares. I invested a lot of time trying to figure out the "right" way to go about giving her a phone. Should it be a flip phone? Should it have limited data?

I wanted to figure out a way to approach these parenting decisions rationally, without coming from the hyperprotective mama-bear place my brain goes when I read about middle schoolers sending nudes, getting bullied, and then killing themselves, or being murdered by people they meet online.

But the hardest part of having my daughter join the Internet was something I hadn't anticipated. It certainly wasn't predators or seventh-grade mean kids on Instagram. It was the fact that almost all the (then) twelve-year-olds we knew got their first phones at about the same time. Things shifted in a dramatic way overnight. The parents of newly licensed teenage drivers have the same slightly stunned reaction. I may have thought that my understanding of my kid and how social media worked could see us through that first year or so, but I was unprepared for the cultural sea change that her entire peer group was about to go through.

So What Does This Mean for All the Kids Getting Phones?

Our experience is pretty common. Most kids in the United States get access to their first smartphone between the ages of ten and twelve.[10] This number appears to be trending down as time goes on. Whether we like it or not, and regardless of whether they're ready or not, this is the new norm for kids in the United States. What's become obvious to me is that there's no corresponding norm for how parents are supposed to handle it. The transition would be so much easier if we were all on the same page, but the truth is, we're really not.

That is especially troubling when you consider that the majority of young teens are getting their first cell phones at the exact same time that their brains and bodies are hitting developmental overdrive. A double whammy of puberty and brain development hits kids hard and effects massive changes in short periods of time. These physical and emotional shifts prime kids to make impulsive and risky choices, more so than at perhaps any other point in their lives. And it's at this precise unfortunate moment that they all get cell phones.

It's critical to remember that every child, no matter how smart and responsible, will make mistakes. It's also important to remember that regardless of the technology involved, whether it's passing notes in 1988 or sending Snapchats in 2018, kids are going to do dumb things they regret, and sadly, that will never change. Many of the behaviors we see online have always been part of growing up. Technology has changed, but kids haven't. Making mistakes and learning how to deal with the consequences of our choices are key developmental lessons all kids need to learn.

Perhaps we should adjust our expectations of how our kids are going to act when we hand them a phone or a tablet, and through it, access to a world of people, ideas, and images they may not be ready for. We can't expect perfection and we should expect missteps. We all make them.

Making mistakes online, however, can result in long-lasting and wide-ranging consequences that very few of us can anticipate. Adults and kids are frequently reminded that online mistakes never really go away. We know that the audience for our missteps on social media is potentially global. The desire to protect our kids from their own blunders is strong and, frankly, reasonable.

The majority of U.S. teenagers are already out there, leaving their digital footprints behind. According to a 2018 Pew Research Center study, 95 percent of U.S. teens ages thirteen to seventeen report having a cell phone, and 45 percent of teens report being online "almost constantly."[11]

THE POPULARITY OF ONLINE PLATFORMS AMONG U.S. TEENS

Percentage of US teens who . . .

	Say they use ___	Say they use ___ most often
YouTube	85%	32%
Instagram	72%	15%
Snapchat	69%	35%
Facebook	51%	10%
Twitter	32%	3%
Tumblr	9%	<1%
Reddit	7%	1%
None of the above	3%	3%

Note: Figures in first column add to more than 100% because multiple responses were allowed. Question about most used site was asked only of respondents who use multiple sites; results have been recalculated to include those who use only one site. Respondents who did not give an answer are not shown.

Source: Survey conducted March 7–April 10, 2018. "Teens, Social Media & Technology 2018." Pew Research Center.

Parents Are Also on Social Media

While the majority of parents are on social media themselves, fewer than you might think are consistently connected with their kids using the same types of platforms. Parents are talking to their kids about making safe Internet choices but are not necessarily out there providing the support and supervision needed to make those safe choices easier. For every family that does their best to provide guidelines, rules, and thoughtful boundaries, there is another that simply hands their kid a smartphone and walks away.

Plenty of adults, including parents, overuse social media and are on their phones too much.[12] Just as parental smoking is an indicator and predictor for whether their children will smoke, how parents use social media and their digital devices sets the standard for what is normal and acceptable in their homes.

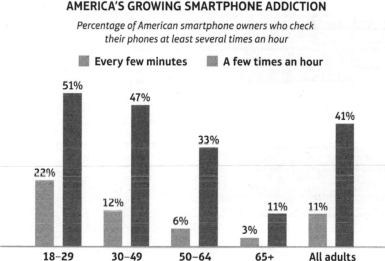

AMERICA'S GROWING SMARTPHONE ADDICTION

Percentage of American smartphone owners who check their phones at least several times an hour

■ **Every few minutes**　　■ **A few times an hour**

	18–29	30–49	50–64	65+	All adults
Every few minutes	22%	12%	6%	3%	11%
A few times an hour	51%	47%	33%	11%	41%

Based on a survey among 15,747 smartphone owners conducted April 17–May 18, 2015.

Source: Gallup

Overuse of devices and Internet addiction are a bigger problem than most want to admit. A 2013 study by Nokia found that we check our phones an average of 150 times per day, and Apple said in 2018 that most iPhone users unlock their phone 80 times per day.[13] Social media and other apps on our phones (I'm looking at you, Candy Crush) are designed to create a cycle that reinforces our continued use, and we're all hard-wired to respond to it. We hear a ping and see an update, cute photo, or message, and our Pavlovian response to that feedback is to keep clicking or scrolling through our feeds, waiting for that next rush of dopamine.

There's evidence in the literature that this cycle could also trigger addiction, interpersonal, and attention issues during critical periods of cognitive development. It may even be impacting how adolescent brains develop. The bottom line is that there are a lot of reasons to be very concerned about the population-level impacts this technology is having, but currently there is simply not definitive evidence in the research to tell us what these impacts are. There is a landmark study currently under way from the National Institutes of Health looking at adolescent and cognitive brain development that in years to come may answer some of these questions.[14]

WHAT HAPPENS IN OUR BRAINS WHEN OUR PHONES GO "DING"

Get a notification.
Pull out your phone.
Click on link.
See picture of cute baby.

Dopamine release. Feel satisfied,
as baby was really cute.
Triggers seeking behavior.
Must. Scroll. Through. Feed.

Suddenly realize you've just
wasted thirty minutes.
Curse quietly to self.
Put phone away.

For most kids there's simply no longer a distinction between their real and digital lives. The generation of young people born after 1995 have tech so entrenched in their modes of learning, working, and communication that it can't be teased out from how they live "off-line." This is perhaps even more true for their social lives, much of which takes place on their phones, laptops, or gaming systems. Researchers describe social media as essentially being a "super peer,"[15] having an unprecedented influence on how teens perceive social and behavioral norms. Instagram and Snapchat have become that super peer, setting the standard for what's cool and normal—from clothes to drinking to dating, and everything in between.

This change in spheres of influence—from parent/family to peers/ friends as the dominant influence—is both a normal part of adolescent development and consistent with our own teenage experiences. However, it's the existence of a super peer that concerns me. As a parent, I know I won't be able to control that conversation about social norms (and arguably I shouldn't), but I at least want to continue to be a part of it.

With that in mind, I began to think about how I could participate in the social lives of my children online in ways that reflected how I would do the same in their real lives. I knew that it was developmentally appropriate for them to want more distance and independence. I knew that I wanted to provide more freedom and opportunities to demonstrate responsibility. I wanted them to know I was there, paying attention and loving them, as they started taking steps out on their own. I knew that in real life, there would be rules, curfews, and consequences. I thought about how to provide similar limits online and to create opportunities to succeed at being responsible and to reward those victories.

In essence, I started by shifting my perspective from "monitoring my kids online" to something that felt more like just "parenting my children." Devorah Heitner, a social media expert and the author of *Screenwise: Helping Kids Thrive (and Survive) in Their Digital World*, calls this approach "mentoring, not monitoring." The latter feels like policing, a job to prevent all the bad things I was afraid of from happening to them. The former is logical extension of what I was already doing in every other aspect of their lives. I started to relax.

My fearful attitude was causing me to focus on preventing bad outcomes instead of on something much more useful. My kids needed me to teach them what to expect and how to behave—life skills necessary to avoid making mistakes. I needed to find a way to teach my kids the mundane task of how to live their daily lives on the Internet as respectful and respectable people—the people I hope they will grow up to be. And then, slowly, to give them the freedom to let them do it on their own.

Fear makes us focus on preventing the bad instead of promoting the good—it's inconsistent with my public health background, where health promotion and disease prevention go hand in hand. We have to do both. Risk factors show us what we need to look out for. Protective factors show us how to draw the map that leads us forward.

You will never successfully solve a public health problem without digging into the data, quantitative and qualitative, to find out what is really going on. Then you have to listen to people's stories and learn what those numbers mean when they are applied to real people's lives. Seeing the data and research through the (sometimes biased) lens of people's real experiences is significant and provides those moments of inspiration—when the pieces start to click into place.

What This Book Is, and What It Isn't

This book sets a course forward that makes sense for families. It takes personal experiences with good and bad outcomes, research data, and expert advice about what works from a diversity of fields, and combines it all into an actionable path forward. Each chapter will start with a personal narrative, someone telling a story that speaks to the theme. In the course of writing this book, I talked to a lot of young people, making an effort to include lots of different kinds of kids, with a diversity of perspectives and backgrounds. I've shared some of their stories here with you. After each story, we'll discuss the issues involved, review the existing data and research, and get advice from teachers, counselors, law enforcement officers, psychologists, researchers, parents, and young adults. Every chapter will end with action steps to get you started with your kids, working with, rather than against, the natural trajectory of their development.

This book isn't going to provide answers to questions like "When should I give my son a cell phone?" or "Is my daughter going to start sexting if I let her get Snapchat?" If your family and the specifics of your situation aren't taken into consideration, how could any generic answer possibly be the right one? Most parents will tell you that one of the most irritating truths about raising children is that they're all different and they're always changing. What works really well for one kid may not work at all for another, even within the same family. What worked perfectly in June may be a disaster in September.

What I can provide is information and a better understanding of how to apply it to what's going on in your family. Let's start by taking a public-health-ish approach and define the scope and nature of the issue by asking some questions. We'll start by identifying things to avoid, but focus on outcomes we want to achieve. What does a kid successfully using the Internet and social media look like to you? Is that the same picture that your child has? Let's find out.

Takeaways . . .

- Think about what responsible digital behavior looks like. Make a list.
  - Why do you think your child should have a phone or a computer? For homework? Convenience? Logistics? Fun?
  - How much should they be using this technology?
  - Think about what kind of social media and Internet person you want your kid to become. What characteristics and behaviors do you most want to encourage?
  - What are you most concerned about? Be specific.

● Review your list.

  • Are these things reasonable? Are they developmentally or age-appropriate expectations?

  • Would you have been willing and able to live up to that list when you were the same age?

  • Are you living up to it now, modeling the behavior you want to see?

● Ask your kids to create a similar checklist.

  • Ask them to describe why they want a phone/device and what they should be allowed to do with it.

  • Challenge them to think about the kind of Internet person they want to be now and in a couple of years.

  • Ask them how they want to be perceived by their friends and classmates based on what they share online.

  • Ask them how they want to be perceived by their teachers, coaches, and parents based on what they share online.

  • Ask them to consider the things they see others doing online that are not cool, reflect badly on them, or have gotten them in trouble. Have them add these things to their list.

  • Have them think about people they know who are doing a good job managing their digital footprint. What are those people doing right? Why do their feeds seem positive or neutral? What kinds of things do they post? How often do they post?

  • Ask them if they have any worries or concerns about being online, and ask them to share what they are.

● Compare the parent list and the kid list and discuss.

● When it's time to give your child a phone, make sure expectations are totally clear to everyone. Collaborate on a family agreement or "contract" outlining specific terms. See Appendix 1 (page 245) for some guidelines.

- Who does the phone belong to and when can it be used?
- Clarify what-ifs: What if you see something you know you shouldn't have? What if you see friends or classmates doing something mean, messed up, or dangerous? What if you made a bad choice and you're not sure what to do next?
- Determine rewards for making good choices and being responsible.
- Determine consequences for bad behavior or inappropriate conduct.
- For every rule, there must be an explanation for why it's there and a consensus that it's logical and based on both parties' best interest.

Social Media and the Imaginary Audience

JACQUELIN'S STORY (AGE NINETEEN)

Eighth grade was the year of ASKfm for me, and probably for a lot of people my age. It was 2012. Heading into that school year, I was so confident. I mean, it was maybe misplaced confidence, but I thought I was pretty and I was nice and everyone liked me. I felt good about myself and my friends. Of course, when I see pictures of myself from that year now, I'm like, "Oh my God, I was the worst," but it's kind of funny, because I thought I was amazing.

So ASKfm is this website where if you have an account, people can ask you questions. Sometimes you can see who they are and sometimes it's anonymous. At first no one had ASKfm, and then, like, overnight, everyone did. The questions were really nice in the beginning. It was great because, I mean, it was just telling me what I already knew, that I was a good person and I had lots of friends. Then after a couple of weeks it started to get mean, and the questions started becoming more and more anonymous.

I didn't have the worst of it. There was this one girl who was bullied so badly. It was just not okay. It went on for months too. The school and her parents got involved—it was bad. Even though things were really mean online, everyone was so nice at school. They were going out of their way to be so friendly and open; meanwhile we all knew the horrible things that were being said online every night. It didn't really make sense, but I was just happy that things weren't worse.

I'm really glad people were trying so hard in person and everything, but it was all a little hard to process. If everyone had been mean in person, at least it would've been consistent. But the same people who were giving hugs and being all like, "Hi!!!" in the hallways could be the same exact people who were telling you that you were fat and ugly and had no friends because everyone hated you the night before on ASKfm. So it kind of made you mistrustful of other people. You just couldn't be sure who was saying what online; you just knew that someone was saying it.

For a while it felt like everyone in the school was reading these things and knew everything about everybody. It was like we were all being watched all the time, and there was nothing that any of us did that wasn't commented on and written about. I remember I walked home from school with a friend (who was a guy), and by the time I got home, people had already posted about it. And I mean, we didn't do anything wrong. We walked home because we both hated the bus and yet . . . It was, like, a big deal.

In the spring of that year, I left school for a couple weeks to do an internship, and I totally checked out of all the drama. When I got back, I was so over the whole thing and I just couldn't believe how much people still seemed to care about it.

I also started to notice things showing up on my ASKfm page that were really mean and also really personal. It was pretty obvious that it wasn't strangers writing these things. Whoever was writing them was someone that I knew pretty well or one of their friends. That whole feeling about not being able to trust people sitting next to you in class or walking past you in the hallways, that people were always watching what you were doing and wearing and saying, it really started to become an issue again.

By the end of the year, I basically had a whole new friend group, which turned out to be really positive. I just couldn't get past the idea that people that I trusted and were close to me would anonymously write those things. I mean, it was either that or they had been talking about me to the people who had done it, because there was no other way they could've known some of the things they wrote about. And, like, trust works both ways. So when it was obvious that I didn't *trust them anymore, they stopped trusting me. At that point, the friendship was pretty much over.*

I wish I could go back and tell myself not to take it so seriously and not to get so upset about it, because it really didn't matter. Most girls in middle school weren't as confident as I was, and I wish I could've kept that confidence longer. It really took a hit that year. I guess that's pretty normal in middle school, but I think it was cool that I felt good about myself even though I was the worst. It's kind of great that I was this happy, confident kid. I'm sorry that I let something as stupid as ASKfm drama make me feel self-conscious and bad about who I was.

I mean, it all worked out fine, and that's the funniest part of all of it. As soon as the school year was over, nobody even cared about ASKfm or any of the things that showed up on it anymore. I wish people really understood that while it feels like a big deal at the time, it's really not. It's just drama and garbage and you need to not let it make you feel bad about yourself. Just keep going, and the next thing you know, it will all be behind you. A year later, you'll be like, "Why did I even care about that? Why did I even think that was a good idea?"

Why Did Any of Us Ever Think Our Eighth Grade Choices Were Good Ideas?

When parents hear about the choices that their middle- and high-school-age kids make (online or in real life), their response can range anywhere from an exasperated facepalm to true heartbreak. Sometimes it's questionable fashion choices (I'm looking at you, crop tops), sometimes it's going on a website like ASKfm (that, while much improved from 2012 when Jacqueline's story took place, can still open kids up to bullying), and sometimes it's much more serious. I still cringe thinking of the stupid things I did and said as a teenager, and it's been thirty years. I'm profoundly grateful that I emerged from my adolescence relatively unscathed and without the digital documentation that defines the lives of teens today.

Kids' behaviors and expectations sometimes seem to be actively working against their own happiness and self-interest. It's often really hard to understand why they make the choices they do. They seem irrational and self-centered, even when you know that's not who they are.

When public health people can't understand the why behind an unhealthy behavior, it means they can't do much to prevent it or the negative outcomes that follow it. We then look to behavioral theories to help us better understand and predict the things people do and understand why they make those choices.

What's Rational Behavior for a Kid on Social Media?

Elizabeth Pisani is a medical epidemiologist who has researched and written about AIDS and sex workers. She knows all about decision-making that is both rational to the person making the choice and irrational to the casual observer. This might not seem relevant to a discussion on how your ninth grader will use Snapchat, but bear with me. Dr. Pisani explains this concept in the context of objectively dangerous health behavior (selling sex and using dirty needles). From my suburban mom perspective, it's irrational to know that HIV can be spread through dirty needles, have clean needles easily available, and yet choose not to use them.

From the perspective of the Indonesian heroin addicts who Dr. Pisani interviewed for her research, the decision to use dirty needles makes a lot of sense. Here's a quote from her TED Talk on the subject, which you should definitely check out: "In Indonesia at this time, if you were carrying a needle and the cops rounded you up, they could put you into jail. And that changes the equation slightly, doesn't it? Because your choice now is . . . I could share a needle and get a disease that's going to possibly kill me ten years from now. Or I could use my own needle now and go to jail tomorrow. And while junkies think that it's a really bad idea to expose themselves to HIV, they think it's a much worse idea to spend the next year in jail where they'll probably . . . expose themselves to HIV anyway. So suddenly it becomes perfectly rational to share needles."

That does change the equation for me. It also underscores the importance of trying to look at decision-making not from my perspective but from the viewpoint of the person making the choice. Understanding what is "perfectly rational" behavior on social media for young teens starts with understanding where most kids are in terms of their emotional and psychological development when they get their first phone or Instagram account. The research tells us that the age at which most kids are getting their first wireless device (about ages ten to twelve in the United States) is the exact point when their brains and bodies may be least able to responsibly handle it.[1]

In the context of making rational behavioral choices, handing an iPhone to a twelve-year-old is simply not the same thing as handing one to an adult. As we know, there is no shortage of examples of adults who have trouble making good decisions when using the Internet. When a middle schooler receives their first phone, that child is not using it in a vacuum. That kid is interacting with their peers, many of whom are also just getting their first phones and many of whom are just as ill-prepared to use them wisely.

Think about it this way: Imagine everyone in your kid's sixth grade class jumping into the same pool at the same time, and they're all still learning how to swim. It's not just your kid in there, clinging to the side of the deep end and trying not to get water up his nose. While he's trying to look cool and not drown, everyone else is doing the same thing— largely without a lifeguard. There's going to be excessive splashing, someone is going to cannonball onto someone else's head (maybe by accident?), and a lot of people are going to stay in too long and get pruny.

Why Middle School Sucks, With or Without iPhones

If our goal is to position our kids to avoid making painful mistakes, it's probably a good idea to start by understanding exactly why that's hard for them to avoid. Many of us look back and remember middle school as perhaps the second deepest pit in hell, and as it turns out, this claim can be validated by decades of psychological research.

Two major physical things happen to kids in middle school (or early high school, depending on the kid) that justify that assertion. The first is that puberty begins, bringing with it overwhelming physical and emotional changes. As if that weren't enough, the advent of puberty usually corresponds with the beginning of a new stage of formative brain development. So in a matter of months, kids' bodies undergo tremendous changes, and then all of a sudden, the way they see the world and perceive other people undergoes a momentous shift.

We've learned a lot about adolescent brain development in the past few years. The development of technology (such as MRIs) that allows us to look at developing brains, combined with advancements in neuroscience research, has really changed the way we think about teenagers. We now know that the parts of the brain (primarily the prefrontal cortex) that govern executive functioning—things like decision-making, self-control, understanding consequences, risk-taking behaviors, and managing impulses—are the last things to develop as people reach adulthood in their early twenties.[2]

Honestly, if human biology was designed by a sentient deity, you have to appreciate their sense of humor. Why else would our immature, still-childlike brains and bodies be designed to hit such critical periods of change at about the same time, making us feel vulnerable, then invincible; overly emotional, then cold; constantly confronted with the changes happening in us and around us, while being virtually powerless to control any of it? Puberty is not for the weak, friends.

Again, consider that when these changes are happening in our adolescent bodies, the same things are happening to all of our peers at the same time. It's a miracle any of us survived it without cracking up. Now that I think of it, my daydreaming and blurting seem like a very reasonable coping strategy.

Say Hello to the Imaginary Audience

The psychology of early adolescence is fascinating in that it describes why and how this process impacts and motivates behavior. In terms of parenting teens and understanding how and why they do the things they do, this is critical information. One psychological construct in particular is really useful in this respect. Although it was created in the 1960s, it almost feels like the perfect, prescient framework to think about the way teenagers respond to social media. It speaks to why young teens feel like they're living in a fishbowl, constantly being scrutinized by their classmates in the hallways and on their social media feeds, forcing them to be "on" all the time. The advent of social media has made this nearly fifty-year-old concept newly relevant. It's called the Imaginary Audience.[3]

It's a productive (but often painful) stage of adolescence, and part of the process of individuation, when kids separate from their parents and form their own independent identities. They do this by engaging in an ongoing loop of behavioral rehearsal, figuring out and practicing who they'll become as adults. Social media is changing the way in which teens interact with the Imaginary Audience and the manner in which the process of behavioral rehearsal takes place. In short, in our collective consciousness, social media has made the Imaginary Audience real.

BEHAVIORAL REHEARSAL LOOP

Observe the cool kids
in the cafeteria or on their
social media feeds.

Adapt to new
behavior/cool hair status.

Discreetly copy what
the cool kids are doing.

Change behavior,
based on feedback:
Post many selfies of awesome
new hair or wear hat for the
remainder of the semester.

Get feedback from people
(good or bad):
"Hey, I really like your new
haircut." Or "Dear God, what have
you done to your head?"

In 1967, a child psychologist and professor named David Elkind wrote a seminal paper called "Egocentrism in Adolescence," introducing the concepts of the Imaginary Audience and its corollary, the Personal Fable. It describes a period of early adolescence that is basically defined by being acutely self-conscious. The Imaginary Audience is the feeling that everyone is watching and judging you, all the time. Though their peers and classmates are real, Imaginary Audience ideation causes teens to overestimate who among that peer group is paying attention to them and how much those peers really care.

Dr. Elkind, the man who created these constructs, clarified this for me by saying that for adolescents, "the issue is not the reality of the audience but rather who it really is, as opposed to who they think it is." The amount of attention that someone perceives is being paid to them, compared to how much attention they're actually receiving—that's the crux of the issue.

It's essentially no different from being in eighth grade and being certain that *everyone* in your class knows about the enormous, humili ating, excruciatingly obvious pimple on your nose. Except that only a few people actually notice, and only a few of them care. The truth is, no one cares about your dermatological misfortunes anywhere near as much as you do, however it might feel at the time.

This phase of development is fascinating because so many things are happening at once. Pubertal changes make young teens hyperaware of their physical bodies and their appearance. Cognitive development allows them to truly understand and appreciate that other people's thoughts exist and are as important as their own. Young teens in the midst of Imaginary Audience ideation are thinking about themselves so much that they believe everyone around them is likely thinking about them too.

Moving On to the Personal Fable, Where No One Understands You and Everything Is Awful

Once teens have experienced the Imaginary Audience for a while and it becomes their new normal, they progress into its corollary, called the

VENN DIAGRAM OF REACTIONS TO AN EIGHTH GRADER'S PIMPLE
(from the Eighth Grader's Perspective)

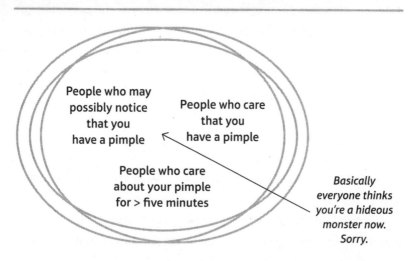

People who may possibly notice that you have a pimple

People who care that you have a pimple

People who care about your pimple for > five minutes

Basically everyone thinks you're a hideous monster now. Sorry.

VENN DIAGRAM OF REACTIONS TO AN EIGHTH GRADER'S PIMPLE
(Reality)

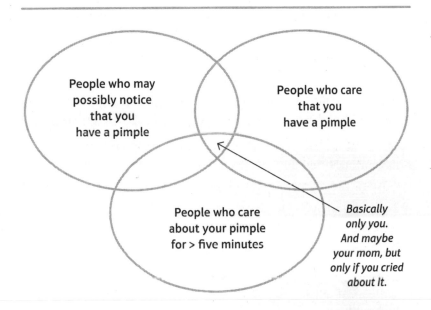

Personal Fable. After believing that you've been continually observed and scrutinized, you start to feel that you must be special, unique, and different. Your awareness of the audience makes you feel unlike anyone else—even friends and family. This emphasis on the self generally decreases with age, as cognitive maturation takes place and a few years of social experiences accumulate, teaching valuable lessons on how to behave. Notably, that we're not the center of the universe.

Teenage Stereotypes and the Imaginary Audience

These phases are familiar to the point of being teenage stereotypes. They're characterized by an obsession with appearance, clothes, and friends, and a marked desire for privacy, as an escape from the audience. You may hear statements like "Nobody understands me," and

"You don't know how this feels," and "That will never happen to me." That last statement is important, because it illustrates the feeling of invincibility that often accompanies the Personal Fable, where risk-taking behaviors may increase.

Examples of these characteristics in literature and popular culture abound. Fifty years ago, when he first introduced these ideas in his research, Dr. Elkind used Salinger's Holden Caulfield and Goethe's young Werther as examples to make these concepts more relatable. They still resonate today, as so many of the most popular young adult protagonists continue to exhibit Imaginary Audience and Personal Fable characteristics. They allow us to identify with being special, to seem normal or ordinary but in fact to be unique, to be able to see or do things that no one else can. From Luke Skywalker to Harry Potter, Katniss Everdeen, Percy Jackson, and Tris Prior, our cultural affinity for characters who meet these innate criteria is well-established.

John Green, author of some truly incredible young adult novels, writes in his book *Looking for Alaska*: "When adults say, 'Teenagers think they are invincible' with that sly, stupid smile on their faces, they don't know how right they are. We need never be hopeless, because we can never be irreparably broken. We think that we are invincible because we *are*. We cannot be born, and we cannot die. Like all energy, we can only change shapes and sizes and manifestations. They forget that when they get old. They get scared of losing and failing. But that part of us greater than the sum of our parts cannot begin and cannot end, and so it cannot fail."

It's easy to overlook that there's something really beautiful and special about this phase of development. So much is happening, our senses are heightened, and our emotions are magnified. There's some neuroscience behind it as well. In adolescence we have more dopamine receptors, which means we experience more intense pleasure. All these things contribute to why so many of us throughout our lives can vividly recall things from when we were teenagers and why we feel such a connection to the music, movies, and experiences of that time. There's actually a name for it! It's called the *reminiscence bump.*

Many kids go through phases in adolescence where they're intense and moody, unbearable and miserable one minute and elated the next, where you don't even know who they are anymore. Then miraculously they slowly come out of it. They're taller and more mature and seem like themselves again—but different. The Imaginary Audience and Personal Fable help teenagers to do that. They enter these phases in the last stage of childhood and they emerge from them as young adults.

Another Way to Think About This

In trying to describe the idea of the Imaginary Audience and Personal Fable to my then eleven-year-old son, I stressed how puberty was a time of incredibly overwhelming biological change. I told him the process of working through all this and of figuring out who you are is called *behavioral rehearsal.* You present a part of yourself to the Imaginary Audience, try out new parts of your personality that feel right or interesting, get feedback on them, pivot in response to that feedback, and present more or less of that part of your newly forming identity until you eventually get a sense of who you are.

This process continues for a long time. For some people, who may become stunted in their egocentric development due to trauma or narcissism, it may last forever. For others, this behavioral rehearsal for the Imaginary Audience is a tool to get through a rough part of puberty. It helps them individuate from their parents, hone how they interact with others, and define who they become and how they present themselves to the world.

I asked what he thought. His response was interesting.

"It sounds about right. I mean, we all feel like that, about the audience. I feel it right now; you said that you did when you were my age a long time ago. It makes sense. It kind of reminds me of this theory I have about puberty. You know caterpillars? Everyone likes caterpillars. They're fuzzy and cute and they crawl around on your hand and it tickles. Then they go into the chrysalis stage. And nobody actually likes a chrysalis. It's creepy and you don't really know what's going on inside of it. It's not fuzzy and cute anymore, but it's not a butterfly yet, either. And it's probably gross—the change from a fuzzy caterpillar to a beautiful butterfly—maybe there's slime, I don't know. So the chrysalis covers itself up. With makeup or the cocoon thing or whatever. You hide what's going on inside. You wear a mask. And then when you're ready, you take off the mask or the makeup and you're ready to be a beautiful butterfly and fly away to a good college or something."

I am taking that excellent analogy and I am running with it. The Imaginary Audience is a chrysalis stage. It's the part of our lives where we hide who we're becoming so we can emerge from it as who we are supposed to be. It's a necessary and productive phase of development, where we conceal our true nature, exposing those parts of it to the world as we are able, conforming to and rejecting elements of our social environment.

But it's only productive if we move past it, and that's where social media comes in.

Social Media Makes the Imaginary Audience Real

These concepts may seem a little out there, but they are incredibly relevant to our understanding of how and why teens use this technology the way they do. At the stage of life when young people are hardwired to be constantly conscious of being observed and surveilled by others, social media not only reinforces that feeling but literally quantifies it in terms of views, likes, follows, and retweets.

This is a big deal.

There are some who may say that the Imaginary Audience doesn't really apply to our digital lives. One could feasibly argue that "friends" or followers aren't imaginary at all but rather real people, most of whom we have some connection to in our real lives. Sure they are, but the research also suggests that while you may have hundreds of "friends" on social media, very few of them are actually paying attention to what you're doing. Research from Facebook itself indicates that most users vastly overestimate how many of their "friends" are paying attention to what they're posting and commenting on.[4] The research is also clear that social media use (Facebook was again the primary platform studied) enhances Imaginary Audience ideation.[5]

We also can't assume that teenagers (or adults) are interacting on social media primarily with people they actually know "in real life." Many with whom we interact or follow online are people we don't know very well. Some may be distant acquaintances (hey there, people from high school I haven't seen since 1995) or even complete strangers. Many of us, young and old, follow celebrities online—athletes, writers, models, or actors. I will even admit to following a few accounts that exclusively feature cute animals. We may feel a connection to these people (or dogs, as the case may be), but that interest is certainly not reciprocated. This point is pretty easy for adults to grasp but is less so for younger teens. Additionally, the relatively anonymous nature of many platforms, combined with the fact that at any point in time we have no way of knowing who or how many of our contacts are paying attention to our behavior online, makes the audience inherently unknown, no matter what it may feel like.

The research tells us that using social media platforms enhances one's interaction with the Imaginary Audience and encourages behavioral rehearsal. The literature also indicates that when it comes to the Imaginary Audience, social media use is a natural extension of what teens are doing anyway—they are using it to make sense of their newly emerging identities and reacting to the social norms they see among their friend groups online.[6]

That Changes the Equation, Doesn't It?

Understanding these developmental phases helped me see that a lot of what I considered questionable behavior might actually seem pretty rational from the perspective of a young teen. The preoccupation with their phones, particularly with their group chats and social media accounts; the self-conscious fear of being left out; the presentation of a carefully cultivated and curated image—one that changes based on the number of likes it attracts; the impulsive decisions to share things in response to negative pressure or positive feedback. These behaviors are all developmentally appropriate and make sense, even if we don't like them very much.

I can't tell you the number of times I've had to repeat that phrase to myself as a mom. "It's developmentally normal, it's developmentally normal." I say it to myself while rocking in the corner, trying not to freak out about the latest teenage problem or drama.

It's not just teenagers who respond to the Imaginary Audience, and it's important for parents to be mindful of that as they observe their children's behavior online. Grown-ups also feel its presence. It impacts how we behave and how we engage on social media, using the medium to learn and adapt, always aware that what we post, share, or comment on is being observed. How we formulate opinions on issues, political candidates, events, movies, and culture are all influenced not only by what appears in our social media feeds but also by how our network of contacts responds to that information. A consistent positive (or negative) framing of an issue may cause you to reevaluate your opinion.

This is a pretty new development, as traditional media did not function in the same way. Historically it has been both a reflector and a director of public opinion, but generally there was no meaningful interactivity. Passively watching a news story on television or reading about it in a book or newspaper is not the same as acquiring that information online. If you leave a comment, click *like*, or share it, endorsing it or rebuking it, you are engaging with the content and with the Invisible Audience, who may be reflecting on you, reflecting on the news story. It's all very meta. This type of social learning is common across age groups and cultures. Now that Facebook is considered the world's most influential news source,[7] more study to truly understand the impact it is having on a population level is called for.

So adults, as well as teens, are influenced by the cycle of self-affirmation and engagement on social media.[8] Our behavior and beliefs are challenged and changed through a social learning process similar to behavior rehearsal. We are made more self-conscious. Certainly we all have that one friend whose behavior on social media is consistently immature and attention-seeking. You may see what she shares and shake your head, thinking how she really needs to stay off her phone after ten p.m. or stop posting song lyrics or cryptic memes in an effort to get people to ask her what's wrong.

So What Does It All Mean?

We're all interacting with an audience that is largely imaginary. Except that it isn't. The psychological impact of this arguably hits young teens the hardest, but it hits us all. Social media is a population-level game changer in terms of ego development during adolescence, and I would argue that it's having a regressive impact on some adults as well, making them feel more self-conscious and concerned about how they present themselves and are perceived by others.

Our kids are supposed to use their relatively brief adolescence productively and move through these phases of development, gaining maturity and insight in the process. They reconcile the Imaginary Audience with a more realistic appraisal of their place in the world, and hopefully outgrow being Holden Caulfield in their own personal fable.

But what happens when that reconciliation can't take place? What kind of impact can this have? I'm reminded of Robert Frost's line: "The best way out is always through." But what if social media use makes it harder for teens to get through this stage of development? What if using social media actually elongates these phases, causing teens to stall out at critical points in their psychological development?[9]

I spoke with Dr. Drew Cingel, a communications professor at the University of California at Davis and a preeminent scholar on the subject of social media's impact on adolescent egocentrism. He feels, as with all new technology, that there are positive and negative outcomes at play. "If the Imaginary Audience is constantly made salient to you, it stands to reason that you would perceive that others are judging you and thinking about you more often. If the message that parents and educators are sending about social media is largely a warning about 'the unseen other' that is out there thinking about you, then it could increase Imaginary Audience ideation. If adolescents fail to progress through that phase of egocentric thinking, that's a negative outcome."

Are We Doing This All Wrong?

This information makes me think that maybe all the ways we're currently trying to keep our kids safe are actually making the problem worse. Educators and parents send kids the overwhelming message that danger is lurking everywhere and everything they share is permanent. We urge caution because you never know who's watching, taking screenshots, or trying to interact with them. One tweet can cost you a college scholarship. One Snapchat story can end a friendship, ruin a reputation, or get you fired. Only a couple of people may really be paying attention to what we say and do online, but there is a potentially global audience for our Internet mistakes. All of these things are true, and because of our awareness of them, we're doubling down on the notion of the unseen other and we're making the Imaginary Audience more salient to our kids. There has to be another way.

So We Should Panic?

The short answer is no, at least according to the experts. Freaking out is generally not that helpful. Dr. Cingel told me that the most common questions he receives from parents are always something along the lines of "Oh dear God, are we all screwed?" He wants us all to know he really believes that it's going to be fine. Dr. Elkind, the man who created the psychological constructs of the Imaginary Audience and Personal Fable, warned me not to jump to conclusions. "We don't have good evidence and we have to be careful to avoid the assumption that because it is new, it is necessarily bad. Dime novels, movies, television—all raised similar questions. At this point we can only speculate."

Those comments resonated with me. I recall very specifically being told that I was a TV junkie and that my whole generation was rotting its brains out and would likely be morally bankrupt due to watching MTV's *Spring Break* and listening to N.W.A.

So How Can Parents Address These Issues?

Dr. Cingel provided a really useful perspective: "The distinction lies in the framing. Is it that there's an 'unseen other' out there that is thinking about you and all of your communications? Or that you should think about how others could potentially use the information that you communicate? I think that's a big distinction and could result in very different outcomes. If teens are taught to consider and predict the potential outcomes of what they do online, that could ultimately be a positive outcome. Parenting and education can have an impact."

Dr. Elkind added, "I would tell the teen that the audience is perhaps a lot broader than they think and might include people they don't want."

Shifting the focus of conversations about Internet safety from being wary of the "unseen other" to helping kids train their brains to think through their choices online before hitting Share is an excellent strategy. Providing consistent positive reinforcement for thoughtful deliberation and responsible decision-making online is a great outcome to shoot for. It can also help young teens progress cognitively and developmentally through adolescence and develop incredibly useful life skills. Life is a chess game, right? Making moves and anticipating responsive countermoves.

We admonish middle and high schoolers to be ever mindful of the consequences of everything they put online during a period when they're developmentally most prone to making stupid mistakes and taking risks. Dr. Deborah Gilboa—a family practitioner, the founder of AskDoctorG.com, and a mom of four—says sometimes it's helpful to discuss *when* and not *if* mistakes are going to happen online. She encourages kids to think through how they would respond, whom they would go to for help, and how they would try to fix problems.

Middle Schoolers and High Schoolers Online

We know intuitively that twelve- or thirteen-year-old kids need more supervision than seventeen-year-olds. There's a huge cognitive gap between those two ages. By the time they're eighteen and legal adults, hopefully they're ready to fly away to a good college or a job or whatever they choose, having been given the freedom to become responsible and independent.

Orienting young teens through their first experiences online is critical to successfully guiding them toward positive outcomes. Young people are getting smartphones at almost precisely the same time that Imaginary Audience ideation begins, without receiving consistent supervision in negotiating that new environment. Studies show that the majority of parents aren't connected with their kids on social media to provide that needed support.[10]

This means that parents need to be judicious about when their kids get that all-important first cell phone and equally thoughtful about how their kids use it in those first couple of critical years. This includes framing how (and how much) their kids should use it, providing clear guidelines and consequences, and having transparency in monitoring their online activities.

Let's explore some suggestions and next steps, beginning with when a kid is ready to get a phone or mobile device.

Takeaways . . .

- Before making a decision about whether to give your child a smartphone, take some time to consider where your child is developmentally and where they're going to be in a year or two.
  - Generally, the longer you can wait for your child to have a mobile device, the better. The same applies to when they begin using social media. The younger the teen, the more supervision and the more restrictions required.
  - Keep in mind that most social media platforms require users to be thirteen.

- Figure out age- and developmentally appropriate expectations to have for your kid's behavior and ability to make choices.
  - The rules should reflect where they are at, not an ideal they can't live up to.
  - Too little freedom and too much can both cause problems.
  - Collaborate with your child to figure out what works best.

- Be clear and up front—not just about consequences but also about asking for help when it's needed. Make sure your child knows they can and should come to you instead of trying to handle something by themselves.

- Provide clear expectations about specific online behavior. Examples include:
  - Do not download apps or open accounts without permission.
  - Do not FaceTime or Skype in bedrooms or bathrooms.
  - Do not take, request, or share inappropriate images, especially of peers or classmates.
  - Do not take or post pictures of people without their consent. Sadly, this happens all the time, even in school. It will probably happen to your child. Ask how they feel about other people taking and/or posting pictures or videos of them without their permission.

- Provide incremental opportunities to make responsible choices.
  - If your child wants an Instagram account, allow them to have an account on your phone. If they make good choices for a few months, move the account to their phone and become one of their admiring followers.

- For any social media platform, app, or account your child has, you need to have their username and passwords. You also need to have your own account and be connected to your child as a friend or follower.

- Talk to other parents or school counselors and teachers about what your kid's friends and peers are doing.
  - Kids will absolutely tell you that they are THE ONLY ONES who don't have new iPhones. This may be true or it may just feel that way.
  - Peer influence can be both positive and negative.
  - Knowing what classmates are up to and how that peer group is using social media will give you insight into the pressures and social expectations your kid is dealing with.

- Think of your young teen's introduction to having a cell phone or mobile device as their orientation to a new world that's now at their fingertips.
  - Try sharing your phone (or gaming/social accounts) with your child for a specified period of time. Having them use your phone means your child has access to the platform and their friends, and you have access to everything they see and do, as you both get used to this new freedom.
  - Try having a "family" phone as a start—a phone that belongs not to your child but to whoever in the family may need it on a given day (for example, on Thursday the oldest takes it to their soccer game; Friday the youngest takes it to a sleepover). The child has the benefit of having a phone, but there is total transparency in how they're using the shared device. Provide the child with the opportunity to use the phone as if it were theirs, aware that it's a test to see if they're ready for their own. This could mean figuring out whether she's mature enough to use the phone responsibly and put it down before her eyes start to cross, or determining if she's prone to losing it or dropping it and cracking the screen. You will also see if your child is sneakily trying to download games or music, thinking you won't notice.

- Make discussions on Internet safety about thinking through and predicting outcomes, instead of drilling down on the idea of the "unseen other."
  - With your kid's first social media accounts, the primary rule should be: You can't post until a parent has given it an okay.
  - When you say yes to a post, praise your child for making a good choice, for being responsible and trustworthy by checking with you, and for posting something cool. Make it a positive experience that you both enjoy.
  - When you say no, specifically explain why without any judgment. It should never be about what you (the parent) like or dislike but rather about objective reasons why sharing that content might result in a

problem or issue. In your explanation, place an emphasis on predicting the responses of people who might see the post and how it might make them feel.

- Over time, you're reinforcing a thought process before every post: Who will likely see this post? How will they feel about it and about me? Should I post this?

• Your family's rules for your teen's social life (whatever they may be) should also apply to their digital social life.

- If your middle schooler has to be in bed by ten, that child's phone should be checked in before then. If your high schooler has an eleven p.m. curfew, the phone should be checked in at curfew time.

• Phones should not be kept in kids' rooms overnight. This promotes better sleep and prevents late-night interactions that should not be happening in the first place.

- Phones should be charged in a common area overnight.

- The older your kids get, the harder this will be to enforce. This point, however, might be the most important advice I can give you, and it's a mountain I'm willing to die on.

Well-Being, Self-Esteem, and Social Comparison in the Selfie Generation

JILL'S STORY (AGE TWELVE)

When I was eleven and in sixth grade, I got tagged in an "Ugliest Person" contest on Instagram. Someone told me about it who went to my school and knew who I was. Otherwise I might not even have known about it. It made me wonder how many other people may have seen it and just not said anything.

Of course I went and checked it out. I don't know who it was who tagged me. I didn't recognize the name or anything. The profile picture was just a blacked-out figure, a bunch of shapes, not a person. And when I looked at their account, they just posted weird and inappropriate things. It was obviously someone's fake account. I still don't know who it was or why they did that to me.

I was a little hurt and angry. I didn't know if this was a personal thing and I actually knew this person. Maybe it's someone I know who did this really mean thing to me, but who? I've thought about it. I also don't know if they just tagged a random account and mine is what came up. I mean, my account is private but . . . It could have just been random.

I didn't do anything about it. I ended up thanking the person who told me about it. I think they just wanted me to know it was out there. I blocked the fake account that tagged me, but that was all I could do at the time. I just wanted to prevent it from happening again. Then I just tried not to think about it.

A year later, though, I can still tell you the exact day it happened. I mean, it was emotional. It hurt. No one wants to get tagged in a list like that.

Honestly, I was really upset at first. After a while I just kind of . . . It just kind of wore off. You see it so much on Instagram. It happens to people every day. It's just always there. That and the perfect people. And you just kind of end up comparing yourself to them, thinking, "Oh my gosh, maybe I am the ugliest person." I never would have thought this way about myself before Instagram. But you see it all a lot and you just get used it.

I still have friends who place so much value on how many likes they have, but I don't do that anymore. And some of them have multiple accounts, I know a girl with twelve accounts. I mean, why? They think it's fine. And it's, like, they're these goofy, funny, nice people, but they only post these things that make them seem so serious and adult and mature and that's just not who they are. I have so many friends who, like, they're not themselves on Instagram. It's like they have two personalities. You just don't know who someone is based on their profile, so why would you get upset comparing yourself to something that's not real?

My mom says Instagram accounts are like movie previews. And the preview is just the best parts, the parts that are supposed to get you to watch the whole movie. But sometimes the preview really has nothing to do with the movie. Like, the preview looks great, but the movie is actually terrible. The preview is happy and perfect, but the movie is actually sad.

It kind of clicked for me when I stopped paying attention to it. For a while I just had to unfollow a bunch of people until I could take control of my emotions and think about how their accounts and their comments were making me feel. I still don't follow as many of them. It just seems so obvious now. If it's hurting you or making you feel bad—just unfollow it. And then take some time to get control of your emotions and figure out what's going on in your head.

There's a girl I know, and we compete in the same sport, and a while ago, we were at the same level. She started training all the time and all the coaches loved her. And she started doing more and more and competing at a higher level, and she just got so much better than me really fast. But I mean, I don't have the money to train the way that she does, and it really just . . . hurt me to see everything and it really just ruined my self-confidence.

But I started to think about it, and I was like, "You know, this is what I have. And I'm grateful for it. And this is what I can do, so I'm not going to take it for granted. I actually feel lucky that I can compete at all. Maybe I don't have everything that other people do, but I have enough. In fact, I have plenty."

And when I think about it like that and don't try to compare myself, it doesn't faze me anymore. I'm past that. So now I'm like, "Hey, I saw on Instagram that you won at nationals! That's great!" And I mean it. And then I just get on with my day because I don't have the time to let it make me feel bad anymore.

The Perfect People on Instagram

Jill's experiences with Instagram are very telling, for a couple of reasons. I related to her story because I think, to a certain degree, we all feel the way that she does. We see other people's best lives play out on social media, and it makes our own feel slightly smaller in comparison. We've become culturally and digitally predisposed to check in on what others are doing, all the time. It can often feel like a contest—whose life is better, more interesting, more attractive.

I've learned how to manage these feelings (more or less). Unlike Jill, I had thirty-plus years of being socially awkward in real life to prepare me for what it would feel like to be off-putting and less attractive than my peers on Instagram. It seems that she learned some hard lessons at a very difficult age. It made me wonder again about the generational differences between me and my kids, and the impact this technology may have on who they'll become. It helped me immeasurably to be a more mature and thoughtful person when I started using Facebook in 2008 at the ripe old age of thirty-five. But what about kids who jump into using social media before they're actually socialized?

The younger the kid, the harder it is for them to understand (and articulate) their feelings, anticipate the feelings of others, and regulate their own responses and behavior. For a sixth grader, Instagram can become a minefield, dealing blow after blow to their self-esteem and well-being.

The Good, the Bad, and the Outcomes

Social media isn't always a minefield. Kids use it to connect with and communicate with one another, find information, do homework, play games, watch videos, learn about stuff they're interested in, and decompress. A lot of the research points to kids having positive experiences online. For some personality types, it allows for easier social engagement. It can help with making friends, reinforcing existing friendships, and building social capital. For some kids with social anxiety, being able to engage via texting or social media is a really helpful tool to build social connection.

Over the past few years, there have been many studies and news stories on how social media makes people feel bad about themselves and can result in a decrease in life satisfaction and well-being. There are also studies that posit that social media causes feelings of loneliness, sadness, and depression, and may be doing so at a generational level. We're going to cover these mental health effects extensively in later chapters.

So what does this all mean? I wish there were easy answers here, but there aren't. It depends on how and how often your kid uses social media and technology. It depends on their personality, how they're doing at a given time, and where they are in terms of their emotional and cognitive development. One thing the research consistently shows is that the teens who use social media the most tend to be the most unhappy and to have the worst outcomes overall.

The question is, what constitutes healthy use? How hard is it for parents, who didn't grow up with this technology, to really know what's normal? How do we steer kids toward positive experiences with technology, while avoiding the negative ones? In the field of public health, we do that by working to enhance the protective factors that lead to good outcomes and limiting risk factors to avoid bad ones. Looking at those characteristics or behaviors that predispose people to good outcomes is simply a way to steer a course. When you study child and adolescent health, the protective factors that help prevent issues ranging from drunk driving to unwanted pregnancy to diabetes are often the same. Enhancing protective factors for one thing often has the effect of limiting risk for a variety of others.

A good example of this is getting enough sleep. For teens, the benefits of a good night's sleep can include improved mental health, eating habits, stress management, and academic outcomes. A chronic lack of sleep in adolescents has been linked to increased risk of obesity, diabetes, heart disease, high blood pressure, risk-taking behavior, suicidal ideation, depression, and motor vehicle accidents.[1] So by focusing our parental resources on this one protective factor, we're simultaneously reducing our kids' risk factors for a plethora of other bad outcomes. By the way, one of the biggest contributing factors to kids losing sleep? Using too much electronic media close to bedtime and sleeping with a cell phone in the same room.

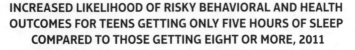

INCREASED LIKELIHOOD OF RISKY BEHAVIORAL AND HEALTH OUTCOMES FOR TEENS GETTING ONLY FIVE HOURS OF SLEEP COMPARED TO THOSE GETTING EIGHT OR MORE, 2011

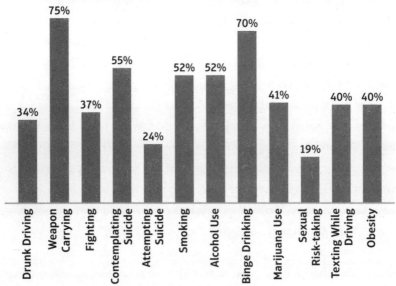

Source: *Preventive Medicine* via *The Huffington Post*

The Social Media Seesaw

In trying to determine the impact that social media and cell phones are really having on young people's well-being, we must look at the data that reflects their experiences and opinions. In almost every large-scale survey asking teens if social media makes their lives better or worse, they answered that *it did both*. It some ways, it improved their lives, and in others, it made them harder. As adults, we know that having smartphones and being constantly connected is both a blessing and a curse, so this should come as no surprise.

Another way to think about this is to imagine social media as a seesaw tipping between positive and negative impacts on well-being, with your child as the base upon which it's balancing. The friendships, connection with others, and real closeness that social media can offer can also start to tip in the opposite direction, bringing with it feelings of loneliness, judgment, or rejection. Browsing Instagram—identifying new people to follow and things to be interested in—may be really fun. But it can also tip toward feeling jealous of other people's "perfect" lives, dissatisfied with your own, or even just irritated that you wasted an hour when you should have been doing homework.

The social media seesaw was conceptualized by Harvard professor and researcher Emily Weinstein. When I spoke to her about this framework, she told me that she had developed it after hearing from young people over and over again that social media was both a good and a bad influence on their lives. Her work on the connection between social media use and teens' well-being[2] is supported by 2018 research findings from Common Sense Media and the Pew Research Center.

The bottom line? Outcomes related to social media use are not binary. We need to move past the idea that it's just one or the other. A much better thing for us to focus on is what tips the seesaw or keeps it stable—namely the characteristics and behaviors that help kids maintain a balanced online life. We need to better understand our kids and their tipping points.

Does Social Media Impact Self-Esteem?

I know how social media, especially when it gets ugly, can make me feel, but I also wanted to understand if it was the same for our kids. For many adults, how the presidential election in 2016 played out on their social media feeds was divisive, stressful, and disheartening. For kids, stress can arise when they notice a party they weren't invited to, a plethora of expensive prom dresses dancing across their Instagram, or pictures of everyone else going somewhere for spring break when they're stuck at home. Research on the generation of kids born from around 1995 to 2012 (alternatively called Gen Z or iGen or the selfie generation) shows that FOMO (fear of missing out) is a real thing, perhaps because they've grown up digitally surveilling what all their peers are doing.

FOMO

For digital natives, FOMO is a big deal. Fear of missing out, or FOMO, is defined as "a pervasive apprehension that others might be having rewarding experiences from which one is absent. FOMO is characterized by the desire to stay continually connected with what others are doing."[3] It may be more succinctly described by the title of Mindy Kaling's 2011 memoir, *Is Everyone Hanging Out Without Me? (And Other Concerns)*.

Social media brings FOMO front and center in the lives of today's teenagers—it was brought up again and again in both the research and the interviews I conducted. It's been linked with increased anxiety and depression in young people, as well as decreases in reported well-being. It's hard to argue with these feelings. Negative social comparisons and feeling left out have always been part of growing up, but the level to which kids are exposed to it now is unprecedented.

FOMO is such a large part of the lives of teens and young adults that David and Jonah Stillman, the authors of *Gen Z @ Work*, have identified FOMO as a defining characteristic of this generation. It's incredibly important that parents start addressing this issue with kids early and often, even before they start using tech. Preparing kids for FOMO and helping them to put the things that they see and feel into proper perspective are critical to raising happy, healthy digital citizens.

Make sure kids (even as young as preschool) understand that not everyone can be included in everything, and that's okay. Share personal stories with them of not being invited to events that others were attending, letting them know that you understood why. Model how you dealt with it—for example, you might have felt disappointed for a little while, but then you moved on. Give clear and understandable reasons why this may happen. Sometimes it's about cost or transportation, or sometimes it may be about wanting to spend special time with a particular friend or friends. Validate hurt feelings and help kids process the difference between intentional unkindness (all too common, unfortunately) and the reality that it's usually not personal, and overall, not being included in everything is really nothing to worry about.

One of the most important ways to manage the social media seesaw in regards to FOMO and overall well-being is time. In a 2018 study, researchers at the University of Pennsylvania found that reducing time on social media to ten minutes per platform per day showed a decline in symptoms of depression, FOMO, and loneliness. It's important to note that this study didn't ask participants to give up social media entirely, merely to cut back. The reduction in time spent engaging in social comparisons online resulted in feeling better overall.[4]

While self-esteem may not be definitively raised or lowered by using social media, high or low self-esteem can predict how and why a person might use it and what they may get out of it. There are not a lot of surprises here. People who were found to have both high self-esteem and high levels of extroversion appear to gain the most benefit from using Facebook in terms of finding satisfaction and gaining social capital.[5] These people also didn't attach a great deal of importance to Facebook, presumably because they were too busy being popular, confident, and outgoing in all other aspects of their lives.

Let us allow the introverts among us a brief moment to sigh and shake their heads knowingly.

People who were introverted *and* had low self-esteem used social media for entirely different purposes. Social media "offers people the chance to connect without many of the threatening aspects of social interaction, such as embarrassing oneself or being rejected. People with low self-esteem may therefore be drawn to appearing on social media."[6]

This is something that comes up a lot in the research and it's kind of a chicken-or-egg conundrum. Kids who have low self-esteem or trouble making friends in real life may struggle in their online interactions and feel the negative consequences of social media use more. The question is, does their already low self-esteem cause that negative outcome, or does the negative outcome contribute to the low self-esteem? We know it's a reinforcing cycle, but what the research rarely tells us is how these kids were doing *before* they got a cell phone.

One thing self-esteem can tell us is how people might behave on social media. People with high self-esteem tend to use social media to express themselves, connect with others, and share things that reinforce their relatively healthy self-concepts. Kids with low self-esteem may be more protective of what they choose to present, guarding their fragile egos more carefully. They may also feel criticism and negative feedback more acutely than their more confident peers. They may engage in more passive online behavior that is largely about observing others. So basically, kids with low self-esteem are more likely to be lurkers.[7] Several studies indicate that people who primarily use their time online to lurk rather than engage tend to experience worse outcomes.

Putting yourself out there and making yourself open to negative feedback is hard. Taking criticism is not something that many young people (or honestly, anyone) find easy to do, and this may be a residual effect of being raised in the shadow of the self-esteem movement. I worried that continued self-esteem hits would create a generation of kids who would doubt themselves and lack the confidence required to become emotionally healthy adults. Like a lot of other people, I may have been looking at this issue from the wrong angle.

The Self-Esteem Movement

For many years, in both the parenting literature and across many other disciplines, high self-esteem was seen as the ultimate protective factor. It was the predictor of future success and happiness that we (and our parents) were told to achieve. High self-esteem would mean avoiding drugs and not sneaking out to meet up with guys named Cheeto. It meant getting into a good college and ultimately having a rewarding, well-paying career. Low self-esteem meant feeling terrible about yourself and eventually living in a van down by the river.

The degree to which our national consciousness has been informed by the self-esteem movement really can't be underestimated. However, it turns out that this movement, at least in the way that many people interpret it and seek to instill it, may have resulted in some pretty far-reaching negative consequences.[8] In fact, several recent studies and well-researched bestselling books have discussed a variety of detrimental effects that our focus on self-esteem may have had on young people. It fostered the culture of participation trophies and grade inflation that has led many young people into an existential crisis as they approached adulthood.

Actual self-esteem is built on personal accomplishment. *Merriam-Webster* defines it as "a confidence and satisfaction in oneself." That satisfaction and confidence are earned when kids take the time to learn skills, practice them, and achieve competence.

Author and educator Jessica Lahey, in her outstanding bestseller *The*

Gift of Failure: How the Best Parents Learn to Let Go So Their Children Can Succeed, describes this intersection of the self-esteem movement with parenting culture and suggests that the logical step forward is "parenting for independence and a sense of self, born out of real competence, not misguided confidence. Parenting for resilience in the face of mistakes and failures."

When children are told they are special or excellent, without having to work hard to earn that distinction, they don't gain self-esteem. It's artificially inflated for a few moments, like air into a balloon. When the air escapes, the child is not left with a feeling of confidence because of what they've learned or accomplished; they're left feeling deflated. Over time, many will begin to seek not the satisfaction of mastery and achievement but the happy feeling that comes from being praised. That praise, however empty, will teach them what it means to feel good about themselves, now and in the future.

Why is this relevant to our discussion about social media? Because kids who crave and search for empty praise will surely find it on the Internet. Looking for admiration via social media can take many forms, some of which are benign. Those that concern me have to do with soliciting feedback from strangers (via open or public profiles and requests for comments/likes), as well as behavior that pivots toward sharing information or images that elicit the biggest response. This could include a more overtly sexual self-presentation or alignment with a peer group to which one doesn't really belong but which brings status and positive feedback. These are exactly the types of behaviors that expose kids to risk online and open the door for risky decision-making in real life.

Kids who use social media primarily for self-affirmation are going to experience disappointment. If how they feel about themselves is based on the number of likes or followers they have, their well-being is built on a foundation that can be toppled by one mean comment. In fact, based on the interviews I conducted, sometimes it's not even what's said that can derail a teen's self-confidence—it's what's *not* said. It's the lack of comments or even properly effusive ones. It's a photo they're not tagged in or a group chat they're dropped from.

There is currently little data on what all this really means. It's a sort of perfect storm—the cultural impacts of the self-esteem movement crashing against a cresting wave of social media market saturation. In a terrific article about the origins of the self-esteem movement and its population-level impact on our collective psychological well-being, author Will Storr writes: "We have a word for people who have become high on their own hollow self-esteem: narcissist."[9]

Narcissism and the Selfie Generation

The relationship between social media and narcissism was aptly described by the term *selfie generation,* which appeared in the popular press in 2014 and took off from there.[10] Rates of narcissism have increased similar to those of the obesity epidemic over the past thirty years.[11]

This tells us two important things. The first is that this is a legitimate problem. The second is that this problem started long before anyone had a smartphone or an Instagram account. The first iPhone was released in 2007, Instagram launched in 2010, and smartphones reached market saturation in the United States around 2012. This means that social media did not cause the increased rates of narcissism that we see today. Perhaps it has worked the other way around. The ever-increasing rates of narcissistic tendencies could have helped create an environment where social media could take root and flourish.

In either case, these changes have been studied by psychologists Jean Twenge and W. Keith Campbell, authors of *The Narcissism Epidemic: Living in the Age of Entitlement.* They explore the role that the self-esteem movement has played in enhancing narcissistic tendencies among millennials.

When I interviewed Dr. Twenge, she said, "If you want to define narcissism concisely, it's an inflated sense of self. Someone who is high in just self-esteem has confidence in themselves but also places a lot of importance on their relationships and having good relationships with others. Someone who's high in narcissism is missing that piece about valuing relationships. There's a lack of empathy and caring. They're willing to admit that empathy and caring are just not their things. They like having relationships because of what those relationships can do for them, but true intimacy, empathy, and caring is something that narcissists do not do well."

According to Keith Campbell: "The data is pretty clear that narcissism predicts and drives social media use. There's some data that says it's self-reinforcing in terms of use; however, social media doesn't appear to increase or cause narcissism. It attracts people with narcissism, who find it really self-affirming, so they may use it more."

So we know that social media doesn't cause this problem and that most people are not and never will become narcissists. However, we do know that social media is all about self-presentation and affirmation. We also know that when most kids start using it, they're already in a developmental stage where they think they're starring in a show for the Imaginary Audience. These things combined can create an environment that doesn't foster self-esteem or confidence but rather just a lot of kids who are really focused on themselves.

HELPING KIDS AVOID BECOMING TOO SELF-FOCUSED

What can parents do to help their kids avoid seeking affirmation on the Internet or from becoming too self-focused? When

Keith Campbell talks to parents about this, he points them toward something he calls CPR—compassion, passion, and responsibility.

One of the risks of kids becoming too self-focused is that they lose compassion for others. Connection and friendship are excellent buffers against ego. He stresses the importance of having friends, but especially of cultivating a couple of close friends. Help your kids prioritize those relationships and encourage them to spend time together in person.

Passion refers to doing things they really love and that really engage them. Being deeply engaged in something they love gives them the opportunity to get excited about sharing their passion with others. That helps them form meaningful connections based on mutual interest, and that enhances compassion. It's easy to push kids into what we think is best for them or what will help them succeed in academic or athletic endeavors. But that's not what this is about. Your kid might be interested in collecting dinosaurs, playing Dungeons & Dragons, or making YouTube videos about eyeliner. Parents may think these things are not the best use of their kids' time (especially when time is such a scarce resource), but it's not about the parents. It's about what the kid loves and is excited about doing.

Responsibility is about really making sure they experience the consequences of their actions, good or bad, which is also an important buffer against narcissism. If kids break rules or do something they know is wrong, they should have to deal with the consequences themselves. If they make a mess, they should have to clean it up. If kids blow off practice, they should miss playing in the big game. If a child cheats on a test, they should take the F. Let them know how much you value taking responsibility and learning from mistakes.

It's Really All About the Process of Social Comparison

The process of social comparison, which is literally hardwired into us, affects our well-being, our self-esteem, and our narcissistic tendencies. It's embedded in our need to be accepted by our peers and allows young people to answer the age-old question that so often plagues them: *"Am I normal?"* There's research on the neural impact of social comparison, which is linked to our brain's reward center. Research using fMRI shows that comparisons in which we do well result in positive rewards in the brain. When we compare unfavorably, it yields negative feelings.[12] In fact, "comparisons constitute central mechanisms of social judgment and, as a result, stand at the core of a whole range of social cognitive processes. Personal perception, stereotyping, attitudes, affect, decision-making, theory of mind, and the concept of self all rely on comparative processes. Over fifty years of psychological research has shown that so-cial comparisons form one of the cornerstones of social cognition."[13]

Social comparisons on social media tend to be the difficult kind. You're almost always comparing your real life to everyone else's carefully curated highlight reel. Though you may understand this intellectually— that the exchange is fundamentally flawed (real versus ideal)—it's still emotionally difficult. This is particularly true for kids who may feel all the feelings but lack the cognitive ability to consistently connect them to what they know to be true. The data indicates that this can eventually erode your ability to find satisfaction in your own life. Most kids are not taught to think critically about this when they're handed their first iPhone.

How Social Media Has Totally Changed Social Comparison

Social media has provided an entirely new way for kids to engage in social comparison, and certainly it's happening on a whole new scale. For us old-timers, an analog-era example of social comparison may have been to look around the cafeteria to see what all the other kids were wearing, in order to gauge whether our outfits were cool enough. Maybe we could look at *Seventeen* magazine, if we were lucky enough to have a subscription, or watch a TV show featuring actors who were about our age. When it came to comparing ourselves to our actual peers, though, that was often done in person and in real time—zits and all.

Kids today may compare themselves to their friends (both in person and on their social networks), as well as to idealized images in the media, just as we did. Research indicates, however, that younger kids are more inclined to compare themselves to others who represent their general age and gender.[14] This makes the peer interaction on social media all the more influential for younger teens. When they engage in this comparison with their friends, it's not just in the cafeteria anymore. This only enhances the problems with social comparison, particularly among young women.

The Culture of Looking Perfect

Social media enhances what's called the *peer appearance culture*, meaning that social comparison, particularly for girls, is often focused on someone's looks and weight. This focus on attractiveness reinforces competition within friend groups that can lead to relational aggression and problems within those groups. It can also lead to a lack of self-compassion, a state of being very critical of yourself.[15] Again, this is a very natural (albeit unpleasant) part of the teenage experience that is heightened by social media.

What you choose to share about yourself on your social media feeds says a lot about what matters to you. Whether it's a selfie or something about a band or a sports team we love, we are sharing elements of ourselves. When we receive positive feedback, it feels good, and the reward center in our brain is triggered, which encourages us to share more. When we receive negative feedback, it feels bad, and we often feel compelled to take an action to protect our ego or the self-concept that has been slighted. For girls, much of this feedback tends to be about their appearance; it can reinforce the degree to which they may become self-focused.

Social comparison when it comes to physical appearance can have far-reaching effects. A 2014 study from the American Academy of Facial Plastic and Reconstructive Surgery (AAFPRS) found that "one in three facial plastic surgeons surveyed saw an increase in requests for procedures due to patients being more self-aware of looks in social media. In fact, 13 percent of AAFPRS members surveyed identified increased photo sharing and patients' dissatisfaction with their own image on social media sites as a rising trend in practice."[16] In 2018, *JAMA Facial Plastic Surgery* published an article about increases in "Snapchat dysmorphia." This condition stems from being able to correct flaws and use filters to alter one's appearance in photos and is related to body dysmorphic disorder, a mental illness on the same spectrum as obsessive-compulsive disorder.

For Boys, It's Function over Form

For boys, social comparison often takes the form of how their bodies function, in terms of strength, speed, or athletic ability. I think this can also be extended to how boys perform in other areas—how well they play video games or how high they scored on last week's test. Comparing oneself in terms of function and achievement can be neutral, positive, or even inspiring. In some studies, when boys compared themselves to celebrities, rather than feel bad about themselves, they felt inspired to emulate what they saw on the screen or the page.

It's a sad statement that girls feel worse about themselves when they make comparisons based on looks and weight, while boys can engage in this upward comparison and still feel positive and inspired. I believe this reflects the gendered response to how boys and girls expect they'll be evaluated (and valued) by society.

Though social comparison is a universal behavior, some personality characteristics are more highly correlated with it than others.[17] For example, people with low self-esteem or depression and those who are empathetic or emotionally unstable are more likely to be oriented toward social comparison. In cultures stressing individualism (like the United States), we again see a gendered response, with women being more likely than men to engage in social comparison. Consider these facts collectively; if your child seems more disposed to negative social comparison, then perhaps limiting their social media use is a course of action to be considered.

Social Comparison and Parenting

Any discussion about social comparison on social media would be woefully incomplete without shining the spotlight on parents for a little while. Many parents are just as invested in the ongoing contest of social comparison as their kids are. And we, as parents, are the models of the behavior we can most likely expect from our kids.

According to bestselling author Julie Lythcott-Haims, we "adorn ourselves with our children's achievements." We do it on the back of our cars with magnets and stickers, we do it with our holiday cards and Pinterest-perfect birthday parties, and God knows, we do it on our social media feeds. We wear sweatshirts emblazoned with the schools our kids will attend or the teams they play for.

Was it always this way? Has social media changed the way we parent? Are we buying into the cycle of social comparison in the same way our kids are? Are we setting that example for them? If our kids see us placing value in the Facebook announcements and the car magnets that reflect their accomplishments, then how do they feel when they don't make the team or get the gold star? They're no longer just managing their own disappointment, they're factoring in ours, as well as the audience we might have shared it with. If we want to raise kids to become more resilient, it might be time for many of us (myself included) to reinforce the idea that both our children's successes and failures belong to *them*. For me, that means looking at where my ego intersects with their achievements (or lack of them) and taking a big step back.

I spoke with family practitioner and parenting expert Dr. Deborah Gilboa, of AskDoctorG.com, and she shared, "My biggest concerns are the false expectations that social media sets up. For parents, it may be the perception they get by scrolling through Facebook. They may perceive that everyone else's family is better fed, better clothed, more attractive, more together. Teens, meanwhile, are chemically predisposed to feel that they're on the outside, that they're different and part of the 'other.' They look at social media and think that no one else in their peer group is feeling like they do, that everyone is doing well. Therefore, social media almost provides them with proof that everyone else is doing great and no one is struggling the way that they are."

If it's our goal to help our kids maximize the positive and minimize the negative impact of social media, addressing social comparison is an important part of the conversation. The research shows that kids can enjoy their time on social media and feel good about it, provided they understand how to view the things that come across their social media feeds in proper perspective.

Takeaways . . .

- Model good behavior yourself. Start by assessing some of your habits:
  - Keep track of how much time you spend on social media (there are apps for that).

- Ask your kids how much time they think you spend on social media (be prepared not to like their answer).
- Talk to your kids about why you use social media (to connect with friends and family, to share and save photos, to watch funny videos, to connect with other people who geek out over *Star Wars*) so they can start to formulate reasons why they use it. It is important for kids to learn to understand their motivations. When we're more thoughtful about why we're doing something, our behavior will often become more intentional. Consider how the act of keeping a food journal can often be a successful tool for encouraging healthy eating, simply because you're forced to be more thoughtful and accountable about what you're doing.

- Talk with your kids about how social media can make you feel, and explain to them how the cycle of social comparison works.
  - Describe how it's risky to compare themselves and their real lives to everyone else's carefully curated social media lives.
  - Ask them if they think it's okay to be "real" on social media, and to look for people who demonstrate that. What kind of feedback are those people getting as opposed to those who show only the highlight reel?
  - Sit with your kid and go through *your* feeds with them, talking about how the things you come across make you feel and why. Go through their feed with them and do the same thing.
  - If there are things in your feed that are not appropriate for your tween or teen to see, consider the nature of the content and how your kids would feel if they accidentally stumbled on your posts or your network's posts.

- Consider who may be more inclined to social comparison and the negative feelings it creates—introverts; empaths; those with depression, emotional instability, or low self-esteem. The negative effects of social comparison are more likely to be felt by younger teens and girls.

- Look out for online risk factors like praise-seeking behaviors in your kids.
  - Examples might include changing their account from private to public, accepting follow or friend requests from people they don't really know (to inflate their numbers), asking for feedback on photos with TBH (to be honest) requests, requesting follows or comments, or shifting the types of content shared.
  - If a kid begins sharing images that are suddenly increasingly sexy or related to a group to which you're not sure they belong, this may also be a red flag or risk factor.
  - Have your parental radar set to high alert at times when people are blasting their "best lives"—holidays, dances and formals like prom, peak vacation times.
  - Remember that social comparison and FOMO are linked. Revisit conversations you had when your kids were little about how it's okay when not everyone is included in everything, and reinforce the idea that it's okay to feel sad but it's important to get on with your day.

- Work with your kids to "talk back" to the social comparisons that create a negative self-evaluation. When they're feeling less than, have them confront those specific feelings and really think about them.
  - For example, your kid might start off with "My friend scored three goals and posted about it on Instagram. He shouldn't brag like that. He's so conceited." Try to guide the conversation to the point where your child understands that "He must have felt really proud because that's a big deal. Maybe he posted about it so he could share it as a happy memory? I haven't been playing that well lately. I don't think I'm scoring at all this season. But I guess every player has slumps. And it doesn't mean I shouldn't be happy for my friend."

- Build high self-esteem, a protective factor, by encouraging your kids to get involved in things that they enjoy and that they're good at. Mastery and competency are keys to building real self-esteem.

- Jessica Lahey, educator and author of the bestseller *The Gift of Failure*, stresses the importance of providing opportunities for kids to grow their competencies (cooking, fixing things around the house, playing sports or musical instruments, etc.) so they can feel proud of their accomplishments and confident that they can do more.
- Parents can also help kids increase their self-esteem by providing warmth, connection, and love. Jean Twenge, psychologist and coauthor of *The Narcissism Epidemic*, advises parents to avoid overpraising and to tell their kids "I love you," instead of "you're special" or "you're smart."[18]

4 | Teen Friendships in the Age of the Internet

MARIA'S STORY (AGE FIFTEEN)

When I was in seventh grade, something happened with Instagram. I was having a sleepover with a friend and we were really bored and it was kind of late. My friend was like, "We should make an account of couples from our school."

So we made an Instagram account and we called it something like "True Pairs" and it had our school's name in the profile. We just thought it would be fun to make a page of people who were dating at our school. We posted some who were going out and some who just liked each other. We would take a picture of one person from their Instagram account and then put it together with a picture of the other person, and then we would tag them in their pictures.

The account was only up for a few hours but that's all it took. Even after we deleted it, people were still talking about it, and they were upset and angry.

I was on a group chat the next day and everyone was asking about who was behind the account. I started to realize that we'd done something wrong. It was all anyone was texting about or talking about at school. At the time, most of my friends didn't know it was me. They were just all talking about the people on the account and who they thought was behind it. I didn't want to tell anyone that I did it.

Things got worse. One of the couples that we posted was two girls. Everyone at our school knew that they were in a relationship. It wasn't a big deal. But it turned out that only one of the girls was out and the other one wasn't. So, like, on campus everyone knew that she dated girls, but in her life outside of school, no one knew. And another person who we posted about was really upset that everyone knew who they had a crush on because they had wanted it kept secret. But I honestly didn't realize it was a secret. I really thought everyone already knew.

I really didn't want to go to school with everything that was happening, so I faked sick. When I wasn't in school, people started texting me, telling me that they knew I did it, that they were going to tell the principal, and that I was going to get suspended. I just didn't want to face everyone.

When I went back to school, I got called into the office and got in trouble. But it was the first thing I'd ever done, so it wasn't too bad. They interviewed a lot of kids about it and made some of us watch videos about social media, and it created this environment where, like, no one trusted each other. That led to other problems, and this just made everything so much worse. When it all added up, it was a lot. There had been other things building up at around the same time, drama with my friends, but I was just pushed out after this. I pretty much lost everyone.

The other girl who I started the account with, the same thing happened to her. For a while we were each other's only friends. But then she left the school. It was kind of hard for me after that to make any friends.

My grades went down. They went from all As to some Cs. It just was really hard for me to make up my bad grades because what was going on was so stressful. It's been a year and I'm still not back to straight As.

I didn't want to go to school then, and it's still kind of like that. It was, like, really bad. When I was in class, I just felt like I couldn't do anything because I didn't want to be there. Even when I was at home, it was hard. I didn't go on Instagram for a while, but it didn't stop. People were really mad. I felt like I couldn't get away from it.

If I could go back in time, I wouldn't have done it. It was childish and it hurt people. I also should have gone to school and faced everyone the next day. It made it seem like I had so much to hide, and really I didn't. But it just was all so much. We never intended the page to be mean. It was just . . . It was late and we were bored and it was stupid. When I didn't just face up to what happened, people assumed the worst about me.

While it was happening, I was so scared to tell my mom. I was worried about getting in trouble and maybe losing my phone. She kept asking me what was going on, but I was too freaked out to tell her. If a kid doesn't have their phone, that kid is totally isolated. They don't have anyone to talk to about what's happening and they don't have any support from their friends. I know you think that by taking away their phone, you're taking away the ability of people to be mean to them, but you're also taking away the people who are there for them. A lot of kids I know don't tell their parents anything because they're scared of getting in trouble and, honestly, they just expect that if they tell their parents something bad that they'll lose their phones.

You can delete accounts and take their phone, but if a kid wants to find drama, they'll find it. I mean, kids need to learn how to deal with drama and how to avoid it, and they need to figure that out for themselves. I had to find a whole new group of friends, but they're really nice and accepting. It's actually really good because we have the same mind-set and things are a lot better. I also started running and that has become so important to me. When things get weird, I can run and it clears my head. I spend less time on Instagram and I'm doing something that's good for me.

"I Pretty Much Lost Everyone"

When I was interviewing this young woman, I could feel her pain when she said those words. We've all experienced social rejection in some form, and it hurts. Moreover, it sticks with you. Remember the story about me passing a mean note in eighth grade and how I was persona non grata for weeks? My friends truly meant everything to me when I was in middle and high school, and when things went badly in those friendships, I felt my whole world crumbling.

These kinds of experiences can have really painful consequences. They happened long before there was social media and I expect will continue, in new and awful fashions, as long as there are teenagers. Although the fundamental ups and downs of kids' friendships really haven't changed, technology has made both connection and rejection easier to come by and harder to avoid.

YOUR RULES, YOUR HOUSE, BUT *NOT* YOUR KIDS

What happens when your kids have their friends over and those friends are constantly on their phones? What if one kid shares online about a get-together at your house, which leads to other kids feeling excluded and left out? What if pictures of your home or your family are posted without your knowledge or consent, even innocently? And what about sleepovers in the age of smartphones and social media? Should kids be allowed to keep their phones?

Education and tech expert Ana Homayoun, author of *Social Media Wellness: Helping Tweens and Teens Thrive in an Unbalanced Digital World*, makes the case for staying consistent and asking your child's guests to stick to the rules of the house. For example, if you host a sleepover and your rule is to charge all devices in the kitchen starting at ten p.m., then that rule should apply to guests as well. Kids should always have free access to their phones in the kitchen, in case they feel homesick or want to call a parent. Homayoun acknowledges that it can feel awkward to enforce this rule, but she also points out that most parents would expect their children to respect the rules of the homes in which they're visitors.

Eliza Harrell, director of education, outreach, training, and prevention at the National Center for Missing and Exploited Children, also advises parents to follow curfew rules and collect phones at the same time teens would be required to be home. And if they want to take pictures or videos of the fun they're having? "They can, but they should be encouraged to 'think before they post' in the middle of the night. Tell them they can always #latergram it in the morning when their heads are a little more clear."

As kids get older, enforcing rules around technology becomes increasingly difficult. I asked a young man who was sleeping over to please charge his phone in the kitchen overnight and he looked at me in shock and fear, as if I'd suggested he permanently detach his right arm. Although I would prefer that all kids, including our guests, check their phones in a common area overnight, it does not always happen when we're hosting. Many kids, especially older ones, are really, really uncomfortable with the idea of not having it right next to them when sleeping in an unfamiliar home.

Having a brief conversation to set expectations with the kids who frequent your house (and their parents) may help ease some of the tension around this. It may also be an opportunity to discuss what the tech rules are when your child spends time with their friends at their houses. Based on what you learn and how concerned you feel, it may be worth it to start asking parents what their rules are about tech before dropping your kid off for a sleepover.

Friendships are critically important as kids mature through their teen years, figuring out who they are outside of the defining limits of their families and their roles within the family unit. The social interactions they have help them "rehearse" aspects of their character and identity, figuring out the kind of person they are and who they want to be. Behavioral rehearsal and interacting with the Imaginary Audience are a central part of this process. What it boils down to is that the friendships and social experiences we have as young people play a big role in who we will become as adults.

When friendships fall apart in adolescence, it usually feels like it's playing out in public. When we factor in social media, that feeling becomes more salient. The dissolution of a relationship can be monitored in real time, as Instagram pictures are deleted or untagged, as people are unfriended or blocked.

It's also painful because of a concept that psychologists call *intimate self-disclosure*, which sounds kind of dirty and sexual, but isn't. It refers to sharing personal feelings and details about your life and is a measure of how close a friendship truly is. Knowing how much to share, when to do it, and with whom are hard skills to learn. Most people—not just teenagers—are reluctant to talk about personal and heartfelt feelings with someone they don't fully trust or who might not reciprocate the same kind of sharing. For many teens, being dumped by a friend represents a betrayal of those first hesitant self-disclosures of their true selves.

OVERSHARING

On the subject of self-disclosure, let's talk about oversharing. Eighty-eight percent of kids have reported that oversharing is a problem among their peers.[1] This is actually great from a parenting perspective, because it means that your kid(s) probably feel the same way. Ask your kids if they think people overshare on social media. Ask for some examples of what oversharing looks like.

- Why is it a problem?
- Does it make people look stupid or like they're trying too hard? Or is it more serious?
- Are there some things that should always stay private?
- What are things that should be off-limits for everyone in the family to post about?
- What are some of the consequences of oversharing?
- Is there pressure to overshare in order to be perceived as "real" or authentic? How do you counterbalance that pressure?
- Have there been times when you or your kids have shared something and then regretted it? What are some things they can do if that happens?

The Social Lives of Teens Today Versus Yesterday

The ways in which teens socialize have drastically changed in the past twenty years. In her 2017 book, *iGen: Why Today's Super-Connected Kids Are Growing Up Less Rebellious, More Tolerant, Less Happy—and Completely Unprepared for Adulthood—and What That Means for the Rest of Us*, Dr. Jean Twenge lays out some stark differences between how prior generations of teens socialized and how kids live today. She categorizes iGen as those born after 1995. They are spending less face-to-face time with their friends and more of their leisure time alone.

"iGen teens are less likely to take part in every single face-to-face social activity measured across four data sets of three different age groups. These fading interactions include everything from small-group or one-on-one activities such as getting together with friends to larger group activities such as parties. They include activities with no real aim, such as cruising in a car, and those that may have more of a goal in mind, such as going to see a movie. They include activities that might be replaced by online convenience, such as going to a shopping mall, and those that can't be easily replicated, such as going out with friends."[2]

This is supported by 2018 data from the Pew Research Center for Internet & Technology, which shows that while 60 percent of teens report spending time with friends online every day, only 24 percent spend time with them in person. The most commonly cited reason for this? Seventy-five percent of teens said either they or their friends had too many other obligations.[3]

Dr. Twenge also observes that for most people who experienced an analog adolescence, the things they're likely to remember most might be a first kiss or a post-prom party or getting in trouble at the mall for some dumb shenanigans. All those things happened with friends and without the direct observation of parents. These experiences are increasingly uncommon for kids growing up today because of both technology and the parenting culture in which we currently find ourselves.

It's Not Just About Tech, It's About Culture

Parents today tend to engage in a certain degree of overinvolvement in their children's social lives, even in middle and high school. While this may currently be the norm, historically this has not been the case. Just at the point in our kids' development when they start to really prioritize their friendships and their social lives, most of them get a cell phone. This can create a difficult moment for parents—phones give teens greater independence and privacy when parents already feel that their kids may be putting them at a distance.

For me, it happened when my oldest daughter was in seventh grade. I refer to it as the year when I stopped controlling the narrative and she started writing her own. It's really, really hard to accept that your kid is growing into her own person, one whom you may not know everything about. She started to make new friends (and I didn't know any of them or their mothers), she listened to music I had never heard of, she started to love scary movies (something I hate), and all of a sudden she cared about clothes. Still, she was the same sweet kid who always did her homework without being asked and made a point of spending quality time with her dog every day.

But she was different—she was growing up. She wanted more freedom to be herself and she wanted privacy from me: her nosy, loving, and bewildered mother. For many parents, especially those who've been really involved in their kids' lives, this push for independence can feel more like a shove. Parents' primal reaction is to hold on tighter, hug longer, and insert themselves even more. Sadly, most young teens just don't enjoy those long (s)mother hugs that much and it just makes them squirm away harder.

HOW OTHER PARENTS MONITOR SOCIAL MEDIA

Every family monitors social media and Internet use differently. Some parents are very hands-off, which drives me a little crazy and makes my job somewhat harder. Other parents are a lot stricter with their rules and oversight. I love those guys and here's why: they serve as a reminder to my kids that (a) I'm actually pretty reasonable and (b) their audience online is often much broader than they think it is. Need an example? Here's a snippet of a conversation I've had multiple times over the years, with multiple children in my house.

Me: I just got a text from one of your friend's moms. She's pretty concerned about the things being said in a group chat that you're in. She asked me to check in with you about it.

Child: [*eyes huge*] WHAT?

Me: Sweetie, you know that other parents check their kids' phones, right? They're sometimes reading your texts and seeing your posts. We've been over this.

Child: [*looking slightly alarmed*] I know that, but . . .

Me: Is everything okay? She seemed worried, and now you look freaked out.

Child: I'm just freaked out because [friend's mom] has been reading our group chat. I kind of forgot that other parents did that. I always just think about you.

Me: Is everything okay, though?

Child: Yes, it's fine. There was some drama, but it's over now and it had nothing to do with me. Thank God. There were some . . . umm . . . bad-language words in there.

Me: Maybe this is a good reminder to you and your friends, then? Because that mom who texted me got a heads-up about it from another parent, whose kid isn't even in the group chat.

Child: Okay . . .

Me: You're glad I mentioned this, right?

Child: Definitely. Can I say something in the group chat about moms reading it? I feel like people forget.

Me: Yes, of course. You always have to assume that some-body outside the conversation might read it. That's just the way it is. That's why we always have to have open commu-nication with each oth—

Child: I know. This is awkward now. Bye.

I think it's really important to have these conversations periodically so our kids can check their own behavior. According to Galit Breen, author of *Kindness Wins* and creator of the parenting tech blog *These Little Waves*, teens' biggest mistakes tend to happen within their inner circles, when their guard is down and they're being careless on private text threads and messages. Sometimes a little reminder to be mindful of your words goes a long way.

Using Tech to Gain Independence

The first smartphone most kids receive provides them with many things, including a certain type of freedom. The unobserved independence that those of us who grew up in the seventies and eighties took for granted is now largely unavailable to our children. Young people still crave new experiences and connection with their friends, as well as the freedom to explore those things away from their parents' observation. Moreover, this independent exploration is required for successfully navigating the transition from adolescence to adulthood, yet for many, it doesn't really exist.

Social media and gaming may provide the only opportunity that many helicoptered tweens and teens have to practice and experiment with ideas, activities, personas, and behaviors without being under their parents' constant gaze. I would argue that kids are unconsciously drawn to this freedom and inclined to keep their (overinvolved but well-intentioned) parents out of the loop. I'm not judging anyone here—I am one of the overinvolved and well-intentioned. Researchers have observed the same thing, noting that "social media may represent an arena where the younger generation can explore and develop their identities and culture without interruption from parents or those in a position of authority."[4]

Convenience, Safety, and Logistics

This tech also represents convenience. It is simply the easiest way for most kids to connect with their friends, especially when free time is an increasingly rare commodity. It is more practical to FaceTime with your best friend than to meet in person when you have only an hour between school and practice and there are hours of homework to be done before bedtime.

There are also the issues of safety and logistics. Say you're in seventh grade and you want to hang out with your friend who lives across town, but your parents are working and unable to drive you. Maybe thirty years ago you would have ridden your bike there or taken a bus or even walked. But now that distance may be considered unsafe. Walking alone or taking public transportation by yourself is no longer socially acceptable. So isn't it a better idea just to play on the Xbox together? Both of you safe in your own homes, connected by a modem, some headsets, and something fun to do?

BUILDING STRONG FRIENDSHIPS

There's overwhelming evidence that strong friendships in childhood and adolescence are an important part of healthy development. So how can we help our kids grow stronger friendships in an age when many of them communicate with emojis?

According to author and psychology professor Dr. Larry Rosen, while many digital natives *feel* like they're more connected, it's less real connection than it is an exchange of pieces of communication. The best example I can provide is the Snapchat streak. Kids will have streaks running for months, meaning they've shared pictures back and forth via the app every day, and they place a lot of value on them. I really can't explain why. But the kids I interviewed routinely joked about how the streaks started and sort of took on lives of their own. Friends might move on and not really talk anymore, but the streak would keep going. One friend might travel somewhere without cell reception and the streak would be broken, and both kids would realize they had almost nothing in common with each other—except a streak that may have lasted for a year.

We can encourage real connection by helping our kids prioritize face-to-face, in-person time with their friends. We can model empathy and compassion in our own friendships and relationships. We can practice our personal communication skills with our kids every day, showing interest and respect when speaking to others rather than being distracted by our phones. We should encourage our kids to find things they love to do so that they can connect with other people who they share those same interests with.

How Kids Socialize Online

Smartphones, social media, and gaming represent the means by which modern communication takes place, particularly among young people. The research consistently tells us that young people use social media and the Internet for many reasons, but paramount among them is communication.

GIRLS MORE LIKELY TO SPEND TIME WITH FRIENDS DAILY VIA MESSAGING, SOCIAL MEDIA; BOYS DO THE SAME THROUGH VIDEO GAMES

Percentage of all teens who spend time every day with friends doing the following...

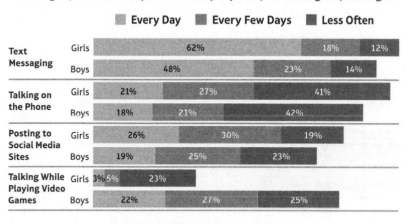

		Every Day	Every Few Days	Less Often
Text Messaging	Girls	62%	18%	12%
	Boys	48%	23%	14%
Talking on the Phone	Girls	21%	27%	41%
	Boys	18%	21%	42%
Posting to Social Media Sites	Girls	26%	30%	19%
	Boys	19%	25%	23%
Talking While Playing Video Games	Girls	3% 5%	23%	
	Boys	22%	27%	25%

Source: Pew Research Center Teen Relationships Survey, Sept. 25–Oct. 9, 2014 and Feb. 10–March 16, 2015 (1,060 teens ages 13 to 17)

That communication facilitates but doesn't always deliver connection with others. Kids who have been surveyed across multiple studies and in many different countries all consistently say that being online helps them make friends and feel connected to their peers. Given that close friendships in adolescence are important keys to healthy psychological and identity development, this is good news.

So how do these friendships form? Kids report making friends on line via social media platforms like Instagram and Snapchat as well as through gaming consoles like Xbox and PlayStation. Some of the first pieces of information that kids report sharing with new friends are their social media or gaming handles. Where we once handed out our phone numbers to potential friends or love interests, young people today share their usernames.

In terms of making friends and staying connected, gaming is for boys what social media (like Instagram) is for girls. Just as girls will share their Instagram or Snapchat username when they meet someone who they may want to become friends with, boys will share their gaming handle.

A 2015 report from the Pew Research Center describes how kids use technology to interact with their friends in a really interesting way—it's as though there's a hierarchy in the different forms of technology they choose to communicate with different types of friends. I have observed this in action and it's fascinating.

Imagine that you're a ninth grader. You probably talk on the phone only on rare occasions, and video chat more often, but only with close friends. You might have several Snapchat streaks with people you like but who are really just friendly acquaintances. You might consistently "like" the Instagram photos of someone you barely know from school because they consistently like yours in return. You might also have multiple Instagram accounts—one that's your more public (and polished) account, one that's about music or memes that you share with a friend, and then one that's your "spam" or "finsta" (fake Instagram) account, where you can post more casually and more frequently because of that account's much smaller audience, comprised of actual friends.

Friends in Real Life

There's a lot of concern over the nature of friendship and social interactions that occur online versus in real life. Specifically, some perceive online friendships as less "real" than those that primarily involve face-to-face interactions, and argue that communication and time spent in person is more meaningful than time spent interacting on social media.

The research indicates that the ties between online friends, or friendships that take place primarily online, are weaker than the connections in traditional social relationships. In fact, sociologists often refer to them as weak-tie versus strong-tie relationships. This is hard for me to accept, as I place an enormous value on my friendships that occur primarily online and feel strongly that these relationships are both real and meaningful. For young people, this may be even more true, as the line between real and digital basically no longer exists when it comes to their social lives.

If your online communication with friends is meaningful, then the resulting relationship is likely to be as well. If the communication is essentially just a Snapchat streak, then it's more likely an exchange of information or pictures rather than a real connection. It's hard for kids, especially those really yearning to connect with their peers, to tell the difference sometimes. That's where parents need to step in and make sure kids understand what constitutes real friendship.

BIG NETWORKS OF WEAK-TIE FRIENDS

Social media, for better or worse, allows us to have contact with lots of people. One aspect of social media that drives its use is the premium placed on the size of our networks. There is much less value placed on the degree of actual connection and support that exists within those large networks.[5]

It's worth asking ourselves and our kids some questions about this. Why do we want to have a big network? Are we spending the same amount of time and effort to build and maintain strong friendships? Do we want to share the things we post with people we don't know very well? Do we see it as an opportunity to collect more likes and followers? Are these people really friends? Are they merely acquaintances? Or something else?

Most social networks built online through gaming or social media are classified as weak-tie relationships, but that doesn't mean that they're unimportant. There is immense value in having a large network, for both adults and kids, and it's one of the most commonly cited benefits of participating in social media.

According to psychologists and tech experts, social capital online is largely derived from acquaintances, not strong-tie friends. Weak-tie relationships can serve as bridges to various groups of people and can help with sharing information, resources, and opportunities. It's important, however, to understand that strong-tie and weak-tie relationships each play their own role and that they're not the same. For adults, this is intuitive. For kids, that concept may be harder to grasp.

People Act Different Online

People communicate and respond differently online than in real life. In-person interactions yield a totally different brain response than digital communications do. Additionally, and this is no small matter, genuine personal interaction not only helps kids strengthen their developing social skills but also serves as an important protective factor against unhappiness.[6]

Most studies of online communication characterize it as less impulsive and more planned. Online interactions, even fairly quick back-and-forth chatting, are described as asynchronous, meaning that these interactions allow those participating in the exchange to pause and reflect before responding. Kids can think through what they're going to say and how they're going to present themselves. Sometimes this is great—it helps shy or impulsive kids consider what they want to do next and encourages them to proceed thoughtfully before hitting Send.

The Bad News

Sometimes the asynchronous nature of online communications is detrimental. It allows kids to overthink situations, to grow anxious about how they should respond or present themselves. Those inclined to harass their peers have the time and space to really hone the most venomous post. This is sometimes called the *cockpit effect*, which refers to how fighter pilots can distance themselves from their targets on the ground. When we communicate in person, we're held responsible for the reaction to our words right there on the spot.

Virtual communication can also be detrimental because reading visual cues and experiencing the other person's reaction to your words help enhance empathy. These skills are critical for success and happiness in life, and from a big-picture perspective, they help foster a more civil society.

In Sherry Turkle's excellent book *Reclaiming Conversation: The Power of Talk in a Digital Age*, she writes: "Without conversation, studies show that we are less empathetic, less connected, less creative and fulfilled. We are diminished, in retreat. But to generations that grew up using their phones to text and message, *these studies may be describing losses they don't feel.*"[7]

The Good News

In many ways, tech can be good. Teens crave contact with their peers, and technology certainly provides that. The feeling of social connectedness and belonging is healthy and helps kids feel better in other aspects of their lives. It's great for people who are shy or who have social anxiety or who feel like they're outsiders in their world. It can help isolated or lonely kids find their people.

Social networks can help kids who are struggling with their sexuality or gender identity find a peer group or role models, kids who are depressed or anxious to find help and support, and kids who have no one to eat lunch with at school to find tons of friends online who also love the same obscure Japanese anime characters. For these young people, social media is a lifeline. Sadly, these kids are also statistically more likely to be harassed or bullied online, which we'll explore in a later chapter.

This is important stuff to understand, because that feeling of belonging comes only from being truly known, and that can happen only when we're brave enough to share who we are with others. Being on social media can help enhance self-disclosure and a sense of belonging, both of which are positive.

What About Empathy?

Although there's a lot of speculation that spending too much time online rewires our brains to make them less attuned to the feelings of other people, the research on this is not conclusive. Empathetic characteristics have decreased while screen time has increased, and those two things are probably related, much like the relationship between narcissism and social media. Like other research on this type of technology, however, these findings are correlative, not causative. Causative implies that one variable (social media) causes a change in another variable (empathy). We do not have a real body of research or evidence that supports this conclusion. A correlative relationship is simply a measure of how two variables are related to each other. That relationship can be negative (meaning that as one variable increases, the other variable decreases), positive (both variables increase at the same time), or neutral (no relationship between the two variables). If we go back to the example of narcissism, there exists a correlative relationship between higher levels of social media use and higher rates of narcissistic tendencies. But we know that social media doesn't cause narcissism, even though the relationship between the two things is strongly correlated.

Studies looking specifically at the connection between being online and empathy found that social media use doesn't negatively affect our capacity to feel or express empathy. Some research does find a connection between slightly decreased empathy and certain types of video gameplay, but we'll discuss this in greater detail in chapter 6, on video games.

What the research does say is that while virtual empathy is real, the type of empathy expressed in person is much stronger. Providing virtual empathy can help people practice articulating support and encouragement to others, something that may not come naturally to everyone. In doing so, it may even help some people express themselves more easily in person and in other forms of communication.

Some people find it easier to express themselves online, enhancing their ability to relate to others or to provide support during a difficult time. According to data from the Pew Research Center, most kids (70 percent) say that using social media helps them feel better connected to their friends' feelings, and nearly as many (68 percent) feel that social media has helped to support them through difficult or challenging times.

Drama and Fighting Online

Social media may in fact be a mirror of how friendships and relationships are functioning in "real life." Mirrors can distort reality just as easily as they can reflect it. This is especially true of drama and conflict, which are hardly new to the teenage experience, but can be magnified and distorted through the lens of social media. When conflicts arise, girls are more likely than boys to block or unfriend, untag or remove pictures. Being erased from a friend's social media feed can be a painfully public experience. This behavior may seem extreme, but this type of digital disconnection after a friendship ends is very common.

Often the drama flows back and forth between online and in-person interactions. Where things can get particularly sticky is when pictures or screenshots of arguments are shared or reposted to others, and can reappear weeks or months later, making old conflict fresh in very vivid ways. According to 2018 data from the Pew Research Center, 44 percent of teens report unfollowing or unfriending people, and the most commonly given reason for this, at 78 percent, is "too much drama."[8]

FROM DRAMA TO SUPPORT, TEENS SEE A WIDE RANGE OF ACTIONS ON SOCIAL MEDIA

Percentage of teen social media users who ever experience the following on social media

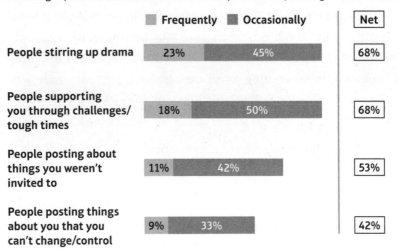

	Frequently	Occasionally	Net
People stirring up drama	23%	45%	68%
People supporting you through challenges/ tough times	18%	50%	68%
People posting about things you weren't invited to	11%	42%	53%
People posting things about you that you can't change/control	9%	33%	42%

Source: Pew Research Center Teens Relationships Survey, Sept. 25–Oct. 9, 2014 and Feb. 10–March 16, 2015 (789 teens who use social media)

Feeling the Pressure

Consider the pressure kids feel to appear attractive, appropriate, authentic, and popular on social media. They want their peers to like what they see, they want their parents to be proud of them, and they feel the constant weight of the permanent digital footprint they may be leaving. And imagine having to balance competing pressure from the adults and kids in your life to have those social feeds meet the "right" requirement for each audience. Now imagine doing this while your hormones are raging and your prefrontal cortex is filled with angry bees.

It's confusing and difficult to coordinate multiple facets of our lives into a coherent whole represented in one social media feed. I'd argue that it's pretty hard for adults to do. This may be one explanation for why kids often have multiple accounts and use multiple platforms.

Digital and social friendships can also start to feel like a job. It can be a lot of work to keep up with all your friends all the time, and there is definitely pressure to do so. This pressure was mentioned both anecdotally in my interviews and in the research. One Common Sense Media study reported that "many teens express an almost adult-like weariness with the pressures of the constant texting and posting involved in their modern lives."[9]

The Rich Get Richer, and
What the Other 99 Percent Can Do About It

One of the recurring themes when it comes to how teens react to social media is this idea that the rich get richer. What does that mean? The research tells us that kids who are good at communicating and interacting with others tend to get the most benefit from social media. And those who use it as a tool to enhance communication and facilitate spending time together, rather than as a substitute for social interaction (strictly for entertainment, lurking, playing games, or browsing), also seem to gain more benefit and are happier socially. Kids who use social media and feel accepted and trusted by their parents also tend to have a stronger sense of identity and higher sense of self-worth. The same is true for kids who already have solid friendships with strong relationship ties. The rich get richer.

Basically this means that happy kids use it to enhance their otherwise happy lives. Popular kids use it to connect with even more friends. Kids with high self-esteem use it and end up finding new ways to feel good about themselves. I'm delighted for these popular, confident (and probably very attractive) young people! That's great for them!

But what does it mean for the rest of us? I'm thinking about this information in two ways. First, it begs the question: Do the poor also get poorer? Do the kids who struggle socially and get picked on at school get bullied more online? Do sad or worried kids get more anxious? We're going to discuss some of these questions in the chapters to come, but sadly the answer is often yes.

Second, this research strengthens the argument for identifying and reinforcing protective factors for all kids and for teaching them to understand their own tipping points. Social skills can be taught, and communication can be improved through encouragement and practice. Help them to be mindful of how they're feeling when they're online, and reinforce how important it is to take breaks when online interaction is negative or stressful. We can also help our kids prioritize face-to-face social time to build up strong-tie relationships.

Takeaways . . .

- Good communication and social skills are protective factors that take practice. Create situations where kids have to interact with people in ways that are slightly out of their comfort zone.
  - Be specific with your children when you discuss communication skills. Encourage eye contact and gauging the other person's responses. Talk about how these skills include reading body language and facial ex-

pressions, interpreting nuance, and understanding changes in tone and manner of speech.

- Make in-person social time a priority for your kids. Carve out time, no matter how busy your family is, for your children to be with their friends in person. It builds important skills and strengthens relationship ties. This is particularly important when kids are not getting along with their friends. Online arguments and misunderstandings are often made worse by the mode of communication.
  - Discuss the importance of having difficult conversations in person and limiting fights that happen via text message, especially on group chats or in comment threads that may be a more public forum. Warn against subtweeting, or calling someone out online without specifically naming them. It's a passive-aggressive play that can cause a lot of hurt feelings and damage a relationship.
  - If you're super busy, and making face-to-face social time a priority is hard, be very clear with your kids that it's a trade-off. Time is a valuable resource and they need to choose how it's spent. They can go to their friend's house or the football game or the birthday party, but that means they lose time on their phone when they get home.

- Discuss the difference between friends and acquaintances. Social media has really changed the colloquial understanding of the word *friend*, especially for young people. It may mean something different to you than it does to your kids.
  - Discuss the importance of both acquaintances and friends. Both are great! Having a network of contacts is a very positive thing, and social media and gaming lend themselves to developing networks of acquaintances.

- Parents should respect both their children's need to be increasingly independent and the importance that they place on their friendships and social relationships. That being said, the younger the kid, the more guidance they'll need when they first go online. Make sure the rules that you use to govern their social lives in real life translate into their digital social lives in a way that makes sense to everyone. Remember to mentor, monitor, and trust.

- The research shows that kids do not want to be observed by their parents online and that they will behave differently if they think they're being observed by adults. This is both good and bad.
  - It's bad because it encourages both kids and parents to be sneaky, kids in their online communications and parents in their monitoring of it. Sneaky behavior can break down trust between parents and their kids. This should be avoided, as trust is an important protective factor.
  - Be honest and direct with kids about how you monitor their phones and Internet use. Remind them again and again that adults might be seeing what they text and post, even if that adult is not you.

- Encourage kids to use their phone or device primarily as a tool to interact with other people, not as a substitute for social interaction.
  - Explain that there's an important distinction between kids who spend hours every day interacting with their phones as passive consumers of content (watching videos, lurking on social media, playing games) and those who use it as a vehicle to engage with other people or with the things they see or read online (texting or making plans with friends, creating content for YouTube, etc.).
  - Several studies have found that using social media as a communication tool enhances friendship quality. Most important for parents, model this behavior yourself.

5 | Digital Dating and Teen Relationships Online

JOHN'S STORY (AGE SEVENTEEN)

Last year, when I was sixteen, I dated a girl for seven months. Almost from the beginning, it was off. She needed me to text her all the time. She wanted to hear from me pretty much constantly, and I felt like I couldn't keep up. It was so much work, and it was a constant distraction from school and classes and sports and my other friends. But I didn't want to disappoint her because that's what she seemed to expect and I cared about her so much.

I knew it was weird. I'd had one other girlfriend, and even though we were a lot younger, even though she texted me a lot, it wasn't like this. It didn't have the same kind of expectations attached to it. I also had friends who were girls and I just knew this wasn't normal.

There was a need for constant attention. I mean, I would come home from spending time with her and she would want to FaceTime with me as soon as I got home. It felt really overwhelming. If I was at a friend's house, just hanging out watching TV or something, she would be texting me the whole time I was there. I thought, "If I'm here, please just let me be here. If I'm texting you the whole time, it's like I don't get to be here with my friends—I'm with you."

When I was upset about school or a game or something, she would text me late at night, knowing I was dealing with things and try to stir things up or start a fight with me. I just needed time to deal with what I was dealing with. If I'd played badly, it didn't have anything to do with her; I just needed to feel bad about it and think about it and get some sleep.

It didn't really strike me just how upsetting and frustrating it all was until it all just fell apart. I was just done. I didn't want to hurt her feelings because I really cared about her, but I couldn't do it anymore. Once I really thought about what it would be like to break up with her, what I would lose and what I would get back, I couldn't let go of the idea. I thought about it for a couple of weeks and I was like, I'm done. I just needed the relationship to be over.

When we broke up, she really freaked out. She kept texting me and said that she was depressed and that I caused her depression. I know she was in pain and that the breakup hurt her, but it was like she was trying to make sure I was feeling pain too. It was scary.

She would also try and start text conversations with me, like, four or five times a day, during school and then again a couple of times after school. She would text me really late at night. It was hard to know how to respond. I wanted to be nice, to be polite, but also not to engage with her. I didn't want to be mean. My responses were really short. I thought she'd get it, but it kept happening.

She got an app that would send texts from a fake number and she would text me and my friends, talking shit about me. At one point she tried to turn my entire group of friends against me by telling them I'd texted her and said that she couldn't talk to them or be friends with them. I had a really good friend who was a girl, and my ex contacted her and called her all kinds of really awful names like a slut and a whore. She tried to get me in trouble with my parents by texting them that we'd had sex. She also texted one of my teachers and tried to get me in trouble with him. He's like a mentor to me, so he came to talk to me about it.

Thank God I saved all our texts, so I could just show people what I'd said and they could see everything for themselves. I feel so lucky that people believed me, that I wasn't being mean to her or trying to hurt her, because I honestly didn't do those things.

I tried to handle it all myself, to keep it as small as possible, but I finally told my parents everything that was happening. My mom texted her mom, but even then, it still kept happening. I'm glad I told my parents, though, because at that point I felt like they could help me handle things because it had started to feel a little out of control. This went on for two or three months. I think it finally stopped when my ex decided she was ready to move on.

Looking back on everything, I think she was texting me all the time because she didn't trust me. It was a way of keeping tabs on me. It was like she worried I might break up with her, and it all just got so weird, that's exactly what happened. I think I know now that if there's an imbalance in a relationship, where one person is secure and the other is insecure, that it just isn't healthy for anyone. I tried to make up for that by giving her the attention I thought she needed, but it didn't make anything better.

I also think I understand now how important it is to take a step back in your relationships and try to have some perspective. Sometimes you get caught up in it and you lose sight of how things are going, and then it hits you all at once. If you have that perspective and you can talk openly about things, it doesn't come to that.

I view relationships really differently now. I'm more protective of my time and of the time I spend with my friends and family. I know that I need a girlfriend who understands that and is okay with it, someone who is independent and busy, who has their own stuff going on. I have a girlfriend now and she gets it. She respects that there are times I need to focus on school or sports, and she does the same.

Digital Dating and the New Normal of Teen Courtship

When it comes to teen dating, the "always on" mentality that defines how so many kids use their smartphones may also lead to a skewed sense of just how much connectedness is appropriate. Is exchanging a hundred texts in a day, plus talking in school, plus FaceTiming for a few minutes at night excessive? Or does it represent a new normal in how adolescents communicate, not just as couples but in general?

One might argue that the three hours a night I spent on the phone with my high school boyfriend was also excessive, and certainly my parents questioned if it was a good use of my time. While so many things are different now, a few remain the same—including the all-consuming and powerful feelings of young love, and of those first romantic feelings reciprocated. More than two thousand years ago, Aristotle wrote: "The young are heated by Nature as drunken men by wine."

Adolescence is the time when children develop their own identities, begin to detach from their loving parents (*sob*), become sexually curious (*gulp*), and form deeper relationships and romantic partnerships with others. These developments are hardwired into teenagers and serve critical purposes.

Adolescent romance and sexuality, however normal these might be, are super awkward for many parents to deal with. Intellectually we know it's an important part of growing up, but it also represents an enormous switch in how we must perceive our kids. If we still view our teenagers as children—and let's face it, in many respects they are—then the very notion of them as sexual beings, both attractive and attracted to others, seems kind of . . . wrong. I struggle with this myself. Through my protective mom goggles, I see the consequences of romance (broken hearts) and sexual exploration (pregnancy and/or infections) as belonging to some far future version of the sweet kids who currently live in my house.

Even though I worked as an HIV/AIDS educator and spoke to thousands of people about safe sex, it's totally different when I need to talk to my own children. I discuss things like hookup culture, unintended pregnancy, sexually transmitted infections, and sexual assault in my classes with my students all the time, and yet when it comes to my own kids . . . it's really hard.

Having "the Talk" or Leaving It to Google

All kids need guidance from their parents on healthy sexuality and healthy relationships, especially because their ideas about what constitutes these things are still forming and are extremely open to influence. It's like anything else we do as parents—if we don't set the foundations for these issues to reflect our values and expectations, our kids will create their own standards. Often those are gleaned with (mis)information from their friends, the media, the shady kid who always sits in the back of the bus, and whatever a Google search turns up. And honestly, even with lots of communication and really good intentions, you're competing with those things anyway.

As hard as we find having talks about sexuality, our kids find it just as difficult. It's so much easier to use the relative privacy of phones, tablets, or laptops to try to get the answers by themselves. Kids use everything from chat rooms to websites to pornography to get their questions answered. As a result, they're increasingly seeing things online that they are not ready for and do not know how to put into context or perspective. This is changing how kids think about sex and relationships, shifting social norms and, for some, changing behavior.

Social Media, Sexual Norms, and Hooking Up

The Internet, social media, and smartphones have drastically changed what it means to be a kid, particularly in the already murky waters of relationships and sex. The consensus among parents is generally that EVERYTHING IS TERRIBLE NOW and we should all be very afraid. I would argue that's only half true. Stick with me, though, because the bad news comes first.

Are more kids exposed to porn at an earlier age, thanks to the Internet? Yes, and there are troubling implications for their developing sexuality. There are also worrisome trends around sexting and harassment that happen online.

I've lost count of the number of articles and blog posts characterizing today's teens as being in sexual hyperdrive, treating intercourse as recreation, switching partners all the time, all while documenting their exploits on Snapchat. Many of these articles shine a light on genuinely shocking and upsetting behaviors, including coercive and abusive relationships, assault, and the sometimes tragic aftermath. Many blame these outcomes on the toxic combination of hookup culture and the pervasive presence of technology in adolescent life.

But understanding what it all means is a complicated feat. To begin with, there isn't a consensus on exactly what a hookup is—it can refer to anything from kissing to sex without the expectation of a commitment or relationship. That being said, hooking up often occurs as a means of starting a relationship or connecting with a prospective romantic partner.

What we now call hookup culture is the landscape in which teens are having relationships. It has a profoundly gendered set of rules and consequences. Girls are subject to a damaging double standard, where their social status and reputation are tarnished while their male counterparts, engaging in the exact same behavior, are rewarded. These double standards are strictly policed and rigidly enforced, by both girls and boys, *and they are not new*. Technology and social media, however, make this landscape more complicated.

So Much More Than Hookup Culture

Our ideas about modern hookup culture don't necessarily represent the experience of all U.S. teenagers. If it were as pervasive as our fears would have us believe, we would be seeing corresponding population-level changes in health outcomes. Based on the headlines, we would expect to see a younger average age at which kids begin having sex and a greater proportion of kids being sexually active and reporting more partners. We would also probably expect more sexually transmitted infections among those aged thirteen to eighteen, as well as more unintended pregnancies, abortions, and teen births.

The truth is that none of those things are happening. U.S. teenagers are having less sex, becoming sexually active later, and having fewer partners, pregnancies, and abortions. This reality may be in stark contrast to what many parents think is happening and certainly to how teenage behavior and sexuality are portrayed in the headlines. The facts remain that today's youth are having less sex and significantly fewer partners than their parents did.

CDC YOUTH RISK BEHAVIOR SURVEY OF HIGH SCHOOL STUDENTS

	1995	2005	2015
Ever had sex	53.1%	46.8%	41.2%
Had sex before age 13	10.2%	6.2%	3.9%
Had more than 4 partners	18.7%	14.3%	11.5%

Digital Dating and Relationships Online

Teenagers are not only having less sex and waiting later to have it, they are also dating less and are older when they start to date. In the United

States, rates of teen dating and relationships vary between 35 percent and 75 percent, depending on the survey. Most kids at some point in their teenage years will explore a romantic relationship. You can be certain that some part of those relationships will happen online. In a 2015 Pew Research Center study, 50 percent of teens identified social media and technology as an important part of developing a relationship.[1]

Studies show that self-disclosure, or sharing personal details about ourselves, is easier online than in person. Combined with the constant connection that so many teenagers have with their phones and their friends, digital dating often promotes a kind of accelerated closeness.

For many young people, what it means to be dating can vary wildly. It really depends on the age of the kids. For example, in middle school and early high school, *going out* can be a label that means actually very little. Some kids text each other and say hello when they pass in the hallway at school, and that's pretty much it. Others spend time outside of school or find ways to be together as much as they can. Once teens start driving, things shift and become more serious, mirroring increases in maturity, social experience, and independence.

Kids use social media as a way to find out more about the person they like and as a means of showing their affection. They may friend or follow someone, or like or comment on their posts as a way of showing their feelings. Everything is significant and carefully scrutinized in this mode of communication. Your choice of emoji apparently can be really important. How many posts you respond to and the types of comments you leave are all subject to unwritten rules that vary based on the platform.

One teenage girl I spoke with told me that "when you're texting your crush, you're also texting a group chat of your best friends about it at the same time. They help you analyze whether their replaying your Snap means anything, find out if the crush is single, find out about their exes, brainstorm opportunities for you to flirt, check out their Instagram, all kinds of stuff. I know it sounds kind of creepy, but that's really what we do now. I mean, I texted my crush a heart emoji and my group chat freaked out and were like, BUT WHAT COLOR WAS IT? Apparently a green or blue heart is much less flirtatious than a pink one. This skill set, to analyze all this stuff—it's like teenage-girl science."

Most teens in a relationship text or connect on social media daily, often multiple times a day. According to Pew, 85 percent of teenagers who are dating expect to hear from their partner daily and 11 percent expect to hear hourly. Thirty-eight percent felt that their partner expected to hear from them at least every few hours. That's pretty significant and speaks specifically to John's story about his relationship.

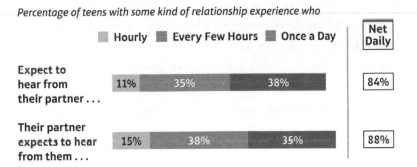

TEEN DATERS USUALLY HAVE SIMILAR COMMUNICATION EXPECTATIONS AS THEIR SIGNIFICANT OTHER

Percentage of teens with some kind of relationship experience who

	Hourly	Every Few Hours	Once a Day	Net Daily
Expect to hear from their partner . . .	11%	35%	38%	84%
Their partner expects to hear from them . . .	15%	38%	35%	88%

Source: Pew Research Center Teens Relationship Survey, Sept. 25–Oct. 9, 2014 and Feb. 10–March 16, 2015 (361 teens ages 13 to 17 who have ever been in some kind of romantic relationship)

Many teens observed that technology is great for keeping them connected but then expressed how that constant connection can also be a source of frustration and hurt. Teens described seeing their significant other online or on social media, interacting with other people or posting content—but failing to text them back. All that connection and surveillance can easily lead to jealousy and arguments. Kids have nearly constant access to one another and to what the other person in their relationship is doing. This leads to some very real issues with boundaries.

One teen I spoke with told me that "text-back culture is *really* intense. Often you're not supposed to text someone back immediately, because that makes it look like you were waiting for them to talk to you, even if you were really just doing something else on your phone and don't want to forget about the message. I've seen people set timers because someone didn't text back for forty minutes, so they're waiting forty minutes too. This is intensified on Snapchat, since you can see when they first read your message, and you don't know what kind of conversation you're dealing with till you open it."

And of course the nature of digital dating is that much of what used to happen privately in terms of communication is now happening in essentially a public space. When arguments happen or tempers flare, it often happens on social media, where it can be observed or commented on by peers and classmates.

Breaking up in the age of digital dating is (as it always was) hard to do. Many young people take the easy way out and use technology to end it the same way they started it—with a text message. According to a 2015 Pew Research Center study, 31 percent of teens report being dumped via text, although the most common way of getting the bad news is in person (47 percent).[2]

After a breakup, many teens end up blocking their former partner, or deleting or untagging pictures. All that constant connection during a relationship can make a breakup feel extra significant and extra lonely. And of course if kids are still connected to their ex on social media, they see all the things they're up to and who they're spending time with. This can make it really hard to move on. According to Pew, one positive component of social media is that 63 percent of teens said that their friends used it as a way to support them and make them feel better once news of a breakup became public.[3]

Unhealthy Aspects of Digital Dating

Some aspects of dating in the age of cell phones and social media can be unhealthy. Much of these start and end with constant contact and monitoring of each other's behavior. There's no consistent definition of what constitutes problematic digital dating behavior, but some of the issues identified in the research are:

- Constant online monitoring combined with possessive behavior
- Threatening to or sharing embarrassing or private material without permission
- Posting abusive, humiliating, or untrue rumors about a partner online
- Demanding passwords or access to accounts
- Looking through a partner's emails, texts, and so forth without permission
- Limiting access to friends and family
- Coercive or aggressive online behavior
- Pressuring to sext or sending unsolicited sexts

- Using texts or social media to coerce a partner into having sex or sexual activities

- Threatening a partner or sending threatening messages

Digital dating abuse (DDA) and harassment are fairly common but hard to quantify. Various studies have found victimization rates range from 12 percent to 56 percent of all teens. Part of the problem are young people's perceptions (or perhaps their misperceptions) of what is and isn't healthy and acceptable behavior. Clearly, aggressive or threatening behavior, sexual coercion, and publicly compromising a partner are unacceptable—and often illegal—forms of behavior.

Where it gets tricky is when it comes to issues around boundaries. Unhealthy digital behavior and how it's perceived can play out in a gendered way. Boys are more likely to report being digitally monitored by their female partners, while girls are more likely to report direct digital aggression and higher degrees of distress. Some studies have shown that girls perceive more frequent contact as a show of caring, as opposed to an intrusion.

There's a somewhat unclear continuum of behavior that the research shows on the context of teens and digital dating—the notion of good/attentive/frequent contact exists simultaneously with bad/possessive/frequent contact. One person's jealous and controlling is another person's protective and caring. The perception of where these things fall on that continuum depends on the person and the nature of the relationship, but it's a troubling and slippery slope.

Behavior that I might consider very intrusive and controlling (hourly check-ins, for example) may be perceived by a teenager as totally normal and conforming to the behavioral standards of their peer group. We're also talking about kids who may have little experience in these

A SMALL SHARE OF TEENS HAVE EXPERIENCED CONTROLLING OR HARMFUL BEHAVIORS FROM A CURRENT OR FORMER ROMANTIC PARTNER

Percentage of teens with dating experience who have experienced the following from a current or former romantic partner

Checked up with you multiple times per day on the Internet or on your cell phone, asking where you are, who you're with, or what you're doing	31%
Called you names, put you down, or said really mean things to you on the Internet or on your cell phone	22%
Read your text messages without your permission	21%
Made you remove former girlfriends or boyfriends from your friends list on Facebook, Twitter, or other social media such as Tumblr	16%
Used the Internet or text messages to try to pressure you into sexual activity you didn't want to have	15%
Spread rumors about you on the Internet or on a cell phone	15%
Demanded to know the passwords to your e-mail and Internet accounts	13%
Contacted you on the Internet or on your cell phone to threaten to hurt you	11%
Used information posted on the Internet against you, to harass or embarrass you	8%

Source: Pew Research Center Teens Relationships Survey, Sept. 25–Oct. 9, 2014 and Feb. 10–March 16, 2015 (361 teens ages 13 to 17 who have ever been in some kind of romantic relationship)

matters except for what they see in their friend groups, on social media, and in more traditional forms of media. In short, they don't always know what they're doing. This is an additional reason for parents to discuss these things—both those that are clearly abusive and wrong, as well as the areas where the lines are somewhat blurrier.

When a Kid Posts Sexy Selfies

The research shows that about 24 percent of teens post some sort of sexual reference or self-representation, with a larger proportion of these being older teens.[4] The posts sometimes come as a surprise to parents, whose perceptions of their kids don't match what they're seeing in their online personas. When teens, especially younger ones, start to post sexy selfies or references to hooking up, going out, and being in relationships, it can be a cause for alarm. Any kind of overly sexualized behavior from a young teen should be viewed as a risk factor or a red flag.

To a certain degree, we all did this pre-Internet, when we experimented with outfits our moms may not have approved of, or wore too much makeup and inadvertently looked like members of KISS. The key is to try to understand when these public presentations of newly emerging sexual or romantic identity are indicators of unsafe activity or just a normal part of growth and maturation.

Some studies have shown that kids who post sexy selfies or references to sex are not actually more likely to be having it, at least not right now. They do report having higher rates of intention to have sex, meaning that these displays are possibly their way of preparing themselves (and their peer group) to potentially become sexually active in the future. The behavioral data is pretty clear: intention predicts behavior. When you start to see cues that intention is shifting, be on the lookout for changing behavior.

What Does This Mean for Parents?

Kids are more likely to post sexy selfies when those images reflect how they feel at that time or how they want to feel in the future. These displays are happening when kids are really susceptible to peer influence and very likely to feel the urge to adopt what they perceive is normal among their friends. Looking at not just what your kid is sharing but also at the social space in which they find themselves is really important. That means we need to observe more than what our kids post; we also need to check in on what is appearing in their social feeds.

Having conversations about this is also critical. Kids who perceive a degree of approval for displays of sexual content are more likely to approve themselves, which impacts intention and ultimately behavior. Depending on the age and maturity of your teenager, that could be either perfectly appropriate or deeply disturbing. Kids who sense that their parents or the community approves of sexual or romantic displays also experience the same positive, accepting shifts toward engaging in those behaviors.

It may also be important to discuss the very gendered response that these types of public sharing can elicit. What is considered appropriate for girls and what kinds of reactions do they receive? Is it different for boys? What about the expectations and pressure girls and boys receive in the types of things they post and share?

Another important thing to point out is that even if a kid isn't interested in having sex or dating or anything, presenting oneself publicly in a sexual way may create that impression of sexual availability. Others may perceive it to be true, even if it's not. As long as there is an awareness of this possibility, no matter how unfair it may be, at least a young person can be prepared for some of the feedback. It may also conform with what they're seeing from their friends, further shifting limits of what's considered normal toward more sexualized content.

Sexual Risk Behavior and How It Plays Out Online

Sexual curiosity peaks in our teenage years, and unfortunately, most kids are now pretty consistent in where they go to find their answers—the Internet. Questions about sex and sexuality are perfectly normal. Looking to the Internet to explore answers and do research is also perfectly normal. Put the two things together? Dear God, get me an antacid.

Some examples of online sexual risk behaviors that the research has identified include searching for opportunities to talk about sex online, seeking sexual partners, sending or requesting explicit images or videos (sexting), or exchanging personal information such as phone numbers and addresses with strangers. If young people perceive that others (particularly their peers) are doing these things without consequence, or if these behaviors are framed as fun or cool, they are more likely to engage in them.

PROPORTIONS OF MALE AND FEMALE ADOLESCENTS WHO REPORTED LIFETIME PARTICIPATION IN ONLINE SEXUAL ACTIVITIES

	Male Adolescents (%)	Female Adolescents (%)	All (%)
Viewed Internet pornography	84.4	46.4	59.1
Received nude or seminude photograph	38.9	23.5	28.6
Sent nude or seminude photograph	14.4	13.4	13.8
Talked about sex online	41.1	41.3	41.2
Talked about sex online with a stranger	11.1	10.1	10.4

Source: L. F. O'Sullivan, "Linking Online Sexual Activities to Health Outcomes Among Teens," *New Directions for Child and Adolescent Development* 144, (2014): 37–51.

Teenagers are not stupid; they know these actions involve risk and can be dangerous. However, this is also the stage at which most young people feel a sense of invincibility. Remember the Personal Fable? Despite being aware of the risks inherent in doing these things, many kids will do it anyway, believing that the consequences that could likely befall everyone else could never happen to them. Research has shown a connection between Personal Fable, perceived invulnerability, and sexual risk-taking online.

Sexting

Most adults, particularly parents, see this issue of teen sexting as somewhat panic-inducing. One mistake, one time, and a kid's entire life can change. And again, the headlines are not helping with our anxiety about this. There are stories about nude pictures going viral, leading to bullying, social ostracism, and suicide. And then there are also the ones featuring bewildered fourteen-year-old boys facing criminal charges for child pornography and the possibility of being a registered sex offender for the rest of their lives.

While sexting is increasingly seen by medical professionals and researchers as a normal part of sexual development for those coming of age in the post-smartphone era, it's still pretty hard for parents to perceive it in that context, given the potentially serious and long-term consequences that could result from it.

It is really important to discuss sexting with our kids. The issue extends beyond educating them on the moral or legal considerations to talking to them about the pressure both boys and girls feel to comply with things they know aren't a good idea. Most kids know that sexting is risky and illegal, and yet some do it anyway. Successful prevention may have more to do with teaching our kids how to withstand pressure from other kids, including their friends and (potential) romantic partners.

Why Do Kids Sext?

The most common reason that teens give for sexting is that they think it's romantic and/or they are in a relationship.[5] Multiple studies support that finding, and show that teens who sext are usually either in a relationship or hope to be, indicating that many teens use sexting as a way to gain romantic attention from someone they are interested in. Others sext as a way of experimenting with their emerging sexual identity, while still others do it as a prank or joke. Worthy of mention is the fact that when youth appeared in or created images, 31 percent included a component like drugs or alcohol, according to the most recent Youth Internet Safety Survey (YISS-3).

Kids who have trouble with emotional regulation and impulsivity may be more likely to sext or share things that either present risky behaviors or expose them to risks. They may be more vulnerable to the disinhibition effect of being online. Kids are often rewarded for increasingly bolder and more sexual content online, and when they receive social rewards or validation for doing so, it can create a feedback cycle where they're inclined to do it more often.

How Many Kids Are Actually Sexting?

The data on sexting, when you delve into it, is somewhat reassuring—at least in comparison with the news stories we see so often. Many of the studies that have generated the most salacious and click-worthy headlines have not differentiated between sexting naked or semi-naked photos versus revealing images that do not include nudity or strictly text messages (with no images) that include sexual content. Many also do not differentiate between receiving these messages and sending them or creating them.

I would argue that there's a huge difference between receiving an unsolicited dirty picture and creating one and sending it out. I would also argue that there's a big difference between sending a text-only explicit message and sharing a nude photo. When you see statistics about teen sexting, particularly in studies that feature kids in late adolescence that purport that half of America's youth are sexting, take those numbers with a grain of salt.

A recent study from the American Academy of Pediatrics showed that 15 to 28 percent of teenagers, with much higher proportions of college-age young people, engage in this behavior. So like sex itself, the rates increase with age. The most recent YISS-3 showed 9.6 percent of respondents (ages ten to seventeen) had participated in some sort of sexting that involved sharing images. Only 2.5 percent had either appeared in or created the image that was shared. According to the YISS, 61 percent of those were girls and 72 percent were ages sixteen to seventeen. That means that 97.5 percent of young people are not taking or sending naked pictures of themselves. I hope that helps you feel better.

According to the YISS-3, about 28 percent of the young people who sent or received explicit images told an adult. In most cases, the person responsible for the image (creating it or sending it) was someone the teen knew in person and someone who was under eighteen. The percentage of kids who forwarded or shared images was also fairly small: only 3 percent when a teen received an image and about 10 percent when the teen was the one who appeared in or created the image themselves. Boys are more likely to request pictures or sexts, and girls are more likely to receive those requests.

What Does the Data Say About Sexting and Teens' Sexual Activity?

If you find evidence of sexting, it doesn't mean that your teenager is necessarily having sex, but it's an obvious red flag and should be a cause for concern. The crux of the link between sexting and sexual activity comes down to one thing—being passive or active. Active sexting is seeking out explicit images by requesting them from other people or by creating them or sharing them with others. Passive sexting refers to when a teen receives an image or a request for an image. It is active, rather than passive, sexting that is positively associated with being sexually active and with other risk behaviors.

As with posting sexy selfies, sexting may not tell us if a teen is actually having sex, but it usually signals a shift in intentions about becoming sexually active. So it may be more accurate to say that just because a kid is caught sexting, it doesn't mean they're having sex right now, but it's an important predictor of future behavior.

As with other risk behaviors, teens who perceive an acceptance of sexual activity (including sexting) among their peers are more likely to engage in the behaviors. They may also then seek out this acceptance and attempt to socially normalize it. There's still a lot of shame involved with this stuff, with girls facing more social consequences than boys, so it makes sense that those who are doing it may be looking for social validation that their behavior conforms to normal standards.

There are different types of active sexting, and some are clearly more problematic than others. Some represent questionable judgment, while others, motivated by malice, are crimes. Coercive sexting, secondary sexting (nonconsensual forwarding or sharing of images or video), taking photos or video during an assault, revenge porn, and sextortion are all examples of how this behavior can be criminal.

SEXTING AND LEGAL CONSEQUENCES

There are no clear-cut laws on how sexting cases are handled. By the end of 2017, only about twenty-five states had laws about it. If a state doesn't have statutes that deal specifically with sexting, then if charges are filed (not a certainty) against a minor, the charges will likely be centered on existing laws pertaining to the creation and distribution of child pornography. Those charges are generally felony sex offenses, which require registration on the national sex offender registry for life. States that have enacted sexting laws generally do so to address the fact that consensual sexting and child pornography are not the same type of offense.

In states where there are no sexting laws, prosecutors may choose to proceed in a variety of ways. Many will decline to prosecute, but some will move forward. In a national study of prosecutors who have tried sexting cases, four main factors explained why a minor might be prosecuted for a sexting charge:

- 36%—If there was an element of malicious intent, bullying, coercion, or harassment
- 25%—When the images or video were distributed, particularly if the minor had been warned to stop distribution but had continued
- 22%—If a large age difference existed between the offender and the victim, or if the victim was very young (under twelve)
- 9%—If the nature of the images was extremely graphic or included violence, including images taken during an assault[6]

Teenagers and Online Porn

The Internet is, frankly, filled with pornography. I was surprised (and horrified) to learn that some estimates are that 4 to 12 percent of the

Internet is comprised of sexually explicit websites. Up to 59 percent of teens ages thirteen to seventeen report having viewed porn on the Internet, though this includes both kids who have sought it out and kids who accidentally stumbled upon it.[7] According to the American Academy of Pediatrics, the number of kids who report "unwanted exposure" to pornography is increasing over time commensurately with the rates of online use.

The research refers to online porn as sexually explicit Internet material (SEIM). Boys are more likely than girls to be exposed to this material. Seeking out and watching porn online increases the likelihood that a teen will approve of sexual behavior, perceive that their peers approve of it, and shift their intentions toward becoming sexually active.

Multiple studies have found links between SEIM use and earlier sexual activity, increases in sexual experiences and numbers of partners, more permissive or recreational attitudes about sex, and more conventional gender role beliefs.[8] Teens who view porn are also more likely to experience decreased satisfaction with their own sexual experiences, have concerns about body image, and have earlier and "more advanced" sexual experiences.[9]

Content analysis of pornographic materials have found that they present a skewed perspective on sexuality, one in which women are frequently objectified and dominated by men, and where sex is consequence-free and casual. For teenagers who are sexually curious and naive, these ideas can easily be perceived as normal. Exposure to SEIM becomes more frequent and socially normal as teens get older, with 70 percent of college men and 30 percent of college women reporting consumption of this material. One study of college-age men and women found that many of them use porn as a resource to learn more about sex. Most noted that it wasn't ideal but stated it was a "singular, nonjudgmental sexual resource in an environment that young adults found to be devoid of alternatives."[10]

LGBTQ Teens

The Internet is really important for kids who are sexual minorities, particularly those who lack social support and community. All kids tend to go online to seek answers to questions, formulate their identity, and facilitate connections with peers, but lesbian, gay, bisexual, transgender, and questioning (LGBTQ) kids may have even greater need of the Internet as a resource for doing that. The Internet can represent a lifeline for some young people. Unfortunately, the very thing that offers hope and information for kids exploring their sexuality online can also represent significant risk.

Many of the things we consider to be online sexual risk behaviors are more commonly occurring among LGBTQ teens. This population of young people is also more likely to go online to get basic health and sexual health questions answered, especially since this is often left out of school-based curricula. Given the stigma and safety concerns many people in this community face, they are more likely to search the web for places to talk about sex or to seek a romantic partner. Educating our kids about safe spaces online to get questions answered is critical, but especially for our LGBTQ kids. It's also important for straight kids who identify as allies, given that teens are more likely to go to a friend for help than a parent or other adult.

Takeaways . . .

- Talk to your teens about appropriate boundaries within a relationship and how much communication or contact might be too much. Figure out what they're comfortable with and what pressure they might be feeling.

- Get a sense of what's normal in terms of dating for your kid's friend group. Talk to your children, their friends, and other parents. Figure out what you're comfortable with and what your kid's expectations are.

- Encourage kids to talk off-line, to get to know each other in person. Provide opportunities for them to spend time together in fun and age-appropriate ways.

- Practice working through examples of what your kids should say in situations that might make them feel uncomfortable.
  - It's pretty easy to say no to someone who is a jerk or a stranger; it's much harder to say no to someone you really like.
  - Offer up practice scenarios to respond to. A male friend texts a girl and says he'll never speak to her again if she doesn't send him a picture. Or a female friend sends an unsolicited nude picture to a boy. How should they respond?
  - Always offer to be your kid's excuse—for example, "My mom would kill me if I did that, and she monitors my phone."

- Spend time with your kids talking about how their friends present themselves online when it comes to romance, relationships, and sex.
  - How has this changed over time? Is it different now than it was last year?
  - Who is navigating their relationship or breakup well on social media? What is it about their posts that makes them good?

- Who is posting things or sharing things that make you shake your head? What is the response to those posts? What is it about those posts that makes you shake your head?

- Red flags to look out for are when young teens post sexy or sexualized content, which may lead to or represent actual risk behavior.

- Kids who spend time online are likely to encounter sexually explicit material.
  - Conversations about explicit material need to start as soon as kids are old enough to go online and interact with content independent of their parents.
  - Understand that kids are going to encounter porn online and make sure they know they will not get in trouble for that. Encourage them to come to you and tell you when it happens so you can help them process the things they saw.
  - Talk to older kids honestly about porn and the ways it can impact relationships, body image, and satisfaction in real-life relationships.

- Talk to your kids about the emotional and physical consequences of sex. Make sure they are 100 percent clear on what your values and expectations are.

- Provide resources and identify places online where kids can safely get questions answered, without coming to you, especially if your child is LGBTQ. If your child is an ally, make sure they know these places so they can support and protect their friends.

- Make sure your kids understand the consequences of creating, requesting, or sharing explicit images or videos.
  - The research shows that kids who spend a lot of time on social media may feel more comfortable sharing things than other kids might. They may experience a degree of disinhibition about posting things, simply

because they post so often. This is yet another good reason to set limits on use, including keeping phones out of kids' bedrooms overnight.

- Whether it comes to sexting or dating, talk to kids about consent and respect. Start these conversations early and have them often.

- Most kids do not tell the adults in their lives when they encounter something creepy online. Try to stay judgment-free and calm, making yourself a safe person to talk to about sexting, porn, dating, and other things they may come across online so they will be more likely to tell you if it happens. Identify other trusted adults that your kids can contact if they don't feel comfortable talking to you.

6 | The Social Culture of Video Games

ANDRE'S STORY (AGE TWENTY-FIVE)

I grew up in a household with my mom, my stepdad, and myself. I was an only child. My stepdad was verbally abusive, and our relationship from as far back as I can remember was just really awful. At a certain point, I internalized everything he said. As a kid, I had emotional issues and I took everything that anyone said about me really seriously. I was kind of antisocial and I had trust issues, so I didn't have many friends.

When I was nine years old, I got a Nintendo 64 from my grandmother and it changed my life. Prior to getting that system, I would just listen to other kids talk about things. I was a bystander and, socially, I was on the outside. But once I got a system and started to play, I did it for hours, and all of a sudden I had something to talk about with other kids. We had a connection and something in common. I started having friends over and going to other people's houses. My friends accepted me and wanted to play with me, and it felt great because I didn't get that acceptance at home.

Gaming was my outlet as a kid, but it was more than that. It helped me overcome a really hard home life. It helped me stay out of my stepdad's way when I was home and gave me a reason to stay out of the house. It just helped me make friends and gain self-confidence. I felt like I was finally good at something. The first game I ever beat all the way through completely shifted my sense of what I could accomplish. I felt like I could actually do things, and once I knew that, my confidence grew.

And I think gaming kind of kept me safe. It helped me escape all the stuff with my stepdad, but it also kept me from getting in trouble. In my neighborhood growing up, it was pretty rough. If you were outside, there was nothing but fights or basketball. Without gaming, that's what I would have been doing, and that would not have been good for me.

It was also the immersive quality of the games. I could lose myself in them and explore different things and ways of being. I could be someone else and I could do these amazing things. I could explore whole different worlds. Games taught me how to make mistakes and they taught me strategy. They showed me different experiences and expanded my perspective and my mind. I mean, my vocabulary changed and grew. Those things were not available to me in my real life. Not at all.

I'd always had creative outlets. First it was poetry and then music. And I knew I was kind of good at it, but I never shared it with anyone because of my fear about getting feedback. I mean, the message I was getting at home was that I was worthless. The first song I ever wrote was about Gauntlet Legends—a game I was playing. It meant everything to me. And as I got older, I felt more confident and I started sharing the music and poetry I was making, and when people liked it, that gave me more confidence.

I was able to make professional connections through gaming. I was able to do shows as a young person because of those connections. Those social connections and friendships have continued ever since I started playing games, it's never stopped. I've met so many people and I'm part of a community, still. Even at twenty-five.

And the thing about gaming is that it really is a community. It's like a family. Those friends you make in the game, they're there for you. When I was in high school, I had gaming friends online help me with my homework, explain math to me, and help me with school. I wasn't getting that at home, but I got it from the gamers I was friends with. We look after each other and close ranks if someone needs us. You have genuine support. And it could be someone who lives in California or Thailand, but they're there for you.

I know it sounds crazy, but that Nintendo 64 really changed the trajectory of my life. I know a lot of people think video games are negative and they're bad for kids. But I haven't had bad experiences. It's been a really positive thing in my life, when I really needed it.

———————————

Gaming and Perspective

The sense of community among gamers is real. I know the importance of that feeling of belonging, and it can be life-changing. "Find your people!" is a kind of rallying cry among bloggers. This young man did that, and it helped him in myriad ways.

While his experiences with gaming are unique, his love for games and his ardent desire to articulate all the ways that they're good were sentiments shared by almost all the gamers I interviewed. I began to notice that people who love video games almost seem to feel a little defensive about it. It then occurred to me that my son is the same way. He loves gaming and doesn't appreciate it when I make disparaging comments about video games. If he already felt that way at twelve, I can only imagine how someone in their twenties would feel.

It reminded me of blogging. As a mommy blogger (a term that is excellent at evoking eye rolls and righteous sniffing), I'm accustomed to people belittling what I do. They may say things that are unkind or untrue, or make generalizations based on one person or one bad situation. Sometimes criticisms feel personal, even when they're not intended to be. I get defensive and shut myself off to the people who are critical of something I really care about and have a lot invested in. Something that they've never taken the time to really understand.

I realized that's what I had done to my kid with video games. His games aren't my favorite. Playing them makes me feel really nervous and stressed out. But he accepts the stuff I like with very little judgment,

MIXED FEELINGS, UNCERTAINTY AMONG GENERAL PUBLIC ABOUT VIDEO GAMES

Percentage of all adults who think the following qualities . . .

	true for most games	true for some games	not true for most games	unsure

	true for most games	true for some games	not true for most games	unsure
Are a waste of time	26%	33%	24%	16%
Help develop good problem-solving skills	17%	47%	16%	20%
Promote teamwork and communication	10%	37%	23%	28%
Are a better form of entertainment than TV	11%	34%	30%	24%

Source: Pew Research Center survey conducted June 10–July 12, 2015

and as far as gaming was concerned, I wasn't returning the favor. As a result, I had shut down conversations before they started. I had also made it a lot less likely that he would come to me if anything upsetting happened while he was playing.

Parents and Video Games

To say that parents are worried about video games is an understatement. While some are supportive and may play themselves, many parents have serious concerns about it. These range from the idea that it's all just a huge waste of time to the idea that video games, particularly violent ones, are harmful. There's also a fairly common misconception that a gamer looks like a solitary dude in his late teens, playing in his parents' basement, cut off from the rest of the world.

Plenty of research indicates that there are positive benefits to be gained from gaming. Whether it's a waste of time depends in large part on the balance of other activities that exist in that gamer's life. Can people game too much? Absolutely, but I would like to point out that problematic use of technology is not just found among gamers but among almost every segment of the population. Walk down the street or look around at a local restaurant—everyone is on their phones. Yet we consider gaming to be a worse way to kill time than, say, watching TV, checking Facebook or Twitter, or playing Words with Friends.

Oh hey, wait. Words with Friends is an electronic game. So are Candy Crush and Angry Birds and a whole slew of other social and puzzle games that millions of adults play on a daily basis. This raises two important questions: What do we actually consider a video game? And who is playing them? The truth is that most gamers are not that solitary, and they're not just teenage boys.

Who Really Plays Video Games?

According to 2017 market data, adolescent boys account for only 18 percent of those who play video games. The average male gamer is actually thirty-three years old and the average female gamer is thirty-seven. According to the same industry data, 41 percent of people who play video games are women (this measure includes all games, such as mobile games like Words with Friends, Candy Crush, and FarmVille). Since 65 percent of U.S. households are home to someone who plays three or more hours a week, it's safe to say they're not all teenage basement dwellers.[1]

As to the notion that gamers are solitary, this is simply not supported by what we know about how electronic games are currently played. Most kids are playing with their friends, either online or in person. Almost all of the top-selling games for the past three years have been multiplayer, meaning that even if a kid is alone in his parents' basement, he's still hanging out with his friends as he plays. The perception that kids who play video games are lonely and antisocial is not really true, because for many, the primary draw of these games is the social nature of play.

Video Games and Being Twelve

A couple of years ago I overheard my sixth grader playing Destiny on the Xbox with his friends, all of whom lived in our neighborhood. They were laughing, joking, and yelling at one another, flushed with the exhilaration of the game. I remembered these same kids, a year before, running through my front yard, shooting each other with Nerf guns, and creating the same loud, happy cacophony. I looked outside and sighed. The days of Nerf gun battles were over. The Xbox years had begun.

I saw clearly that video games had displaced all that wonderful running around the neighborhood. I also recognized that finding free time to play with friends, all of whom were incredibly busy, was becoming almost impossible. The boys had also reached a point where it felt awkward and maybe a little embarrassing to have scheduled play. They wanted to hang out, but they wanted their privacy. So more and more they played together online, away from their parents and the expectations of grown-ups.

For some of them, it was the first time they'd ever had that kind of sustained interaction with their peers that was completely free from adult observation and intervention. They got into fights and they worked it out. Friendships formed, evolved, and fell apart. They won and lost, got frustrated and pushed past it. When I realized this, I knew I needed to reevaluate the role that video gaming played in the lives of kids.

Video Games and the Social Lives of Teens

According to a 2015 Pew Research Center report, gaming is a critical component of teenage boys' social lives, playing a role that is the equivalent of social media in their female counterparts' lives. As is true with Instagram or Snapchat, gaming can be an opportunity to connect with people and reinforce those connections. It becomes the means by which communication takes place and the mode of spending time together. Eighty-four percent of boys say they feel more connected to their friends because of video games. About half of all teenage boys play video games with their friends on an almost daily basis, either online or in person. Among boys, 38 percent share their gaming handle as their primary contact information, making them five times more likely than girls to do so.

Kids who play these games frequently are also more likely to make new friends online. Seventy-four percent of kids who play online daily have made friends that way, and 37 percent have made more than five friends through online gameplay.[2] While building social capital and making new friends are generally pretty positive activities for a teenager, gaming also raises concerns about interacting with strangers online.

Safety in Video Games

The most popular games that teens play are generally online and multiplayer, meaning that they will be playing with both friends and strangers alike. While chatting or direct messaging with strangers has been identified as an online risk behavior, it's also very common for a lot of young gamers.

Chat or direct message features within games, including massively multiplayer online role-playing games (MMORPGs), can be another source of risk. Again, interacting with other players is normal gaming behavior, particularly for games where cooperative play helps win missions or level up characters. MMORPGs are incredibly popular and are usually played on PCs. World of Warcraft, Clash of Clans, and Roblox are online games where millions of players interact with one another within the context of virtual worlds. Many of these games are known for being fairly gender-neutral spaces, where it's not unusual for boys and girls, men and women, to all play together.

There have been cases, many of which have received significant press coverage, where younger players have been harassed, stalked, or sexually solicited via the chat functions of these games. As a result of one such case, in 2012 New York state attorney general Eric Schneiderman deployed Operation Game Over, coordinating with Microsoft, Sony, Disney Interactive Media Group, Electronic Arts, and other gaming companies to shut down the accounts of more than 3,500 registered sex offenders in New York. In fact, the personal story that sets the stage for chapter 9 (about safety, predators, harassment, and bullying) is all about how a young girl encountered a predator while playing an MMORPG.

While this is scary stuff, it's important to note that there are relatively few such cases compared to the large number of American households playing video games every week (65 percent, to be exact). While the risk of encountering a predator online is real, the risk is relatively small. In order to minimize risk, families can use parental controls, set up appropriate "child" accounts via consoles like PS4 and Xbox, monitor gameplay and communications, and become familiar with the games their kids are playing—not just to make sure the content is appropriate but also to get a better understanding of how communication is happening with other players and if it's required for a good gaming experience.

KIDS WATCHING OTHER KIDS PLAYING VIDEO GAMES

Many parents see their kids spending hours and hours watching other people play video games on YouTube or Twitch (a livestream platform for gamers, owned by Amazon, that as of 2017 had 45 million users). A lot of parents really don't get it. Actually playing a game? *That* they might understand. But wasting hours watching other people play? That makes less sense.

I spoke with industry veteran James Casey, who teaches video game design at George Mason University, and he says that watching other people play is a logical choice. "If you look at the major sports out there today, how many people watch football religiously every week? People watch the draft and all these other things that are ancillary to the sport. And they don't actually play it themselves. Watching video games being played is the same thing; you enjoy seeing somebody do well at something you're familiar with. If you ask someone why they watch football, they'll say, 'Well, it's fun! It's exciting to see,' and I would respond that kids are getting that same kind of enjoyment out of watching gamers compete."

When kids watch other people play video games, it may seem passive, and of course, compared to playing, it is. But there are other things going on. There's observational learning of a higher level of play. Tips and strategies are being inferred and actions being anticipated. There are also communities that form around this. For every gamer who has thousands of subscribers, there is a community of those subscribers who connect and identify with one another.

Video gaming as a spectator sport is not going anywhere. In fact, 2017 market data shows that professional competitive gaming, called esports, is growing by 40 percent per year.[3]

Esport championships are now routinely broadcast on television, and networks like Disney XD are investing in producing blocks of content specifically for gamers, including a thirty-minute show starring successful YouTuber Parker Coppins, who spends that time cracking jokes and making commentary while playing video games. Between the growth of esports, the success of Twitch, and the movement to broadcast video gaming on TV, watching other people play may just be the next logical step in the evolution of video gaming.

Video Games and Gender

Data from the Gamer Motivation Profile, a large national survey of people who self-identify as gamers (i.e., not of the general public), shows that only about 18.5 percent of hard-core gamers are women. Among core gamers, gender plays a role in what and how people play games. In the Gamer Motivation Profile survey, women were more likely to play games like the Sims and Match 3 puzzle games. This seems pretty consistent with what the young adult gamers I interviewed described. As we talked, one of them scrolled through Twitch, seeing who was playing what, and pointed out which games were popular and which weren't. While doing so, he noted the ones he perceived as being "more for girls."

He described games like the Sims as ones that girls and women would often play but that guys would mostly avoid. He told me, "Some video games are considered girl games, and guys would really never play them. Other games are considered guy games, and when girls play them, it's fine but . . . It would be like a girl playing baseball in high school. She's welcome to try out, but she better be good. And if she makes the team, that's great, but she needs to be aware of the fact that when she walks into the dugout, she's probably going to be the only girl there. The environment is going to reflect the fact that it's mostly guys. The language, how people talk to each other—it's all based on dudes interacting with other dudes. That's kind of the culture of it. Some games like League of Legends and Overwatch are pretty gender neutral, and everyone plays. I really like those games. Though there are roles within those games that most guys avoid. Like if a guy played a support in Overwatch, he would totally be mocked for it."

This is actually a really concise evaluation of how gender often plays out in gaming, even for girls who identify as core gamers, and is supported by the research. One study found that girls who favor first-person shooter games tend to be more confident and have higher self-esteem.[4] Developmentally, girls tend to be more open to identifying with masculine traits in gameplay by early adolescence, but boys do not increase their identification with feminine characteristics in the same way.[5]

Experiences of Female Gamers

Video games, particularly action games and first-person shooter games, historically tend to feature more male characters and to oversexualize female characters. This trend appears to be changing, as more women play and as the industry responds to widespread bad press. There's been a lot of coverage in the media about the way women are treated (and sometimes targeted) in video game culture—including a series of incidents collectively referred to as Gamergate, in which death and rape threats were directed toward women working in the video game industry. It brought to light a deeply misogynist subculture within the gaming community.

After interviewing female gamers, reading essays and first-person accounts, and reviewing countless Reddit threads where female gamers discuss their best and worst experiences, I found that women who play video games are well aware that depending on what they play, they may be in a space largely dominated by men.

One overwhelming theme in the accounts of women and girls is their love for the games themselves. Like other gamers, they seemed protective of what they loved and reassured me that gaming really is for everyone. Several of them were also adamant that in their experiences, the media's reports of gender-based harassment were overblown. And even those who may have had a negative experience or two weren't going anywhere.

PARENTS SHOULD PLAY VIDEO GAMES WITH THEIR KIDS

Some studies have shown that when parents co-play video games with their kids, it can improve their relationships. Dr. Christopher Ferguson, who teaches and researches the psychology of video games at Stetson University and is a coauthor of *Moral Combat: Why the War on Violent Video Games Is Wrong*, suggests that parents play with their kids for a variety of reasons that benefit everyone.

"First, it's good social time to spend with your kids. It demonstrates that you're getting to understand their hobby and showing them you're interested in them, even if video games really aren't your thing. You're also becoming informed and learning about what your child is doing, seeing how the games and the technology work. Maybe you'll see something you don't like, in which case you will have a lot more credibility in setting limits or ruling that something is not appropriate. You may also find that you're reassured by what you see." Ferguson says that parents should pause before restricting media or making judgment calls about media that they don't take the time to understand. It's better to come from a place of being informed.

Trash-Talking and Bullying

One manner of communication that is ubiquitous in the world of gaming is trash talk. Some kids think it's hilarious and fun and don't take it seriously. Others find it hard to take. Most see the trash-talking as part of the culture. Some games, and some genres of games, are worse than others, where the trash-talking and language can border on abusive.

Depending on the sensitivity of the player, trash-talking can ruin the experience. I interviewed several young adult gamers who work in the industry. Their perceptions of trash-talking reflected their many years of playing. One of them told me, "It can get really bad, but you can't take it seriously. You hear things like 'Kill yourself'; 'Go drink bleach'; 'Your mother should have swallowed you.' I mean, those are *normal* comments in some games. You would hear that every day."

What that gamer found to be normal, I found to be pretty darn upsetting. It raises concerns about younger kids hearing these things, especially if the comments are directed toward them, and not knowing how to handle it. Depending on the games your kids decide to play, it may be worth becoming familiar with the norms of the games they're playing and how likely it is for them to encounter this. When I mentioned this to some middle schoolers I know, I asked them if those types of comments were fairly common, and one boy's response was to say,

"Where? In games? Yeah. But, like, also in the cafeteria." Hearing a statement like "Go kill yourself," which most of us would find pretty horrifying, is an increasingly normal experience for many young people, whether they are gamers or not.

Sometimes the trash-talking is a strategy. It can put players off their stride, causing them to lose momentum, react emotionally, and make mistakes. This is called *tilting*. It's not unlike catchers in baseball, muttering things to players at bat to distract them while they're trying to get a hit. The experienced gamers I talked to explained that it's just how things work—another tactic people use to win, and one more thing you quickly learn not to take personally.

That being said, there's a difference between players flaming or trolling each other (being jerks) and a pattern of repeated harassment, especially when multiple players are attacking one person, if the victim is known to be young, or if the nature of the harassment is racially or sexually motivated. A 2017 study conducted by an anti-bullying organization called Ditch the Label found that 57 percent of young people had experienced bullying when playing games and 22 percent had stopped playing a particular game as a result.

This bullying can happen with strangers, but as with other forms of cyberbullying, it is more likely to happen with people the victim knows in real life and to carry over into their real lives. Gaming is so closely tied to the social lives of teens that relational aggression is inevitably going to be part of the social experience of gaming. When friends are fighting in real life, their gameplay is likely to be acrimonious. When kids are feeling socially excluded by their friend group and the group plays together online, that exclusion will carry over. This is very similar to the experience that many young people have when they find themselves bullied over social media by classmates or former friends.

Games and Aggression

One major concern parents have about gaming is the violent nature of many of the games and the influence that this may have on kids. These concerns led to calls for research, some of which indicated that there were associations between violent video games and aggression and anti-social behavior, as well as reductions in academic performance and empathy. This led to legislation in California to ban the sale of violent video games to young children. The law was contested by the gaming industry and ended up before the Supreme Court (*Brown v. Entertainment Merchants Association* in 2011), where the high court struck down the law. The court, in examining the law's constitutionality, found fault with some of the underlying research that linked negative outcomes to video games, stating, "These studies have been rejected by every court to consider them, and with good reason."[6]

The Supreme Court was not the only authority to question the existing research on the impact of video games. According to a 2015 study on video games and aggression: "In 2005, the American Psychological Association (APA) released a policy statement implicating links between violent video use and subsequent player aggression. By 2010, the APA appeared to have qualified that position, however, having declined to participate in the U.S. Supreme Court case *Brown v. EMA*, citing inconsistencies in the literature."[7]

This study also points out that if video games were as harmful as many parents have been led to believe, we would have expected to see increases in youth crime commensurate with the growth of the video game market since the mid-1980s. However, youth crime, according to the Justice Department, is at a forty-year low.

NUMBER OF SERIOUS VIOLENT CRIMES COMMITTED BY YOUTH BETWEEN AGES 12 AND 17 YEARS IN THE UNITED STATES FROM 1980 TO 2015 (PER 1,000 YOUTHS)

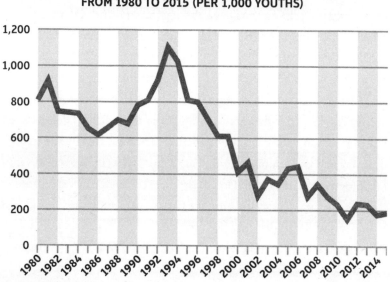

Source: U.S. Department of Justice, Bureau of Justice Statistics (https://www.childstats.gov/americaschildren/tables/beh5.asp)

Risk and Impacts of Video Games on Kids

Though the Supreme Court and the APA have walked back their support for the evidence that gaming can be harmful, this is not to say that video games pose no risk to kids and that they have no impact on kids' behavior. Any form of media that kids interact with consistently will have some measure of impact. To really understand how all the pieces fit together, we need to look at why our kids are playing and what is motivating them to stay with it. For some, it's about having fun and building friendship and community. For others, it's about the challenge and immersive quality of the games—possibly offering an escape from stress or problems at school or at home.

What the data does imply is that for video games, the effect is nuanced and contextual. Some children—especially those with conditions like ADHD, autism, or depression—will react differently to technology than their typically developing peers. Parents must also consider how much time their kids are spending on games. The more hours per day they play, the greater the presumed response. The research indicates that moderate users fare the best, experiencing positive outcomes associated with gameplay, while the heaviest users fare the worst.[8]

Even when video games are removed from the equation, aggression (along with risk-taking behavior) peaks during adolescence and then declines. What drives kids to play Grand Theft Auto (see what I did there?) may be a more important factor to consider than how much they play. One study found that boys with lower rates of educational success were more attracted to violent video games than their peers with higher levels of academic success, who were more likely to choose multiplayer social games. As with poor outcomes related to social media and measures of well-being, there are definitely some chicken-or-egg factors in play.

I'd also like to mention that games in general can bring out our competitive sides, and perhaps not our best behavior. Competition can lead to relational aggression. As anyone who watches professional hockey can tell you, talking trash and being aggressive are not limited to Call of Duty. I'm not proud of this behavior, but I once looked at my beautiful, beloved daughter and told her coldly, "There is no family in air hockey," and took a lot of pleasure in winning two games out of three. Aggression and trash-talking may just be a function of gameplay, and not specific to video games.

Problematic Gaming Versus Engagement in a Game

Problematic video gaming is something that almost every parent of a tech-savvy kid has encountered at some point. We will cover this and the issue of video gaming addiction in greater detail in the next chapter.

Problematic use can range from what I call the "It's time to stop playing Minecraft monster" admonition to the "Dear God, how long have you been playing that, and when was the last time you ate human food?" exclamation of horror that many teens have heard.

Problematic use and engagement in video games are not the same thing. Problematic tech use is generally defined as "an inability to control one's use of the Internet which leads to negative consequences in daily life."[9] It's very common for parents to see kids get so sucked in to their games that they become really irritable and snappish when they have to stop playing. If that happens enough, parents may conclude that their child has a problem.

However, it's absolutely possible to have a kid be intently engaged with a game, every time he plays, to the point that he is completely oblivious to the world around him. This does not mean he's addicted. He could just be hyperfocused on what he's doing and need a few minutes to transition from playing to whatever activity comes next, during which time he may be really cranky. Once his brain resets and he moves on to the next thing, he may be fine. This is not an addiction but an immature brain with low to moderate impulse control being told to stop something it enjoys doing in order to do something that is less desirable. Consider what it can be like to get a little kid to leave a playground before he's ready—same type of meltdown.

Conversely, a kid can play a game all the time and not be deeply engaged with it, and yet the nature of their play is mindless or compulsive. I found myself playing Candy Crush almost automatically, without any real awareness that I was doing it. Was I engaged in the game? Not at all. I ended up deleting it from my phone because I found that I was unable to self-regulate how often I was playing and I was losing time to it every day.

SETTING LIMITS

Setting limits around playing video games can be a really good way to prevent problematic use. The key to limits? Consistent enforcement. If you create a set of rules and then don't follow through with them or follow through only some of the time, the lines between what is okay and what isn't become fuzzy. When parents then step in and try to hold kids accountable, it may seem arbitrary or punitive. When new rules or limits are first established, you should expect pushback and testing of boundaries. That's when it's most important to be consistent.

Many of the experts I spoke with also recommended creating rules and limits collaboratively with your children. For example, you and your kids may decide to abide by guidelines such as these: "I can play only after homework is done"; "On nights when I have a game or a practice, I can't play video games." These are fair rules that prioritize schoolwork or a kid's commitment to a team. Kids may not love these restrictions, but they will understand the reasons behind them and may be likely to buy into rules they helped establish.

One study found that competitive sports reduced the risk of gaming addiction.[10] Kids who are busy and engaged with other things may just have less time to play video games. But in doing so, they're prioritizing what they want to do and setting limits on how much they're gaming. If you see your kids doing that, discuss it with them. Frame it in a positive way—say that you're proud that they're making thoughtful choices about how to allocate one of their most important resources: their time.

Research findings also indicate that kids who had gaming systems in their rooms tended to play more hours per week than kids who had to play in common areas. The study suggested that one way to limit access was to make sure kids played in shared areas of the house and not in bedrooms, where it was also more likely to impact much-needed sleep.[11]

Another study found that when parents discussed cyber-safety with their kids, those kids played video games fewer hours per week, perhaps because parents set limits as a result of safety concerns, or perhaps because kids understood and approved of the reasons why their parents were creating the rules. The same study found that good communication between parents and kids led to a decreased likelihood of risky online behavior.[12]

Are Video Games Meeting Needs?

I mentioned earlier in the chapter that young teens' need for privacy, independence, and unobserved time with their friends might be one of the reasons why they're so drawn to social video gameplay. Many kids face an incredibly competitive and high-pressure environment at school. They may feel inadequate because they failed to make a team or pass a class. Or maybe they're succeeding in school but don't derive any satisfaction from being good at algebra. Video games may be meeting this need, allowing them to achieve competency at something they enjoy that permits them to be autonomous and independent.

What are some other needs that may be met by gaming? One theory I have involves evolutionary psychology. Humans are hardwired during adolescence to take risks and are likely to display dominance behaviors, including aggression, to establish themselves within perceived hierarchies. Video gaming may represent a prosocial outlet for young humans to be aggressive, to dominate, and take risks. The social environment in which most teens find themselves often makes it really hard for them to express those very natural feelings and impulses. Gaming might actually be meeting that need in a very direct way.

Video games also teach kids one thing they desperately need to learn today—how to fail. Being a gamer means you're going to make mistakes, sometimes big ones that make you feel terrible and embarrass you in front of everyone. When that happens, gamers have a choice. They can quit or they can try again.

Games are inherently frustrating, especially as you learn to play a new one. The rules are unclear; you don't know where enemies are coming from or how to find the allies you need to accomplish your goal. And for a while, you're not very good at the game. And here you have another choice: You can quit or you can work through the frustration and apply yourself to learning how to succeed.

Gaming can instill resiliency. In order for kids to benefit more from the games they already play, they need to be made aware of their benefits. Talk to them about the lessons learned when they play games. Ask them to think about those lessons and how they can be applied to challenges and problems they face in other areas of their lives. You may need to give them the vocabulary to do this. Help them to develop a framework for thinking about gaming in a more analytical way so they're conscious of the best things gaming has to offer and can make the most of them.

Takeaways . . .

- Get familiar with family and privacy settings for gaming consoles like PlayStation and Xbox. Setting up family accounts can be time-consuming, so have your kid help you. You can talk through all the options available and make decisions together about accounts, access, and settings.

- Some ideas for setting limits:
  - Decide what the rules should be with your kid.
  - When making rules, be sure your kids understand why you feel they're important.
  - Keep gaming consoles in common areas, not bedrooms.
  - Try to attain balance between school, extracurricular activities, social time, outside or exercise time, and time spent in the digital world.
  - Be consistent in your enforcement of the rules.
  - Revisit the rules every so often, being open to change what isn't working.

- Take the time to learn about the games that your kids are playing, as well as the ones they want to play.

- Learn about the Entertainment Software Rating Board (ESRB) system. It's pretty straightforward but it's best to understand the standards that are used to classify games.

- Use Common Sense Media (the website or the app) to research games your kid is interested in. This free resource might already be on your radar, but if it's not, you will definitely thank me. They evaluate video games (and a ton of other media) for areas that may be of concern to parents, and also allow for kids and parents to add their own reviews. It's a great way to learn about a game before you buy it.

- Watch videos about the game, including a few minutes of what it's like to play the game. Often the most popular reviews of new video games are on YouTube, where players take you through some of the game. This is something you can do with your kids, both to let them know you're making a real effort to be informed and also to help them do some critical thinking about the game.

- If you're worried about safety, here are some questions you can ask to get a conversation started with your kid:

- Is it a multiplayer game?
- Are the people who play generally pretty nice?
- How do you communicate with other players on what you're doing?
- Does this game have a chat feature?
- Do you talk to other players on your headset or chat with them? If yes, are these people ever strangers?
- What would you do if someone started raging or targeting another player?
- Do people trash-talk in the game?
- How do you feel about trash talk? Does it make you uncomfortable? Do you think it's funny?

- Try playing video games with your kids. Some research indicates that it can improve family relationships, especially with girl gamers.

- When you play with your kids, one of the first things you'll figure out is that you can't pause online games. Asking a kid to pause means they will probably have to bail out of whatever they're doing. If a player bails out of enough games, their whole account can get banned. Instead of asking a kid to pause, ask them to finish what they're doing and wrap it up as soon as possible. Sometimes it might take them a few minutes, but they will appreciate that you get it, and it may help them transition from one activity to the next.

- Try to spend time observing and talking with your children about why they're into gaming and what draws them to the games they choose. Understanding the why behind the behavior, for both you and your children, can be really helpful in terms of figuring out how to set limits and what the impact of playing may be on your children overall.

- Identify lessons that specific games may be teaching your kids, like strategy, resource management, collaboration, or situational awareness. If they lack the vocabulary to describe these things, then talk them through it. Discuss how these skills can be useful in the real world and how they can be tapped when problems arise.

- If you're struggling to find some of the positive lessons in the games, then search for them on the Internet. I guarantee you that there is a message board or a blog post discussing the exact game you're researching, no matter how random it might seem.

- Video gameplay, especially at night, has been shown to interfere with sleep. Like other kinds of electronic media, games are stimulating, making it more difficult to fall asleep once you stop playing. Gaming may also simply displace sleep, as time spent playing is a trade-off for time young people could be in bed, recharging their batteries.

- If you suspect your child has a problem with gaming addiction, don't be afraid to get help, starting with your pediatrician.

HOPE'S STORY (AGE EIGHTEEN)

When I was in middle school and in high school, I was pretty rebellious. In fifth and sixth grade I could just be a kid. I wore cutoffs and sneakers and played on the playground with my friends, and it didn't matter if they were girls or boys. Then I got to middle school and it felt like a war.

All of a sudden, what you wore mattered. The type of sneakers you had mattered. Your hair should be straight. And if I hung out with boys, even the ones who had always been my friends, I was a slut. It was hell.

I was also one of the few kids in that school that didn't have a phone. I didn't get a phone until my freshman year of high school. Before that, I had an iPod. I had some social media accounts on my iPod, like Instagram and Facebook. I wasn't allowed to have a Twitter, but I went and got one behind my mom's back in eighth grade.

It was weird to have social media and have an iPod but not a phone at that age. It's like I was half in and half out of everything that was going on. I remember people asking me if I had a phone, and saying no and, like, feeling ashamed. They'd be incredulous: "What do you mean, you don't have a phone?"

Social media was still pretty new then and it was so important to be a part of it, and I saw just enough of it when I was at home on the Wi-Fi to want that. I would see what people were doing, crazy things, and I wanted to do those crazy things too. And I had to hear about it at school and it made me feel like I had to try that much harder to make up for the fact that I wasn't part of it, because I didn't have a phone.

That included doing things to be accepted that I knew I shouldn't have done. I mean, looking back on it, it was so dumb. We would go to this outside shopping center on Friday nights and we'd walk over to a wooded area where we couldn't be seen and smoke weed. To be considered cool and popular, that was the kind of thing you had to do.

People would talk about it constantly at school, those Friday nights, and there would be group chats about it. There would be private Twitters—they were a really big thing. Vape pens were another huge thing in eighth grade. I would vape in the bathroom with my friends, because if you were cool, that's what you did. They would post pictures of themselves doing it to group chats and to Twitter. Not actually vaping, but it would be clear to people who knew what was going on that they were smoking or vaping. I'd snap pictures too and share them with people so they would know I was part of it.

When we hit high school, things got . . . I guess we just did more. Like before football games, we would smoke or drink in the woods by the school. By sophomore year, the parties started, and people started going out and hooking up more.

There was so much pressure. Pressure at school telling me this is what you need to be. Pressure on the other side from my parents for me to be something I knew I wasn't. And I just pushed back against that. I always wanted to please my parents, but at the same time, I wanted to push back against their expectations and rules because they weren't always fair.

It sounds crazy. But for a while it felt like because I couldn't please my parents, it became about pleasing my friends and trying to be cool and trying to win that game. Social media was a part of it, part of how you played the game. It caused even more problems with my family—especially with pictures I posted of myself and my friends. But not being on social media wasn't really an option, so I kept doing it.

My youth pastor tried to talk to me about it. And she saw how hard I was *working to be cool and how unhappy it was making me. I was losing myself, trying to be someone I wasn't, and one day she just asked me: "Is all of this worth it to you? Are you actually happy?" It made me pause.*

I wanted things to be different, but it took me probably another year before I was ready to change things. Around the beginning of senior year, something switched for me. I was like, I have to get my life together if I want to go to college. But it wasn't until I matured a little bit, got more engaged in school, and started trying hard. I stopped doing things for the people around me and for my friends. I also deleted some of my social media accounts and stopped spending so much time on my phone.

Now that I'm at college, it's weird to look back on everything. I cared so much about being popular, and it was so destructive. Everyone was consumed by doing what other people expected of them, even when that meant partying and blowing off school and posting pictures and just being so dumb. Even when it hurt their relationships and made them really unhappy. I think maybe it's worth making mistakes when you learn from them and end up in a much better place.

Understanding Adolescent Risk Behavior

There are a handful of concerns that parents have about teenagers online that seem to always be there, ubiquitous threads running through our whispered conversations and the headlines we see. We seem to share the fear that one bad decision, made impulsively and played out online, can come to define a young person's whole life.

Our concerns about teenagers doing risky, impulsive things are actually well founded, and this behavior is certainly nothing new. In Shakespeare's *The Winter's Tale*, a shepherd says: "I would there were no age between sixteen and three-and-twenty, or that youth would sleep out the rest; for there is nothing in the between but getting wenches with child, wronging the ancientry, stealing, fighting—Hark you now! Would any but these boiled brains of nineteen and two-and-twenty hunt this weather?"

Teenagers are risk-takers. The prefrontal cortex—the part of the brain that controls planning, executive function, the ability to predict consequences and control impulses—is not fully developed until humans reach their early twenties. In every category of risk-taking behavior, teenagers are substantially overrepresented.[1]

When kids begin puberty (around twelve), they often start to become aware of the Imaginary Audience, and the phase that follows is the Personal Fable. This is the stage of adolescence characterized by a sense of invulnerability and risk-taking. So a year or so after our awkward kids get iPhones and Instagram accounts, they start to think and act differently. According to the research, all this tends to peak in eighth grade. Interestingly, this is the same period that several school administrators and educators told me was the prime time for serious problems with cell phones and social media.

Teens and Friends and Risky Choices

When I was in ninth grade, I had a best friend, and though we were both objectively smart and responsible kids, we were capable of enormous acts of stupidity when left alone together. We once paddled a canoe so far out into a lake that we got stranded and lost. My friend's father would look at us, shake his head, and say, "When you are together, one plus one does not equal two." I neither understood nor appreciated the wisdom of that statement until I became a parent myself.

It turns out there's a substantial body of research supporting this theory. When teenagers are with their friends, one plus one does not always equal two. At a time in their lives when they're most likely to be impulsive, they're even more likely to engage in risky behavior when their friends are present.

There's a famous experiment on this, conducted at Temple University.[2] Young adults ranging from their teens to their early twenties were asked to complete a driving simulation, at first alone and then with a couple of friends. Can you guess what happened?

Teenagers were markedly the worst drivers, taking more risks when their friends were with them. The college age group felt some of the same effect with their friends present, and to an even lesser degree, the adults did as well. The teenage group, however, was substantially riskier, leading the researchers to comment that the adolescent group was more likely not only to take risks around their friends but also to perceive the risks as being potentially positive. When their peers were watching, the kids shifted their thinking to focus less on the negative consequences of taking a chance and more on the potential social rewards if that risk worked out.

We discussed in earlier chapters how many of the mistakes that teens of every generation have made are now being made online, where there is (potentially) a much bigger audience and a greater sense of permanency. But consider all this again given that *their friends are always there*, right in their back pocket. When you think about the overwhelming pull they feel to share and document every aspect of their lives, is it any wonder that kids are doing dumb things online? Is it maybe a miracle that it isn't much worse? And if we're being honest with ourselves, is there a single one of us who grew up in the seventies, eighties, or early nineties who hasn't thanked their lucky stars that there were no cell phones around when we were young and stupid?

Online Risk Behavior from a Kid's Perspective

An important public health precept is looking at behavioral decision-making from the perspective of the person doing it. Let's take a hypothetical example that's increasingly common. An otherwise smart and responsible teenager shares a photo of himself smoking weed on Snapchat. This seems like an objectively dumb thing to do. Smoking marijuana is generally illegal for healthy teenagers under eighteen, and the picture could result in consequences ranging from getting kicked off a sports team to being suspended from school, fired from a job, arrested, or grounded by their angry and disapproving parents.

But this kid may see the risks and consequences differently. My social reference point for the image is one that matches my perspective— as a suburban mom who would be really upset by both the act of smoking pot and the lack of judgment inherent in making it public.

The social reference point of our hypothetical kid reflects that of his own peer group, which is one of the ways he decided if this was a risky or a safe choice. His peers might not consider the image to be controversial. They may in fact see it as completely normal, or possibly as kind of edgy and cool. Is weed considered edgy anymore? I have no idea. I drive a minivan and buy my jeans at Costco, so I'm not the person to answer that. In any case, the basis for deciding what's expected and acceptable is likely totally different for this teen than it is for me.

Social Reference Points and Risky Choices

We use social reference points (SRPs) as a comparative basis for weighing our decisions. SRPs can be divided into three categories: those that yield social loss, those that are socially neutral, and those that provide social gain. The size of the SRP is also important—the bigger it is, the more relevant it becomes to decision-making. Comparing yourself to a big group yields a more meaningful result than comparing yourself to a small group.

One study found that the social standing of the decision-maker was a key factor in making risky choices.[3] If a kid had high social standing, any decision that might lower their status, especially as compared to a big group, made the kid risk-averse. Conversely, if the kid in question had low social standing, they had less to lose by taking a risk that could improve their status in front of a large SRP. Those kids were more likely to take risks because the social benefit outweighed the potential loss.

There are a lot of lessons to be learned here in understanding why kids may be posting risky or controversial content, or why they care so much about the number of followers or likes they have. Kids feel better when they compare favorably against a large group, and much worse when they fare poorly. Increasing the size of the social reference group amplifies the good or bad feelings, the sense of gain or loss. In the complicated landscape of making choices online as a teenager, SRPs add an interesting dynamic.

Social Media and the Funhouse Mirror

When studying the effects of social media, especially on teenagers, I keep coming back to this image of a funhouse mirror. It both reflects and distorts what's really there to look completely different. Our perception of risk can also be manipulated. A lot of observational learning takes place online. When kids watch their classmates publicly post risky behavior, they're also watching for the response that this behavior receives. Do those photos get a lot of likes? Or do they get mean comments? Do they immediately get taken down? Are screenshots taken and passed around? Do there appear to be consequences for sharing them, good or bad?

If you were to see your peers consistently post about illegal behavior, with seemingly no repercussions, your perspective on how risky those acts are may begin to shift. According to researchers, "the subtle distinction between opportunity and threat seems vulnerable to social influence, and could be easily biased unconsciously in a social context where people take their cues from the gains and losses of others."[4]

Let's look at our hypothetical kid again and think about how this might apply to him. Let's say he's having a bad week, there are some issues with some of his friends, and he's spending a lot of time on his phone by himself. He starts to feel some FOMO (fear of missing out). So he goes to a friend's house and smokes weed and then Snaps a picture of it to a couple of people who aren't there—just to let them know he's out on Friday night having fun. If these types of pictures are commonly shared within his friend group or commented on favorably by others, then sharing that picture may not feel like a risky choice but rather a socially neutral or even an advantageous one, at least in the moment when he decides to do it.

Looking at teens' decisions in the context of SRPs and the funhouse mirror of social media helps us to understand their actions in a way that teens themselves may not be able to articulate. If you were to ask our hypothetical pot smoker why he would share that picture, the answer would likely be "I don't know," followed by a shrug. If you were to ask me and my friend in ninth grade what we were thinking when we paddled our canoe into the middle of nowhere, we probably would've answered that we weren't thinking at all. We were just doing.

When Risky Behavior Becomes Socially Normal

We've discussed the concept of the social media super peer effect. What we see in our social media feeds, the content created and shared by the people in our networks, becomes one of the standards by which we measure what's normal. It's human nature to measure how we're doing compared to everyone else, and now we use social media to do that.

What's most interesting to me about this is that what we post ourselves or what our children post is telling only one part of the story. Parents place a lot of value on what their kids are sharing, and that's usually what most parents monitor. We look at what they put out there and ask: Is my child behaving badly, being inappropriate, or displaying any red flags? These are important things to keep an eye on, and there's plenty of research that tells us that what kids post online is indicative of what they're doing or is a meaningful predictor of what they're thinking about doing. But what our kids post is only one part of the picture. What they see on their social media feeds is a critically important driver of their choices around things like drugs, alcohol, sexual self-presentation, and self-harm.

According to the Social Norms Theory, our perception of what's normal is sometimes more important than what actually *is* normal. It also tells us that people, especially teenagers, are more likely to overestimate the degree to which their peers are accepting of and engaging in risk behaviors related to drugs and alcohol. Several studies have compared what college students see online to how it impacts their behavior. All have found (with differing degrees of influence) that the more positive images around drugs and alcohol that one sees, the more likely one is to actually drink or use drugs. As parents, we need to be looking at not only what our kids post but also what they're seeing online.

A PUBLIC HEALTH NOTE ABOUT UNDERAGE DRINKING AND SUBSTANCE USE

Alcohol and drug use are less common for teenagers today than for earlier generations, including their parents'. Attitudes toward underage drinking vary quite a bit in the United States, ranging from "Well, they're going to do it anyway, so they may as well do it here," to "Over my dead body, young lady." Regardless of where you may stand on this issue, the public health data on teens who drink regularly and who binge-drink are pretty conclusive.

Underage drinking is correlated with many, many bad outcomes. Some (but not all of them) include increased risks of injury, accidents, and death; unprotected sex, unwanted pregnancy, sexually transmitted infections, and sexual assault; physical altercations; problems with parents; issues with law enforcement; worsening of mental health; and decreased school and work performance. In addition, the younger a teen is when they begin drinking, the more likely they are to develop an alcohol-use disorder or other addiction as an adult.[5]

We also know a lot more now than we did even twenty years ago about adolescent brain development and the specific impact that drugs and alcohol have on developing bodies.

Social Marketing and Influencers

Until recently, I honestly hadn't considered the degree to which the content that fills our social media feeds isn't created by our "friends" but by strangers, bots, and brands trying to sell us stuff. Marketing and advertising is increasingly showing us carefully selected images and messages, tailored to our specific and personal interests, sometimes in ways that feel downright creepy. There have been times when I've thought about buying a product and, moments later, an ad for it appears in my Facebook feed. Is it black magic of some kind? Someone should ask Zuckerberg. These messages may come directly from advertisers and brands or through social media influencers, who are paid to integrate sponsored content into what they share with their followers.

I should note that I'm considered a social media influencer, so none of this should have come as a surprise to me. Perhaps because I'm an adult, I'm able to separate the messages I see from friends and family from what I perceive to be advertising. Or maybe because of my advanced age and uninteresting demographics, the marketing messages targeted to me have to do with comfortable shoes and laundry detergent. I certainly am a sucker for a well-placed ad, but I hadn't considered the impact such an ad could have on my behavior.

Sponsored content can take many different forms, some more direct than others. A young person may like or follow a brand account for beer or liquor because that brand works with really cool celebrities, posts funny videos, makes cool commercials, or hosts giveaways of stuff they'd like to win.

Sometimes kids may be interacting with sponsored content in more nuanced ways. If a brand is working with an influencer, particularly someone whose followers include a lot of teens, the content may be designed to look like everything else that influencer shares. In fact, making sponsored content feel "authentic" to the influencer and his or her audience is generally the hallmark of a good campaign. It doesn't feel like a hard sell; it feels like your very cool friend recommending something to you. But when a model on Instagram, with millions of teenage followers, casually mentions how much she loves drinking a cold [insert name of beer] on a hot day at Coachella, that sponsored post may reach teens without their necessarily knowing it's targeted advertising.

Positive messages about drinking are everywhere online. We may think because drug use is illegal, that similar messages are more covert (they are) and less readily available (they are not). Positive messaging around drugs and drug use are extremely common online, both user-generated and as marketing material. In many places in the United States, marijuana is legal, and the cannabis industry uses social media to connect with their customers the same way any other business might.

Isn't Marketing to Kids in That Way Illegal?

You might wonder if kids are "allowed" to follow brands or products that they're not old enough to purchase or use. The answer is (mostly) yes. Sometimes there's a function where kids must verify their age before gaining access to content (this is usually on a brand's website), but on social media accounts or through influencer campaigns, usually there isn't. These online advertisers do little in the way of verifying the age of the eyeballs seeing their content, while doing an excellent job providing engaging content to those they consider to be consumers of their products. There's little federal regulatory oversight for this, in contrast to traditional media advertising, which is strictly regulated.

Something else to consider is that the age requirement for most social media platforms is thirteen. We know from both the data and anecdotally that millions of users (often with the permission of their parents) misrepresent their age when setting up their social media accounts because they're younger than the terms of use permit. Perhaps advertising should be part of the decision-making rubric when parents consider whether to allow their children to get their first account. The privacy and marketing considerations of this decision often don't come up beforehand.

The Greatest Risk Behavior May Just Be Using the Phone Itself

The greatest risk behavior that many kids face may not come from exposure to online content related to drugs and alcohol, but from the means through which all that content is delivered—cell phones. It's easy to understand why we're all so attached to our screens. Our brains release happy little dopamine hits whenever we get a positive reward from our phones. A new text message—*ding!* Someone retweeted me—*ding!* In a 2017 TED Talk about technology, award-winning journalist and podcaster Manoush Zomorodi joked that "the only people who refer to their customers as 'users' are drug dealers and technologists."

The truth is, most tech is designed to keep and capture our attention on a neurological basis. One of the most successful app development companies in Silicon Valley is Dopamine Labs, for Pete's sake. The neural feedback you get from Facebook, Snapchat, or Candy Crush is intermittent, variable, and unpredictable. The positive reinforcement you receive from social media is very addictive and linked to pleasure centers in the brain. It encourages patterns of behavior like waiting for and seeking that unpredictable reward. People will continue to engage in this behavior again and again until they're exhausted—until they want to stop but can't quite get themselves to do so.

Dr. David Greenfield, assistant clinical professor of psychiatry at the University of Connecticut and director of the Center for Internet and Technology Addiction, compared Internet use to gambling: "You don't know when and where you'll get positive reinforcement, so you feel compelled to wait for that response and to seek it. The whole Internet operates on a variable ratio reinforcement schedule, which is a fancy way of saying that the Internet is like a slot machine."

What Is Tech Addiction?

Tech addiction has been defined in many ways, related to different types of use. Common Sense Media describes it as problematic media use, enumerating the ways in which phones, gaming, social media, the Internet, or other types of tech are used compulsively or in an addictive manner. Studies have placed the rate of Internet addiction worldwide at about 6 percent, with rates for North America at 8 percent.[6] Compare this with rates of alcohol use disorder, which are at about 6.2 percent in the United States.[7]

It's not just kids who have a problem. Every tech addiction expert I spoke to said that parents often do too. According to Common Sense Media, 54 percent of kids said they thought their parents checked their devices too much, and 32 percent felt unimportant when their parents were distracted by their phones. Take a minute and really think about what that says about us collectively.

There has been a lot of research on problematic gaming, Facebook and social media use, Internet and chatting, and pornography addiction. Although tech addiction is widely considered to be a problem, the only form found in the *Diagnostic and Statistical Manual of Mental Disorders*, fifth edition (*DSM-5*), is "Internet gaming disorder," which is listed not as a diagnosis but as a "condition for further study." This kind of addiction is different from being addicted to a chemical substance. It's a behavioral addiction, one that shares more similarities with problematic gambling than with cocaine. As a result, the clinical definition for Internet gaming disorder was based on the language used to define gambling addiction.

Dr. Clifford Sussman is a child psychiatrist in Washington, DC, who specializes in treating Internet and video game addiction. He explained to me that "the biggest backlash against digital addictions is from people who say we're overpathologizing the excessive use as an addiction. The whole definition of addiction hinges on how the behavior is impacting your whole life. If it's not a problem in your life, then it's not really a problem. Our society as a whole is dependent on technology. This should probably be viewed as a continuum that includes problematic use and addiction."

Defining addictive or problematic use starts with understanding "normal" use. The bottom line is that people consume an alarming amount of media and technology each day. Part of this is related to how we work, study, and communicate. Technology has become so integrated into those functions that it's hard to tease out what is functional use and what is excessive.

WHAT ARE THE "SYMPTOMS" OF TECH ADDICTION?

Tech addiction can mirror other types of substance abuse in terms of the symptoms you may see. Are grades dropping? Are your kids sleep deprived? Do they have trouble waking up in the morning? Are they performing poorly in social situations? Do they experience withdrawal symptoms when they have to stop using technology? Do they blow off everything else to be online, even in the face of negative consequences?

It may be helpful to look at how gaming addiction is defined in the *DSM-5*: "repetitive use of Internet-based games, often with other players, that leads to significant issues with functioning." Five of the following criteria must be met within one year:

1. Preoccupation or obsession with Internet games.
2. Withdrawal symptoms when not playing Internet games.
3. A buildup of tolerance—more time needs to be spent playing the games.
4. The person has tried to stop or curb playing Internet games but has failed to do so.
5. The person has had a loss of interest in other life activities, such as hobbies.
6. The person has had continued overuse of Internet games even with the knowledge of how much they impact their life.
7. The person lied to others about their Internet game usage.
8. The person uses Internet games to relieve anxiety or guilt—it's a way to escape.
9. The person has lost or put at risk an opportunity or a relationship because of Internet games.

Social Media Addiction

A lot of research has been conducted on the addictive nature of social media specifically, with most of the research focusing on Facebook. This research has consistently shown that women are more likely to be addicted to social media than men, and that younger people are more likely to be addicted than older people (no surprise there). Some research shows that people who aren't in a relationship are more likely than those with partners to be addicted to social media as well. The researchers who developed the Facebook Addiction Scale also concluded that people scoring high in extroversion and neuroticism (people who are more moody or anxious) and low in self-esteem were more likely to overuse social media.

According to *Adweek*, social networking accounts for 28 percent of all media time spent online, and those between ages fifteen and nineteen spend at least three hours per day on their social media feeds. Additionally, 18 percent of Facebook users can't go more than a few hours without checking it, and 28 percent of iPhone users check their Twitter feed before getting up in the morning.[8]

Addressing Problematic Tech Use in Your Family

If you think that someone in your family has a potential tech addiction, it's important to address it. There are tools that you can use to assess how serious a problem it is, like the *DSM-5* diagnostic criteria for online gaming addiction included in this chapter. It's also important to get help. For kids, starting with their pediatrician is a good idea. Meeting with a psychologist, psychiatrist, or addiction expert to get a better understanding of the problem and to help manage the process of recovery is ideal. Unfortunately, the cost of tech addiction is often out of pocket, as most insurance companies don't pay for it.

When families start to address problematic use and enforce rules around limits, they should expect a certain degree of defiance. Teenagers are often genuinely torn between wanting to change and not wanting to change, and this is consistent with what we know about other types of addiction. Even when kids know they have a problem, it's not easy for them to stop.

According to Dr. Sussman, "Addicts will be irritable, they will lie, they will sneak around and hack into phones and computers if they need to in order to get their fix. Parents should expect these kinds of behaviors, especially when families first start setting limits and being consistent. Try to ignore the irritability and attitude that come with this. It's important not to feed into it and allow it to become a trigger for fighting. Try not to provide reinforcement for that behavior. You can put kids in a kind of time-out, even teens, by making them have some quiet. A reset, even just for a few minutes."

TAKING TECH BREAKS AND RESETTING YOUR BRAIN

Many of the experts I spoke with recommended taking technology breaks to help reset your brain and break bad habits. This can be really helpful for both adults and kids, but it can also be pretty challenging given how dependent we are on technology to work and study. While shutting your phone or laptop off for a few days (or weeks) is definitely good for you and something to strive for, it may not be possible.

Start by giving yourself a fifteen-minute tech break every hour or two, especially if you find yourself compulsively on your phone or the Internet wasting time instead of doing work (or homework). Here are some things you can do:

- Go for a walk around the block.

- Wash your face or take a quick shower.
- Have a conversation with someone, face-to-face.
- Do a quick chore (for me, the psychological benefit of crossing something off my to-do list is huge).
- Sit outside and enjoy nature, making an effort to really observe your surroundings.
- Write down ten things you're grateful for (on paper, obviously).
- Listen to some music.
- If you play an instrument, practice for a few minutes.
- Read a book, magazine, or comic book—something printed on paper.
- If you have a dog or a cat, go tell them how good they are and get some snuggles in.
- Do some deep breathing, stretching, or mindfulness exercises, if that's your thing.
- Draw or doodle something.
- Drink a refreshing glass of ice water and sit in a comfortable spot.
- Go ride a bike or shoot some hoops, or do something to get your heart rate elevated.

Tech breaks can also take the form of stepping back from apps, games, or social media for a day, a week, or for good. I mentioned needing to delete the game Candy Crush off my phone. I've also deleted Facebook several times, which was tricky due to my role as a social media manager. It meant I had to be much more mindful about how I used it (on my laptop only) and how often (once or twice a day as opposed to pulling out my phone and mindlessly scrolling every few minutes).

Another important thing about tech breaks is being honest and open with your family about your efforts to keep your technology use in check. When I'm working from home, I always keep my phone in another room and I tell my kids why—I'm not great at managing distractions. These conversations come in handy when I see them struggle with homework as texts from their friends come in. They know I'm not trying to punish them by requesting they put their phone away, or even asking them to do something I'm not doing myself.

Willpower, Delayed Gratification, and Marshmallows

A famous Stanford University psychology study began in a nursery school in the early 1960s. Four-year-olds were given one marshmallow and told they could eat it right away. They were also told that if they could wait a little while to eat it, then they could have two marshmallows. Can four-year-olds delay gratification in pursuit of a greater reward? The answer for most was no. Only about 30 percent of the kids could wait, but those who could fared well in the long term: "The four-year-olds who could delay gratification longer went on to receive significantly higher SAT scores. They also developed better social cognitive and emotional coping skills. Today, the study participants are in their forties and fifties, and recent research indicates that the children who were better at delaying gratification back in the day continue to enjoy numerous advantages. They excel in education, have a greater sense of self-worth, manage their stress better, and are less prone to drug abuse."[9]

The Stanford marshmallow test has become synonymous with the importance of willpower and the ability to delay gratification. While willpower may be easier for some people than for others, it's a skill that can be developed like any other. The ultimate goal with social media, gaming, and tech use is for kids to be able to self-regulate and use technology in healthy and productive ways, thereby avoiding addiction and problematic use. Several of the experts I spoke with discussed the importance of helping kids and teens practice delayed gratification around tech use to teach them how to self-regulate. Early termination, or stopping tech use before they're quite ready to, is another way to help kids learn how to do this.

The best way to improve early termination and delayed gratification? Practice them. Explain to your kids why early termination, while super annoying, is something they need to be able to tolerate and is actually a really helpful life skill. One of the teenagers I interviewed for this book practiced this herself and told me, "When delayed gratification works, it comes with a sense of smugness just as strong and heady as dopamine hits. We need to weaponize that." In our fight against the technology trying to capture and keep our attention, we need all the weapons we can get.

Takeaways . . .

- Help teach your kids how to self-regulate, remembering the hard truth that you are their most important role model when it comes to tech use, drinking, drug use, and any other kind of risk behavior.

- Practice delayed gratification and early termination. If your teens want something right away, ask them to wait fifteen minutes. Ask them how they can productively use that time. Model the same behavior yourself. Maybe you want to raid the Halloween candy; tell your kids that you're dying for a candy bar but you're going to set a timer for fifteen minutes and see how you feel then.

- Learn about mindfulness or meditation with your kids and see if this can help them refocus when self-regulation is hard. I will state for the record that I am *terrible* at mindfulness, but I keep trying.

- Gamify delayed gratification. If it's around tech use, make it a contest in your family to see who can go the longest without looking at their phone. Keep track of when and what kinds of tech everyone is using and set goals for starting that use later and ending it earlier, with rewards attached for achieving these goals.

- Let your kids know that while it's really hard to disconnect, certain things are not allowed. For example, if asked to put their phones away or stop playing a video game, they can't throw the remote down, shout at people because they're feeling grouchy, slam a door, or call anyone names. It's okay to sigh, roll their eyes, or be irritated for a few minutes when they have to stop in the middle of something before they're ready.

- Acknowledge that it takes your brains a few minutes to reset from one activity to the next, and give kids that time. Ask your kids to think about how they feel during that reset time.

- Give lots of warnings that a transition is coming, for example: "We're turning it off in five minutes!" This works well for some families but not others. I know that I can often completely tune out the world around me when I'm engaged in a game or reading something on my phone; I might not even hear my husband calling me or the dog barking.

- With younger kids, set up a system of rewards for making good choices and self-regulating their behavior. Dr. Clifford Sussman suggests making rewards immediate and tangible. If kids shut off the device the first time you ask, they get five tickets. If you have to ask twice, they get four, and so on. It's about shifting that gratification from the game to the reward. Then they can trade in tickets for a toy or a fun experience.

- Set limits with older kids and teens (with their input), and then think about immediate and tangible rewards that will appeal to them to help with the transition. One strategy is to have something enjoyable that they can transition directly into after getting off their phones, like getting a coffee (oh, wait, that's a reward that I want) or listening to music.

- Have family discussions about what it means when kids post online about drinking, drugs, or other risky choices. Discuss how social media posts are often seen as evidence of such behavior, even if the kid is only thinking about doing those things.

- Discuss how posting about risky choices contributes to a culture or a social norm that encourages other people to engage in those risky behaviors too.

- Remember that when kids see risky behavior play out online, seemingly without consequences, it shifts their perspectives about the potential harm. Remind them that just because they may not see the negative consequences, it doesn't mean there aren't any.

- In any discussion about underage drinking or drug use, parents must remind kids of the facts about:
  - the negative impact of alcohol on young brains and bodies.
  - the negative outcomes associated with underage and binge drinking.
  - potentially serious drug interactions (if they or their friends take medications, prescribed or recreational).

- Talk to kids about advertising and marketing and what it means to follow or like a brand on social media. Discuss the more nuanced ways in which advertisers may try to reach them, through influencers and celebrities or hashtags and campaigns where people are encouraged to post content and participate.

- Protective factors to reduce the risk of underage drinking and drug use include teaching refusal skills. Teach kids how to say no in ways that don't come with huge social costs. Remember that risks are often perceived as opportunities by teens anxious to maintain or improve their status within social groups.

- This also translates to online behavior. Talk through ways kids can respond to friends who post about risky behavior. What's the best way to handle it? Ignore it? Privately message them? Speak to them about it in person? There are a lot of choices.

8 | Growing Up Online with Anxiety, Depression, ADHD, or Autism

SAMMY'S STORY (AGE TWENTY-FOUR)

It's been almost two years since I started #TalkingAboutIt. That's absolutely wild to me, because my life was completely different back then. I was twenty-three and living in Pennsylvania in 2015, a few months after I graduated from college. I was living in my own apartment, and I was pretty miserable—for fairly good reasons, honestly. I was tied to the area solely because of my boyfriend, and the relationship wasn't working out. My depression and anxiety kept me confined to my bed, only getting up to write a quick article (I was a freelancer at that point).

I remember scrolling through my phone, mainly Twitter, feeling like every ounce of my body was weighed down—that it was impossible and pointless to do anything. I'd see tweets of people doing amazing things and changing the world, and I remember thinking how wild it was that they could do . . . well, anything, while I could barely get up to get a shower. And then I saw a tweet from my friend, who had a bad cold and was planning on spending all day on the couch watching the Hallmark channel. It was a semi-joking tweet, and it was that humor that made me realize I'm doing pretty much the same thing she is, except it's because of my anxiety instead of a cold. Why can't I talk, tweet, joke about my anxiety that way?

I'm in a position of privilege where I can speak openly about my mental health without fear of persecution in any way, from my loved ones or from my employer, so I decided from then on that I'd talk as openly about my mental health as I would my physical health, both in real life and online—but with the latter, I'd use the hashtag #TalkingAboutIt.

"I feel it's important to say that my anxiety has been more difficult than ever, because if I was physically sick I'd sure as hell tweet about it," I posted on December 13, 2015. "I've spent a lot of time in bed recently because of anxiety. Sharing that makes me fearful, but if it were due to a cold, I wouldn't think twice. If you feel comfortable, talk about your mental health the same way you'd talk about your physical health. Joke, share, be raw and open. When it comes to mental health—and many other issues, really—the only way to end the stigma is to keep the conversation going. In fact, if you want to join me, I'm going to make more of an effort to talk about my mental health with the hashtag #Talking AboutIt."

At the time, I figured that if my friends joined in, it would be nice to see all the tweets in one place to remember you're not alone. But I had no idea how it would blow up. At first it was just my friends and me, as I'd predicted, but it quickly gained steam, and it started getting covered by major publications, including Cosmopolitan, The New Republic, and Metro. I started working with To Write Love on Her Arms, a mental health organization I've loved since high school, and I did a Facebook Live chat for MTV on mental health. I'm no expert whatsoever, which just shows how such a simple concept—talking about your mental health without shame—resonated with so many people.

Since I've started #TalkingAboutIt, I've felt so much less alone. That sounds cheesy or like some weird, gimmicky "social movement" crap, but I promise, it's true. On days where I don't even have the strength to tweet about it, I scroll through the #TalkingAboutIt tweets, and it's become exactly what I had hoped it would be—a perfect mix of "I'm not okay" and "Today is a good mental health day" to remind you that what you're going through is valid and real, but that it doesn't mean that it's unending. There will be bright days along with the dark ones—the two can coexist; both are valid and both are okay.

I also have tweeted right before spiraling into a panic attack and have found that people who use the hashtag are excellent at talking me down and reminding me of the important things in life, or telling me to stop what I'm doing and go have a glass of water or watch an episode of my favorite show or something, anything to distract myself from continuing down the path my brain is taking me. But at the same time, people who use #TalkingAboutIt don't condemn the brain. It's not about trying to change who you are or "just deal with it"—it's about learning to live with the brain you have, learning how to cope with feeling too much in what can often feel like a cold society.

As someone who doesn't go much more than an hour without checking social media, and as someone whose entire professional life is pretty much built on social media, I still think there are ways to make it healthier. The problem I currently see with social media is that you see only the curated highlights of someone's life. You see only the best moments, the fantastic vacation photos, the photos from the fun night out with friends. And when all you see are everyone else's good moments, OF COURSE you're going to feel lonely and you're going to compare your life to others' lives. Doesn't matter if you have a mental illness or not—that's just human nature. But when you have anxiety, depression, or another mental health condition, social media can often be completely overwhelming.

If everyone used #TalkingAboutIt the way I've imagined, we would also share the hard moments. Like, imagine if your friend tweeted that she had a panic attack shortly before going out because her body dysmorphia made her think that all her clothes didn't fit. She still had fun out later, but you'd see the other side of the coin too—that life can be hard and life can hurt, but it can be beautiful too. Really, my biggest goal for #TalkingAboutIt was to make social media a healthy place to be.

———————————

Is Social Media a Healthy Place to Be?

Most people who use social media understand that it can have a pretty profound impact on how we feel. On several occasions, I've felt bad enough that I've had to log out for a few days or even a few weeks. It just didn't feel like a healthy place for me to be, and it turns out I'm not alone. A 2017 study by AP showed that almost 65 percent of U.S. teens had taken a social media break, and most of those were done voluntarily. Those who chose to step away felt positive about the decision, experiencing relief. Those who were forced to take a break (by their cruel and interfering parents) felt anxious and disconnected from their friends. Both cases are a powerful reflection of how social media can affect our mental health.

This chapter looks at research on tech use and kids and teens diagnosed with autism spectrum disorders (ASD), attention-deficit/hyperactivity disorder (ADHD), anxiety, and depression. For kids with these conditions, time spent in front of screens can have even more of an impact. There is a lot of research showing that these populations can both benefit from and become at greater risk for problems associated with screen use. There are some clear social and educational benefits for these kids but also some serious potential risks to mental health and well-being, including a heightened likelihood of problematic use or addiction.

PERCENT OF POPULATION WITH THE FOLLOWING CONDITIONS

Condition	Percent of population	Data source and age of population
ADHD	9.4%	NSCH, as of 2016, ages 2–17
ASD	8.5%	CDC, as of 2012, all 8-year-olds
Any anxiety disorder	25.5%	NIMH, as of 2010, ages 13–18
Depression	12.5%	NIMH, as of 2015, ages 12–17

While these four conditions are all very different, they're what public health people call comorbid, meaning they occur together frequently in a way that is statistically significant. These four conditions combined also represent a significant proportion of young adults in the United States, meaning that many of us are raising families (including my own) where one or more of these conditions are present.

The Mental Health of U.S. Teens

The state of adolescent mental health in the United States is a growing and significant problem. Data from multiple long-term population-level studies indicate serious increases in depressive symptoms and major

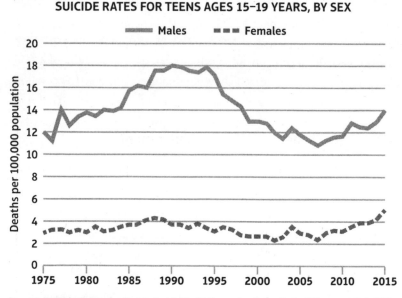

Source: Suicide Rates for Teens Aged 15–19 Years, by Sex—United States, 1975–2015. MMWR Morb Mortal Wkly Rep 2017;66:816. DOI: http://dx.doi.org/10.15585/mmwr .mm6630a6

depressive episodes. A study in 2010 from *USA Today* found that "five times as many high school and college students are dealing with anxiety and other mental health issues as youth of the same age who were studied in the Great Depression era."[1] Since 2010, those numbers have only gotten more troubling.

It's not just feelings of depression that are increasing. There is a corresponding increase in rates of suicide and self-harm. According to a 2017 analysis from the Centers for Disease Control and Prevention (CDC), the suicide rate for teenage girls has hit a forty-year high. The rate doubled for girls and rose by more than 30 percent for boys from 2010 to 2015. In the UK, a 2017 study found a 68 percent increase in self-harm among teenage girls from 2011 to 2014.[2]

The data is difficult to argue with. A generation of emerging adults is facing a mental health crisis, one that our health care delivery system seems woefully unprepared to effectively manage. There is no way of knowing if this trend will continue or will revert back to previously "normal" levels or will get even worse. Frankly, as a parent, this scares the shit out of me.

Have Smartphones Destroyed a Generation?

In Dr. Jean Twenge's bestselling book *iGen*, she discusses the startling shifts in teens' reported well-being, happiness, and mental health since 2012. This is approximately the same year that cell phones reached market saturation in the United States. Are the two connected? Have cell phones "destroyed a generation," as her viral article in *The Atlantic* asserted?

A ton of data links heavier Internet use with various measures of loneliness, depression, anxiety, and stress. In almost every study linking mental health declines to social media use, the kids who are using it the most are experiencing the worst outcomes (these results also translated to time spent gaming). These findings are based on some of the best data we have in the United States, culled over more than thirty years from the experiences of millions of Americans.

Dr. Twenge explains that her conclusions are correlative. In other words, increases in cell phone usage coincide with declines in mental health, but it's difficult to prove that one definitively caused the other. *iGen* is a fascinating discourse on the ways in which this new generation is different from its predecessors; it describes a culture of individualism that underscores many of the beliefs and behaviors that drive young people today.

But we shouldn't look at the mental health crisis our children are facing and decide it's just about iPhones. Attributing a cause to just one thing fails to consider or address all the other issues in play that remain contributing factors. Culture, policy, economics, and technology all change in tandem and in response to one another. Young people are depressed and anxious in unprecedented numbers, and there is no question that cell phones and social media are contributing to that. But they're also stressed out because the culture of childhood has changed, economic and political realities have created elevated stress for the adults in their lives, our education system has become more high-stakes and test-driven, and opportunities to release this stress by being physically active are now more limited, competitive, and expensive, with 70 percent of kids losing that physical outlet and quitting organized sports by the time they turn thirteen.[3]

In "Teen Depression and Anxiety: Why the Kids Are Not Alright," a 2016 cover story for *Time* magazine, journalist Susanna Schrobsdorff writes:

They are the post-9/11 generation, raised in an era of economic and national insecurity. They've never known a time when terrorism and school shootings weren't the norm. They grew up watching their parents weather a severe recession, and, perhaps most important, they hit puberty at a time when technology and social media were transforming society.

"If you wanted to create an environment to churn out really angsty people, we've done it," says Janis Whitlock, director of the Cornell Research Program on Self-Injury and Recovery, also in this article. "They're in a cauldron of stimulus that they can't get away from, or don't want to get away from, or don't know how to get away from."

Our notion of what it means to be angsty, anxious, or depressed is also collectively shifting, with a slowly growing acceptance of neurodiversity and mental health conditions, and a commensurate diminishment of the stigmas attached to them. While there is still a long way to go, positive changes can be seen every day. One of the things driving that change, ironically, is the Internet.

FINDING FRIENDS AND COMMUNITY WHEN YOU'RE A DIFFERENT KIND OF KID

One of the main benefits of cell phones and technology for kids with a mental health diagnosis or who are neurally atypical is that it opens doors for them socially. Connecting with people online via games like Minecraft, or through social media, Tumblr, or YouTube communities, can be an amazing opportunity to make friends. There's the chance to build connections with other people like them, who understand their ups and downs in a way that their typically developing peers might not. While this is also true for everyone on the Internet who feels socially awkward, it's especially true for stigmatized groups. Finding community in an environment where there is less judgment and more understanding can be literally lifesaving.

Of course this is also the Internet we're talking about. While it has the potential to connect people with communities that are supportive and affirming, it also has the potential to connect vulnerable people with those who would cause them harm. This population of kids is more likely to report feeling excluded and lonely and to be bullied. Particularly in the context of young people who may not have the ability to discern good intent from bad or to process feelings resulting from tough situations, it's important that the trusted adults in their lives work with them to assess the safety of the online communities they become a part of and the friendships they make.

One of the young people I interviewed told me that "people will make memes about feeling suicidal and they get shared around in depression communities online, where everyone can relate to them. Sometimes they become more mainstream and you get average people joking about wanting to kill themselves over little things, minimizing the experience of depressed people and creating a culture where hating yourself isn't a cause for concern but makes you cool and relatable. People know they're messed up, but instead of seeking help, they make jokes about their terrible coping mechanisms. It normalizes depression, which I guess is good—but does it in a bad way."

Social Anxiety on Social Media

Socially, the Internet and platforms like Facebook and Instagram can be helpful for young people who have various forms of anxiety. For all the same reasons anyone might find this type of communication easier than face-to-face conversations, people with social anxiety are especially drawn to online exchanges, where they can take their time and not be put on the spot. Some studies have found that socially anxious teens find the Internet to be helpful in terms of managing intimate self-disclosure, which leads to more communication and closer friendships.

On the other hand, it can also become a means of avoiding things they don't want to deal with. Several studies pointed out how, especially with social anxiety, tools that make our lives easier can also become maladaptive strategies for coping. People with anxiety might use the Internet and social media to avoid things like in-person social encounters with friends and family. That trade-off can hurt them in the long run, as spending face-to-face time with friends is a protective factor and a valuable tool to build relationships and improve communication skills.

Another measure that moderates the impact of social media use on levels of anxiety and depression is how emotionally invested kids are in using it. If kids feel deeply distressed when they can't check their feeds or log on to their accounts, that may indicate an unhealthy level of investment. Those teens who were the most invested in using social media tended to have the worst outcomes related to anxiety and depression.

This makes a lot of sense, doesn't it? If a photo posted on Instagram doesn't get a lot of likes or comments, for some kids it may be disappointing, but they shrug and get on with their day. For a kid with anxiety, the same experience may cause genuine distress. It may be a good idea for parents to work with anxious teens to help put the importance of social media into perspective. In general, help them prioritize and place value on other things in their lives: sports, activities, hobbies, academics, and face-to-face time with friends. Ask them to articulate why the particular situation feels like such a big deal. Don't dismiss their feelings, but help them to look at the situation more objectively. Ask them how they'd discuss the situation with a friend who was having the same experience.

WHAT DO WE MEAN BY *ANXIETY*?

Anxiety is a blanket term used to cover a variety of different conditions, including social anxiety disorder (SAD), generalized anxiety disorder (GAD), obsessive-compulsive disorder (OCD), post-traumatic stress disorder (PTSD), various types of specific phobias, panic disorder, and several others.[4] Anxiety disorders impact more than 40 million Americans each year, or more than 18 percent of the adult population. According to the National Institute of Mental Health, the prevalence of an anxiety disorder experienced at some point during their lifetime for thirteen- to eighteen-year-olds is 25.1 percent, with 5.9 percent experiencing severe disorder. For the purposes of our discussion, when referring to anxiety, I generally mean the conditions of SAD and GAD.

Can Cell Phones Directly Cause Anxiety Symptoms?

One example of when cell phones can clearly be shown to cause or worsen anxiety symptoms is when that device is taken away. I've both felt it myself and observed it in others, notably among the undergraduates I teach. There's research to support this as well.

One study looked at college students and how they responded to being separated from their mobile phones. There was an expectation that those who used their phones the most and potentially had problematic use issues would report having the most anxiety. That's exactly what happened, although symptoms of anxiety increased across the board. Over time, the anxiety that the heaviest users experienced escalated in a manner that was similar to the withdrawal symptoms that an addict might experience. Rather than characterize this reaction as addiction-related, the researchers noted that "a more appropriate classification might be separation anxiety."[5]

Most parents are familiar with that phrase. To me it connotes vague uneasy memories of my babies crying for me or clinging to my legs as I tried to leave them with a day-care provider so that I could go tearfully to work. Separation anxiety is specific to close relationships, where the perceived loss of the connection feels traumatic. I interviewed one of the lead researchers of this study, Dr. Larry Rosen, and he explained that the students treated their phones like they were an appendage or an extension of themselves: "When the device is taken away or placed out of sight, people who rely on this technology more will undoubtedly feel separation anxiety or 'lost' without it. Light users, on the other hand, would not feel this loss because of less reliance on the device."

Communication overload is another form of anxiety linked to cell phone use. This refers to how many of us feel bombarded with information in the form of texts, updates, emails, and calls. We get notifications, sometimes hundreds a day. This has been shown to cause psychological distress and often feels just plain overwhelming. All of the data coming in, most of it signaled with a sound or image, elicits a Pavlovian response from us, requiring us to be in a constant state of attention. What is important? What can go unread? What is truly urgent? This is a cumulative cognitive burden that stresses people out.

Anxiety is also linked to FOMO, which in addition to being worried that you're missing out on social experiences has a distinct subtype called disconnection anxiety. This means that stepping away from your phone, your emails, or your social media feed, whether it's voluntary or imposed by unkind parents, triggers anxiety symptoms. I think disconnection anxiety also explains why I feel kind of uneasy when my phone's battery is super low and the nice, relaxed feeling I have when it's fully charged. Just me? *Never mind.*

Depression and Digital Media

There is an extensive body of research that links digital media use, particularly high levels of use, to an increased risk of depression. Again, while social media can enhance feelings of connectedness and well-being for people, it can also tip people in the opposite direction, making them feel isolated and lonely. Those who struggle socially and exhibit depressive symptoms are more likely to find that using social media makes them feel worse.[6]

The impact of social media and tech use on a young person's depression risk depends largely on the person's temperament and personality. In chapter 4, we discussed the "rich get richer" theories around social media use, and it's certainly in play here. Popularity was actually a moderating factor in predicting whether social media could make a young person feel depressed. Popular kids did well, while unpopular kids felt depressed.[7]

Passive social media consumption, or lurking, is also correlated with an increased risk of depression. Using the Internet and social media for the purpose of direct communication has been shown to have some benefit to well-being. Lurking, however, had the opposite effect.[8] A 2018 study found that undergraduates with higher baseline depression scores who reduced their time on social media to about ten minutes per platform per day for a month saw a significant reduction in their depressive symptoms.[9]

All this information collectively tells us that kids with anxiety and/ or depression need to limit their tech use. Perhaps more important, they should learn to be super aware of their tipping points, and when things start to feel negative or stressful, they need to train themselves to put their phones down and take care of themselves.

EMOTIONAL CONTAGION THEORY

Several studies have noted that emotional states can be spread through social networking sites and other online communication. There is evidence that both positive and negative emotions can be spread throughout social networks, with people largely unaware of the influence that it can have.

A study conducted by Facebook and published in 2014 demonstrated that by manipulating users' newsfeeds to show them more or less positive, negative, or emotional content, users would then change their content to reflect the "mood" of the information that they were interacting with. "These results indicate that emotions expressed by others on Facebook influence our own emotions, constituting experimental evidence for massive-scale contagion via social networks." This is a prescient and somewhat disturbing finding.

Emotional contagion theory has long been applied to the study of depression and happiness. Infectious disease models have been mathematically applied to understand how these emotional states spread, using epidemiology to better predict their course. The relationship between online social contagion and suicidal ideation has been well established.[10] Infectious disease pathology has also been applied to things like eating disorders and self-harm communities online.

These communities can form around hashtags, user accounts, memes, websites, or message boards. Often they provide connection and support for people struggling to make healthy choices. There are also many communities that connect people who are engaging in unhealthy behavior, by providing #Thinspiration or #ProAna Pinterest boards for people with anorexia or body dysmorphia disorders or providing (intentional or unintentional) self-harm triggers for people who are cutting themselves.

Can we help?

Posts with words or tags you're searching for often encourage behavior that can cause harm and even lead to death.
If you're going through something difficult, we'd like to help.
Learn more

[Show posts] [Cancel]

If you search Instagram for a phrase or hashtag that has been flagged as potentially harmful, you may see this in response.

As parents, we should discuss with our teens the concept of emotional contagion online, if only to heighten our collective awareness of its influences. When you encounter it yourself (Facebook seems to provide us with innumerable opportunities for this), use those examples to explain this theory to your kids. It's also worth considering the sometimes blurry line between finding online support and community for conditions like depression, self-harm, or eating disorders and the potential for online emotional contagion to trigger or worsen those conditions.

Social Comparison and Depression on Social Media

Social comparison comes up again and again as an important factor in how depressed and anxious kids experience social media. Directly related to social comparison was the finding that the number of strangers followed on Instagram was a predictor of loneliness and depression. When the strangers being followed are celebrities, two problems arise. The first is the nonreciprocal nature of the relationship. The second is that comparing your own life to the lives of celebrities will almost certainly lead to feelings of envy and disappointment.

Following celebrities today is more nuanced than you might think.

Often teens are fans of people who are, for example, "YouTube famous" and whose fans form a community that consistently engages with both the content and the person creating it. When these communities are relatively small, fans feel like their support is really important—that their likes and shares and comments are really making a difference and are valued by the content creator. To a certain extent that's true. There's a degree of personal investment and identification with the influencer that may not make a lot of sense to someone who is unfamiliar with this part of Internet culture.

When you pair the urge to compare yourself with a search for feedback and affirmation, it presents another risk factor for depression, particularly for girls. One study looked at it through the lens of excessive reassurance-seeking behavior. This can take many different forms. Kids might post photos and then ask for comments on how they look. They might use sites like ASKfm (where users ask and answer anonymous questions), or they might solicit feedback and affirmation using the acronym TBH (to be honest).

SEEKING AFFIRMATION WITH A HASHTAG

The TBH hashtag, or the variation #likeforfollow, is commonly used on Instagram. People may use it as a form of currency, as a means of getting people to like and comment on their posts. And as most parents know, the number of likes and comments a post gets can make or break a kid's day. A TBH is a flattering or nice comment often paired with a like, left on someone else's post, that says something nice like "TBH you're really pretty" or "TBH I think you're nice." And it can also serve as a means of building social capital.

The phenomenon continued to explode through the fall of 2017, when an app called tbh became the number one download on the app store. Designed as a bully-proof way to provide positive anonymous compliments to friends (you authorize the app to access your contacts), the app quickly spread like wildfire. In nine weeks, it had 50 million downloads and 2.5 million active daily users, and had been purchased by Facebook for somewhere in the neighborhood of $100 million.

"The company decided to build something at the intersection of the positivity it saw lacking in anonymous apps like Secret and Yik Yak, and the honesty teens craved as seen in the TBH trend where social network users request candid feedback from their friends: tbh was born. 'We shipped it to one school in Georgia. Forty percent of the school downloaded it the first day.'"[11] Despite its initial popularity, tbh lacked staying power. By the summer of 2018, Facebook made the decision to sunset the app due to reported decreased usage.

ADHD and the Internet

In some ways, the quick-clicking online environment is almost perfectly designed for the ADHD brain. This is both good and bad. The bad news is that ADHD is highly associated with Internet and gaming addiction. Given how the technology is conceived and carefully engineered to be distracting and to reinforce use, it's remarkable that it isn't a much bigger problem for the estimated 6.4 million kids who have ADHD.[12] In fact, it's truly a testament to how hard many of these kids are working every day to find strategies and solutions to integrate technology into their lives in healthy ways.

The relationship between this technology and ADHD is being studied from many different angles. In 2018, a preliminary study from *JAMA*, the journal of the American Medical Association, suggested that young people who are frequent users of technology (using tech to do many different activities many times per day) were at increased risk of developing ADHD symptoms. While we can't use this study to say that tech use causes ADHD, we can add it to a very long list that tells us the kids who use tech the most are having the worst outcomes.[13]

ADHD Brains and How Tech Affects Them

Child psychiatrist Dr. Clifford Sussman explained to me that "kids with ADHD have a smaller amount of dopamine receptors than a typical kid. That's why drugs likes psychostimulants help them. When their brains are really stimulated by something, like gaming or videos, it exacerbates the underlying condition. These kids are constantly seeking out stimulation, which is what they're wired to do, and tech really provides that."

The wiring issue is also why it's hard for them to stop their tech use, either on their own or when they're directed to. In ADHD brain development, the prefrontal cortex (which you'll recall is the part of the brain that oversees things like planning, executive functioning, and higher level reasoning) develops more slowly than in typically developing youth. As a result, self-regulation is more difficult, and impulsiveness is more common, almost like the behavioral default. ADHD specialist Dr. Edward Hallowell describes these brains as being very powerful and fast, like a Ferrari, but having bicycle brakes.

Helping ADHD Kids Be Tech-Positive

Jessica McCabe runs a successful science-based YouTube channel called How to ADHD and creates content to help young people better understand their ADHD brains. She talked to me about how technology can adapt information to make it appeal to people whose brains process information differently. "For example, it can be great for helping ADHD kids learn Spanish or Italian, because they've 'gamified' the learning process. That is a really powerful learning tool that helps maintain focus."

In addition, she says that using the Internet for project-based learning and research is fantastic. Kids who would normally struggle to wade through material in textbooks now can get on the Internet and find so much information in so many different formats.

Jessica also works with teens in the production of her YouTube channel, and she's learned about how they use technology to support their academic and social pursuits. "They use Skype to do homework, as a way of having accountability or helping each other out. Connecting like that can give them a sense of purpose. They can also use YouTube or other platforms to connect with each other. Through this, they find a community, and that's a huge issue for ADHDers—not feeling connected and feeling alone."

Jessica says that tech can be a good way for parents and kids to better relate and empathize with one another. One of the reasons she began making videos was to help young people understand and process what it meant to have ADHD. "Parents are able to use it as a tool because kids don't always understand what they're going through or what they're feeling, but if they see somebody on YouTube going through it and say, *Oh, that's me, that's what I'm feeling,* and parents can understand a little bit better, then the whole family has a place to start conversations that help them know what everyone is dealing with. It can really help kids feel more confident."

Autism Spectrum Disorders

Symptoms of autism spectrum disorders (ASD) can vary widely from child to child, even within the same family. Autism is often described as a cluster of symptoms, which can group together in unique ways. This makes looking at neural and behavioral responses to technology for the entire population of ASD kids especially complicated. Like those with ADHD, kids on the spectrum tend to have a lower density of dopamine receptors, as well as delayed processing and prefrontal cortex development. They're more likely to have issues with executive function and self-regulation. Essentially their brains are more susceptible to the negative effects of technology and may be less able to rebound from those effects. They're also more likely to struggle with problematic use issues.

Every parent I know has at some point asked their child to stop playing a video game or watching a video, only to have their lovely child morph into a snarling, angry beast. This experience is heightened in children whose brains are more sensitive to stimulation (like ASD and ADHD kids). There are numerous benefits to using tech, but two of the brain-related side effects are hyperarousal and dysregulation. And those side effects can result in behaviors that are really challenging for parents to manage.

This poses a problem for many families. Tech is part of our way of life. For ASD kids, it may be more than that. Many of the studies I read observed that kids on the autism spectrum displayed a powerful preference for electronic media, noting that the preference for video games was "particularly striking."[14] There are many reasons for this. Kids with autism love electronics for all the same reasons any other kid does—it's fun and immersive. Some kids on the spectrum use screen time to decompress (also like many other kids) and self-comfort after a long day or a stressful situation. It's also socially normalizing. What kids don't like to play online or watch YouTube videos?

ASD kids, however, may have a different neural response to tech. For families who manage challenging behaviors related to their child's diagnosis (tics, self-injurious actions, or aggression), using tech can bring some temporary and much-needed peace. Kids may also use it for learning and exploration. They may use it to create things online, Minecraft being an excellent and commonly cited example of this.

Are There Social Benefits to All This Time Online?

Kids on the spectrum often experience problems connecting with their neurotypical peers, reducing opportunities to develop friendships with classmates and neighbors. One of the consistently cited benefits of social media and cell phones is that it can help kids build friendships.

Dr. Clifford Sussman told me: "Social issues can be a problem for [ASD] kids. The myth is that they don't need that socialization, which couldn't be further from the truth. They're often lonely and depressed, especially when they reach the age when they start to be attracted to others and to really seek contact. The Internet can become a more level social playing field. They can interact with other kids in a way that's more comfortable. They can master certain things; they can share the things they're good at and that they create online."

While the Internet provides social opportunities for many kids, that may not always be the case for the ASD population. The data indicates that most ASD kids don't use tech in a manner that facilitates communication with others or that builds social capital. In general, these kids use less social media, and when they play video games, which can be an excellent opportunity to connect with others and make friends, they are significantly more likely to play by themselves, both in person and online. This is the opposite experience of typically developing children, the majority of whom play video games with others on a regular basis. Sadly, these findings imply that some of the social issues that ASD kids experience in person are also occurring online.

Takeaways . . .

- There is significant evidence that the more people use social media, the worse they feel, and the greater the negative impact on their emotional well-being and mental health. For kids already dealing with mental health issues, there should be limits in place to help them manage their condition.

- Make sleep a top priority. While sleep is an issue for all kids, it's a bigger deal for families with kids who are neurally atypical or who have a mental health disorder. These kids are significantly more likely to have a sleep disorder (between 40 and 75 percent), depending on the condition. Lack of sleep can cause a worsening of severity in symptoms, as well as contribute to a host of other behavioral problems previously discussed.

- Observe your kid's use of social media and assess how emotionally invested in it they are. Remember that the research shows that the kids who are the most emotionally invested and get the most upset when they can't get on social media are also the ones who tend to have the worst outcomes related to anxiety and depression.

- ADHD expert Jessica McCabe suggested that the most important thing with tech is to be consistent and outsource the rules.
  - Have the rules physically posted where the kids can see them, and if the rule is "You can't be on social media until after your homework is done," that's the rule. You can't have your phone back until your homework's done.
  - Use timers, apps, or parental controls for agreed-upon time limits, which can shift the "blame" from mom and dad to a more neutral enforcer.

- Reward and praise kids every time they transition from tech time to nontech time smoothly or follow the rules without being reminded. Acknowledge all the things they do right.
  - Have realistic and reasonable expectations about where your kid is at on any given day; some days it might be really hard for them.

- Kids with ADHD need choices. Ask what their goals are and start from there. Ask them: What's distracting you? What is reasonable to you in terms of setting limits or consequences? If you cocreate the rules, kids will be more open to following them than if the rules feel arbitrary.

- When it comes to kids with ADHD or autism, or those who struggle with anxiety or depression, it's even more important to monitor and take an interest in what they're doing online. Even if you're not personally comfortable with technology or find Minecraft or their latest YouTube obsession mind-numbingly boring, listen to what your kids are saying about it. Participate in the conversation.

- If you're concerned that your special-needs child may have a tech or gaming addiction or a problematic use issue, ask your pediatrician to screen them by discussing their phone, social media, or gaming habits during check-ups.

- One clearly identified risk factor for depression is low self-esteem combined with high intensity of social media use. If your kids exhibit signs of feeling bad about themselves, work together to set limits that allow them to still feel connected but also give them a break.

- Excessive reassurance-seeking behavior online, especially for girls, is a red flag for parents when monitoring kids online.

- Take a look at who your kids are following on their social media feeds. Whose stories are they seeing on Snapchat? Whose pictures are they viewing every day on Instagram? If a significant chunk of what they're seeing is being posted by strangers, consider that a good opportunity to have a conversation about social comparison.

- Talk to your kids about what they're seeing and how to put this information into an appropriate context. Remember that the people who populate their social media feeds become super peers, capable of wielding a lot of influence and setting social norms. Perhaps the Kardashians are not the role models our kids need.

9 | Safety, Predators, Harassment, and Bullying Online

KATHERINE'S STORY (AGE TWENTY-ONE)

When I was eleven, I met and developed a relationship with an online predator. I am lucky that my mom figured out what was going on before anything happened to me physically, but it was still a traumatic experience. It took my family and me a long time to recover, and part of what helped us to process everything was to write about it. My mom wrote a fictionalized account of the story in a novel called Who R U Really?

I met this guy in an enjoyable online role-playing game. There are tons of these popular games out there. It is easy to get immersed playing, and I was an eleven-year-old having fun; the potential for danger never crossed my mind.

At first he and I went on quests together to level up our characters, which was a typical thing to do within the game. My brother joined us for a time before he got bored and stopped playing. We used the chat box to communicate about the quests, and after a few missions, our conversations began to move away from the game. He told me he was eighteen, and I told him I was eleven. Soon we were talking openly about what was happening in our lives—normal things, like how our days were going and how excited I was to be skipping sixth grade. Feelings of friendship quickly grew.

Eventually he persuaded me to give him my cell phone number. We went from chatting during the game to constantly texting each other. Over time we went from being friends to something more. He convinced me we were madly in love. I believed him, and I loved the feeling of being in a secret intimate relationship. The focus of our conversations became planning the future together.

This went on for about a year and a half.

I finally told my middle school best friend, about a month before my mom found out. Other than that, I followed his recommendation of keeping it secret from people, because "they wouldn't understand our relationship." The people closest to me had no idea what was happening.

He and I never met in person, but we had established a general plan without a specific date. It would be after one of my sports practices at school, before my parents would pick me up. Our first meeting would be "quick," just for us to see each other. I had built up that moment in my mind with anticipation, but now I am thankful it never happened.

One family game night, my mom discovered the text messages on my phone. Everything came out. She called the police and set off a nuclear explosion inside of me. The cops investigated, and I was told the man I loved was actually forty-five years old. Because he never touched me physically, he was never charged with any crime. The police could not prove he had crossed state lines with the intent to harm me.

He is still out there.

I never had contact with him directly after that. The abrupt halt in our communication was caused by my mom, who took away my phone, computer, and fairy tale. Everything I thought was true was actually a lie. It was hard to accept what had happened and what might have happened.

I struggled to recover from the experience. I fell into a deep, dark depression for about six months after that game night when the police came to my house. My mom knew I was in a bad place, but she did not know how to help me. So, she put me into counseling. I resisted at first. About three months into it, I attempted suicide but failed. That was a wake-up call for me. I had several realizations in therapy that helped me put my experience into perspective, and I began to move on. I came out of my depression but made the mistake of letting this experience define who I was for a long time.

About this time, my mom proposed the idea of writing Who R U Really? *We talked about the what-ifs of the story and decided that writing the book would be a good healing activity for us, while providing a warning to others. We wanted to* create a story that would help at least one person. If we could do that, then the book would be a success. As the book was written and published, I went back to therapy a couple times to process the thoughts and feelings that arose from thinking about everything and working through it. During that time, I finally distinguished myself from the experience I'd had. I was able to say, "Yes, this happened to me, and it sucked, but that does not define me. This is who I am now."

There are several pieces of advice I want to give kids so they can stay safe. I would advise them to be as honest as they can about who they interact with online. Do not share unnecessary personal information with others, especially if you do not know them in real life. One thing the police detective told me that I often still think about is [that] the only real friends we have are the ones we interact with in person. We can't actually know if people are who they say they are on the Internet. It is far too easy to lie or make up a fake identity when interacting with someone just online. We also need to trust our parents; though it is frustrating at times, they typically have our best interest in mind.

To kids who have been lied to online or targeted by someone or had a terrible experience like I did, I would say, "Hold on. What has happened is hard, and it is going to push you to the breaking point, but I know who you become on the other side of this, and you will be okay. Ride this wave the best you can, and forgive yourself as soon as you are able. Having gone through this, you are going to help so many people, and you will be able to better empathize with them. Don't regret it, live with it, and make the most of it."

Every Parent's Worst Fears

When it comes to my kids and the Internet, Katherine's story represents some of my worst fears. It elicits the same bone-deep panic we feel when our toddler darts away from us in a crowd, when our teenagers miss curfew, or when we hear about something terrible happening to a child. These feeling are so deeply ingrained in me that I use special capitalization to describe The Fear.

Many of us read or watch coverage of tragic stories, and we struggle to process them. How are we supposed to keep our kids safe from all the bad things that are out there? It's incredibly overwhelming, and there are days when I wonder if life wouldn't be better—or at least simpler—if things like cell phones and social media simply didn't exist. While cases like Katherine's represent only a very small percentage of kids' experiences online, and cases that lead to abduction or assault are fewer still, many kids (about 9 percent) will experience some degree of sexual solicitation online, and many more (20–40 percent) will report being bullied or harassed online.[1]

These things trigger The Fear in me, so I try to remember that fear doesn't drive great decision-making. When The Fear has taken over my brain, I'm not thinking rationally. Often The Fear causes us to either freak out or shut down (fight or flight). When we shut down, we ignore the really complicated environment in which we're raising our kids. And that's a real problem—because then we do nothing.

And doing nothing means our kids have to figure it out for themselves instead of having us there to guide them through it. If we want to teach them how to keep themselves safe, we have to do this with them.

Who Is Out There Targeting Our Kids Online?

When we think about the people who pose the greatest risk to our kids online, our perceptions are often dictated by what we see in the news media. Many of the researchers and child-protection experts I spoke with felt that media coverage of these issues was a problem, that it should better reflect what's actually happening and encourage families to think through ways to stay safe rather than evoking a fear response that's more visceral than thoughtful. We're also informed by prevention and education messages about predators and pedophiles, and we pray that no one we love will ever encounter them.

However, online abuses are like any other type of child abuse—the reality of who is actually committing these acts is often more complicated than we might think. We're likely to be aware of "stranger danger" and to discuss this with our kids, and while those risks are real, our fear of strangers may distract us from where the real danger is more likely to come from. In the case of both in-person and online abuse and harassment of youth, the most likely culprit is not a stranger; it's other kids and people known to our children in real life. One study showed that 58 percent of the aggressors in incidents of online harassment were kids who the victim knew from school or in their community.

In fact, the 2014 iteration of the Youth Internet Safety Survey found that the risk of online predators was real but comparatively small. For example, the greatest single source of sexual solicitation came from other kids (42 percent), which also accounted for 59 percent of the sexual solicitations victims characterized as "aggressive." Over half of these incidents took place on social media sites.

This chapter will look at a few different kinds of online danger, including cyberbullying, online abuse or harassment, and online sexual solicitation. In all cases, the perpetrators are other kids (more often) and adults (less often). In all cases, the offenders are both people your kids know in real life (more often) and strangers (less often). In many cases, there are characteristics and behaviors that may place a young person at higher risk of these dangers. It should go without saying, however, that under no circumstances does any young person deserve to be bullied, harassed, or solicited online.

WHAT ARE SOME RISK FACTORS FOR VICTIMIZATION?

Anyone can become a victim of online bullying, harassment, or solicitation, but there are certain characteristics and behaviors that increase risk.

Age
Almost all victims are between thirteen and seventeen years old. About half are thirteen or fourteen.

Gender
The majority of youth who self-report being victimized online are female (65 percent).

Social Media Use
Kids who use social media are more likely be victimized, bullied, or harassed online than kids who do not use social media. The majority of harassment incidents (82 percent), for example, took place on social media sites.[2]

Kids Who Spend More Time Online
Kids who spend more time online are more likely to encounter abuse or harassment. This isn't surprising, as more time online means more opportunity to run into something or someone negative.

Kids Who Post Aggressive or Mean Things to Others Online
Young people who say they make rude or nasty comments or frequently attempt to embarrass or humiliate other people online are twice as likely to report that they were victims themselves. I'm inclined to make a sarcastic comment here about taking what you dish out, or to make a reference to Wheaton's Law,[3] but you're probably already doing that yourself.

Boys Who Are Gay or Who Are Questioning Their Sexual Identity
Young people who are struggling to understand their sexuality may encounter both exactly what they need (peer support, role models, facts, and answers) and precisely what their parents fear most (threats, solicitation, explicit materials they may not

be ready to process). This dichotomy is particularly relevant to LGBTQ teens. Using the Internet and social media forums to explore issues of sexual and gender identity can be tremendously helpful to many young people, particularly if this type of information or support isn't available to them in their communities. However, it also exposes them to increased risk. Boys who are victims of Internet predators are generally targeted by male offenders.

Young People with a History of Sexual or Physical Abuse

From a 2012 report about online predation of children:

> Abused youth are more at risk for sexual victimization and exploitation in a variety of ways. Abuse history could make some youths less able to recognize inappropriate sexual advances. Some may be vulnerable to online sexual advances because they are looking for attention and affection. For some, prior abuse may trigger risky sexual behavior that directly invites online sexual advances. Moreover, delinquency, depression, and social interaction problems unrelated to abuse also may increase vulnerability. Adolescents of both sexes who are troubled with depression and related problems are more likely than other adolescents to form close online relationships with people they meet online.[6]

Young People with Depression or Other Mental Health Problems

Young people who suffer from depression or other mental health issues may look to connect with people online for support and community, or to avoid the potential stigma or judgment of disclosing their problems to people they know. This can backfire, because anonymous communication increases the risk of encountering abuse or harassment.

Youths Who Have Poor Relationships with Their Families
Teen boys who report low levels of parental monitoring and teen girls who report a high degree of conflict with their parents are more likely than other teens to develop close relationships with strangers they meet online.

Other Important Risk Factors
Kids who report meeting people via multiple platforms (for example, on different social media accounts, on comment threads, or in chat rooms) are associated with higher rates of being harassed or victimized online. Youth who add strangers to their friends, followers, or contacts lists are also at increased risk, as well as those who talk online about sex, particularly anonymously. There is a noteworthy overlap with other risk factors

Online risk behavior	Percentage of youths engaging in risk behavior
Posting personal information online	56%
Interacting online with unknown people	43%
Having unknown people on a buddy list	35%
Using the Internet to make rude and nasty comments to others	28%
Sending personal information to unknown people met online	26%
Downloading images from file-sharing programs	15%
Visiting X-rated sites on purpose	13%
Using the Internet to embarrass or harass people one is mad at	9%
Talking online to unknown people about sex	5%

Source: M. L. Ybarra, K. J. Mitchell, D. Finkelhor, and J. Wolak, "Internet Prevention Messages: Targeting the Right Online Behaviors," *Archives of Pediatrics & Adolescent Medicine* 161.2 (February 2007): 138–45.

here. Kids who have trouble at home, have a history of abuse, have mental health problems, are LGBTQ, or engage in off-line or online risk behaviors are more likely to visit chat rooms or anonymous spaces where they can interact with people. They may rely on these interactions and the friendships that develop there to offset social and emotional deficits stemming from problems at home or at school. About a third of teens who are sexually solicited online received those solicitations in chat rooms.

An Interesting Note

One survey found that more than 40 percent of risky online behaviors occurred when kids were using the Internet with their friends. Remember the study on risk behavior, where teens were significantly more likely to drive unsafely in a simulation when their friends were present compared to when they were alone? This is another example of kids making riskier choices when their friends are around and further evidence that off-line behavior translates to online behavior.

If your otherwise intelligent child gets dumber in the presence of their friends, then maybe it's a good idea to collect phones if they're all sleeping over at your house. Is your responsible daughter going to a friend's house where you suspect there will be excessive giggling, no sleeping, and too much free time? Maybe discuss with her that she needs to be mindful of the choices she makes with her phone, and shoot her a text halfway through the night to remind her how proud her responsibility makes you.

What Katherine's Story Can Tell Us About Online Danger

I shared Katherine's story with the law enforcement and child-endangerment experts I spoke with, and they all agreed that it's an almost textbook case for how many online predators work. In most cases, young adolescents are the primary targets, and they're made to feel special, unique, and different from everyone else. Consider the age when this is most likely to occur—around age thirteen or fourteen, when kids are developmentally primed to respond to these tactics due to the Personal Fable.

Numerous studies confirm that the adults who perpetrate these crimes tend to gain the trust of the kids they're communicating with. Their initial goal is not abduction or assault or to extort graphic images from them, but rather to develop a relationship and rapport with their victims. That feels pretty cool to a young teen. Over time, that person no longer feels like a stranger. They've been talking online for a while now, so how can it be dangerous? Often the child truly values the relationship with the predator. One study of law enforcement data showed that half the victims in cases of online abuse either thought they were in love with the perpetrator or described having a close connection with them.

While many of these predators lie about their age, only 5% pretended to be the same age as the victim. From a report on Internet-related sex crimes: In some of the cases, the offenders started off saying they were teens, but later introduced that they were older. Another 25% of offenders shaved a few years off their true ages, but still presented themselves as much older than their young victims. For example, men who were 45 told victims they were 35.

Deception about sexual motives was also uncommon. Although 21% hid or misrepresented their motives, most of the deceivers were open about wanting sex from their victims . . . most representations involved insincere promises of love and romance.[5]

Laura Parrott-Perry, cofounder and CEO of Say It Survivor, told me, "What predators do in the grooming process is fill a need. They will identify what it is a kid needs and then try to fill that need. They may do this because they know the child, or they've spent time talking to them, or they've gleaned information about the child from social media or some other source. Is a kid being bullied? Are things hard at home? Do they want a boyfriend? Or just a friend? When that need is being met, the child feels beholden and connected and becomes vulnerable."

This is significant for several reasons. First, if a victim has been manipulated to believe the relationship is real and the child values the connection they felt with the perpetrator, the child is much less likely to report it to someone. Such victims are also less likely to cooperate with medical or mental health providers, law enforcement, or their families out of feelings of allegiance to their abuser.

Second, while our perceptions about these types of predators often connote abduction or violent assaults by strangers, this data suggests that we pivot our thinking about risk. In most cases, victims are manipulated to think the predators can be trusted, so our discussions about this with our kids need to change. Most of the victims described in these studies were not snatched from their rooms or forced to meet with their predators but typically agreed to meet them in person, knowing that the adults were "romantically" or sexually interested in them. To the victims, these were not strangers, even though they had not met in person. Our discussion about safety should reflect the reality of how these people target kids so that they're better able to identify predators if (God forbid) they should ever encounter one.

Parrott-Perry, a child sexual abuse advocate, said, "The object shouldn't be to instill fear in your child; it should be to provide tools. [To teach them]: 'Trust your gut. Even if it's someone you know and trust, if that voice inside you says danger—listen.' The very best defense you have against this type of abuse and predation, though there is by no means a perfect defense, is your relationship with your child. Is there trust and communication? Is your child being heard by you? Do they know they can come to you, no matter what?"

WHAT IS SEXTORTION?

Sextortion is a type of crime where a criminal uses sexually explicit images of a victim to blackmail them. Frequently, what the blackmailer wants in exchange is more images—usually increasingly explicit images or videos. Sometimes the request is for money or sex. According to the Brookings Institution, 71 percent of victims are under eighteen years old. Every prosecuted offender in the United States, as of 2016, has been male. Ninety-one percent of victims were targeted on social media sites, while 43 percent had their computers or devices hacked.

The Brookings report states:

> The average teenage or young-adult Internet user, however, is the very softest of cybersecurity targets . . . They often "sext" one another. They sometimes record pornographic or semi-pornographic images or videos of themselves. And they share material with other teenagers whose cyberdefense practices are even laxer than their own. Sextortion thus turns out to be quite easy to accomplish in a target-rich environment that often does not require more than malicious guile.
>
> It is a great mistake, however, to confuse sextortion with consensual sexting or other online teenage flirtations. It is a crime of often unspeakable brutality.[6]

Like other sexual predators, sextortionists are generally repeat offenders. If they've successfully coerced one victim, it's likely they've done so many times.

The offenders can be other young people or former romantic partners of the victims. The concept of "revenge porn," which is the nonconsensual sharing of explicit images or videos of the victim in retaliation by a former romantic or sexual partner, has received more attention in the media.

Sextortion is a sex crime where the victims, who are primarily teens, are sexually coerced and menaced. Because of the fear and shame involved, many young people comply with the perpetrator, which generally exposes them to increasingly greater risk and trauma. It's critical to talk to kids about how being scared and panicked might lead them into making decisions that put them in more danger. If someone threatens them or tries to blackmail them, the best course of action is not to comply with the person trying to harm them but to get help right away. This may make total sense to parents, but frightened teenage brains don't always know how to respond in these situations.

We also need to have frank, realistic conversations about taking and sharing explicit pictures. Though this is increasingly normal behavior for teens, there is a threat that these images could be used against them. This is true even if the picture was taken only to satisfy their own curiosity and never shared with anyone. Once the image exists, it can be stolen, hacked, or accidentally discovered by someone who might use it against them.

How Do Kids React When Harassment, Bullying, Solicitation, or Abuse Happens?

The good news is that about half the kids (53 percent) who experienced a sexual solicitation online told someone, with 69 percent telling someone about the situation if it were aggressive or distressing.[7] The bad news is that a significant proportion of young people do nothing and tell no one about what happened. Friends are the most likely audience when kids decide to talk about this, followed by parents at a distant second.

Several different surveys report similar findings. The number of kids who tell anyone what is happening is distressingly low, but those numbers are improving over time. One survey found that of the kids who told their parents, 66 percent said it made the situation better.[8]

ACTION STEPS YOUNG ADULTS (AGES 14–24) REPORT TAKING IN RESPONSE TO BEING HARASSED, BULLIED, OR SOLICITED ONLINE

■ Made the situation better   ■ Made the situation worse

Changed passwords

Changed address, screen name, or number

Deleted social networking profile

Told parent(s)

Asked a friend for help

Asked a brother or sister for help

Called a help line or found an online help forum

Told a trusted adult who is not a family member

Reported person to Internet provider or website

Asked another family member for help

Asked person to stop

Reported person to police

Ignored person

Retaliated against person

Did nothing at all

0   10   20   30   40   50   60   70   80

Percentage of those who took action in response to digital abuse

Source: The AP-NORC Center for Public Affairs Research at the University of Chicago

Many kids don't tell parents about what's going on because they're afraid of getting in trouble or losing their phones or devices, which they see as their lifeline to their friends and the rest of the world.

This data highlights the urgent need for parents to discuss these issues with their kids. Many parents have an agreement with their teens about drinking and driving, where teens won't get in trouble if they prioritize their own safety by calling home for a ride. These agreements are predicated on survey data indicating that many kids would rather drive drunk or get a ride with someone who has been drinking than risk getting in trouble with their parents. There's a huge difference between providing your tacit consent or approval to a behavior and giving your child a way out of a bad or unsafe situation. You can be clear that you strongly disapprove of sexting, but still provide a safety net for your child (or one of their friends) if someone attempts to use an explicit image to blackmail them.

The data also tell us that kids are often likely to find themselves in the role of crisis counselor in these situations. Peers are more likely to be the support or resource for friends than parents, older siblings, teachers, the police, or the Internet service providers who host the site where the solicitation took place. Is your middle schooler ready to help a friend who's been sexually solicited or bullied online?

Discussing all this with our kids and creating an emergency plan of sorts can be really helpful. Have them think through what they would do and identify some places and people they can go to for help. When kids experience some kind of digital abuse, they often take the steps described in the chart on the previous page to try to make the situation better.

What to Do If Your Child Is a Victim of Online Bullying or Abuse

All the people I interviewed for this book, whether they worked in child protection, as educators, or in the tech world, were unanimous in advising families to do one thing if they suspect their child is being targeted: *document everything.*

You may want to block the person harassing your child, but it's important to document and take a screenshot of everything before doing so. Once blocked, you are generally no longer able to see the things they have posted, even the things they've already sent to you or that you may be tagged in. So collect evidence before blocking.

Take screenshots, keep a file with hard copies, send emails with attachments of the images in order to time-stamp when events occurred. Posts, tweets, images, even whole accounts can be deleted. Without a record of what happened, there is no evidence—only one person's word against another's.

When Families Contact Their Child's School After an Incident

If an incident occurs that involves kids from the same school, families may report the situation to school authorities. When this happens, there are many factors that affect how things are handled. Did the online abuse take place on school property or during school hours? Are the identities of all the kids involved known, and are they all students? Does the incident impact the students involved as learners and their safety in school? Is there evidence to substantiate claims or defend against them?

School administrators and staff are not criminal investigators, yet they're frequently tasked with finding out what happened in somewhat murky situations, with varying degrees of cooperation and little jurisdiction to discipline students (particularly if the incident occurred outside of school hours and off school grounds). While teachers and counselors are usually the first to flag incidents as they're unfolding, it's generally school administrators like principals or vice principals who are responsible for managing these incidents.

There is some personal discretion involved in how these things get handled at the school level, based on the administrator's experience and knowledge of what's involved (for example, the technology, the kids, and the details of what happened). There are some individuals who handle these situations really well, with empathy and tact. There are others who make matters worse. Based on the comments of families who've reached out to me on these issues from across the country, the type of response you can expect from the school is largely dependent on the school administrator that you're dealing with.

This is a policy gap, and one that should be addressed. It's certainly difficult to write policies around this when the technology is quickly evolving and each case must be treated carefully and on an individual basis. Currently, most administrators use the rules of their school district and state, as well as whatever student code of conduct or athletic team or extracurricular activity participation agreement that may govern the students' behavior, to assess if rules have been broken and determine how to deal with them.

Again, the rules and laws governing codes of conduct, school districts, and municipalities vary from place to place. What will get you expelled in one district may be simply frowned upon in another. Most schools will try to keep incidents fairly quiet, for a variety of reasons. Often this is perceived as "covering things up," and certainly this is sometimes the case. But the administrators I spoke with also said that it was generally their policy to keep things under the radar because it protected the victims. The more people who know about cyberbullying or sexting incidents, the greater the demand there is to know what's going on. As the audience grows, so does the drama and, frankly, the trauma that can result from it.

How Common Is Cyberbullying, Really?

There is no real consensus about just how pervasive cyberbullying is. One comprehensive study published by the American Medical Association in 2015 reviewed and analyzed findings from thirty-six other studies and placed the prevalence of cyberbullying among children and teens at about 23 percent.[9] You may have seen numbers much higher or lower than this. Bullying generally peaks during middle school,[10] while cyberbullying specifically peaks in seventh to tenth grades.[11]

The term *bullying* itself is subjective, and there's no widely accepted definition that researchers, educators, and policy-makers all use. As a result, when you are trying to determine how often bullying happens online and how serious it is, the numbers tend to vary based on whom you talk to. Some of the educators I spoke with said that efforts to increase awareness of the problem of bullying have resulted in some parents labeling unkind or mean behavior as bullying when technically it's not.

There's significant research that indicates that rates of bullying may have actually decreased over the past ten years, though that may not align with many people's perceptions. Again, this may be due to successful efforts to raise awareness of the issue. When we look specifically at rates of online bullying, we may see increases, sometimes drastic ones, over the past ten years. However, we need to take a step back and consider how the role of technology has grown. Remember that the first iPhone was released in 2007 and that Instagram didn't exist before 2010. When we see teenagers report an increase in conflict online, many researchers assert that it represents a shift in how teens now spend their time. The conflicts are different, but not new. They've migrated with teens, away from phone calls and arguments at the mall after school to group chats and FaceTime.

What Do We Mean When We Talk About Online Bullying and Harassment?

The Cyberbullying Research Center (which is a really excellent online resource) defines cyberbullying as "willful and repeated harm inflicted through the use of computers, cell phones, and other electronic devices." I like this definition because it's simple but places importance on a few key issues. The abuse is willful, meaning it is done with intention and not accidentally. The definition also stresses that the behavior must be repeated. One instance of cruel behavior online can be really awful, but it's not bullying. What makes bullying so harmful is the fact that the victim is targeted again and again.

Some of the specific behaviors that researchers include in the definition are name-calling, using hate speech or hurtful remarks, spreading gossip and rumors, making threats or sexual comments, or sharing images, videos, or personal information without consent. The type of bullying that is often the most upsetting involves pictures or videos that someone was coerced into taking or sharing, or that was taken or shared without their consent or knowledge.

Effects of Cyberbullying

In some ways, cyberbullying is more intense than traditional bullying. It's more difficult for the victims to avoid their perpetrators, the means by which the harassment is occurring can be shared and spread quickly and widely, and, of course, there is a degree of permanency to some forms of cyberbullying that is both daunting and traumatizing. Images and taunts out there on the Internet are always out there, threatening to come back at some future date and cause harm.

Perhaps these reasons account for the relationship between cyberbullying, self-harm, and suicidal thoughts. The data is clear that cyberbullying hurts the relationships that the victim has with family and friends. From the interviews I conducted on this subject, I can tell you with certainty that cyberbullying doesn't just affect the kid—it impacts the whole family. In short, cyberbullying is very serious stuff and not to be minimized or dismissed.

Victims report emotional distress, anxiety, depression, avoidance, symptoms such as headaches and stomachaches, and alcohol and tobacco use. It's also correlated with aggressive tendencies, anger management issues, reduced academic achievement, and increased school absence rates. However, it's not always clear in the research if cyberbullying precedes these issues, worsens them, or occurs as a result of them.[12]

What Are Some Risk Factors for Online Bullying and Harassment?

Anyone can be the victim of online bullying. Often it has nothing to do with the child who is being targeted; however, some kids experience a greater likelihood of being bullied. This is particularly true for kids who are atypical in some fashion. In many cases, relational and social problems that kids experience at school and in person carry over to issues they deal with online. Girls are more likely than boys to experience online bullying, as are gay or questioning youths. Across multiple studies and surveys, kids report being bullied online because of their race, religion, and appearance. Some studies have noted that cyberbullying tends to take a disproportionate toll on vulnerable populations, which can also include kids who have mental health or other developmental problems.

With traditional forms of bullying, it is easier to identify times and places that represent elevated risk and to create some protective strategies to address them. The walk home from school, lunchtime in the cafeteria, and the parking lot after football games might be more high-risk environments. It's more challenging to avoid digital harassment, but it's still important to think about the times of day and spaces on the Internet where abuse is most likely to happen and to develop some strategies for addressing the behavior when and where you're most likely to encounter it.

What Are Some Coping Strategies That Work?

The research also tells us that when kids perceive a problem as "controllable," they are more likely to take action to solve it. When they feel that a situation is out of their control, that there's nothing to be done about it, then they seek to avoid it or minimize the impact of the emotions associated with it. We want to teach our kids that if they're bullied, it's not their fault and they can control the situation.

We need to let our kids know that they always have a choice and there are always actions they can take. Reinforce that, at a minimum, there's the choice to do something or do nothing. Externalize the situation—remind your child that someone else's unkind behavior is not on them. They're responsible for their own choices, not other people's actions.

Dealing with the problem directly can happen online or off-line. You can change passwords or accounts. You can investigate online. You can respond. You can block users or remove suspected aggressors from your social networks. You can lock down your account to make it harder for them to contact you or view your content.

Off-line, you can seek out social support from friends or family by telling someone what's happening. You can confront or respond to the person harassing you. You can go to the authorities (parents, teachers, school administration, law enforcement). You can also retaliate against the bully—not a strategy I would advise, but something kids report doing in the research fairly frequently.

Seeking social support has been identified as the most effective "buffer" against the ill effects of bullying. In short, telling people and asking for help works. It's the best thing you can do to protect yourself and deal directly with the situation. I would add that if the first person you tell isn't helpful or supportive, then tell someone else. The research says that younger kids are more likely than older kids to seek social support and tell their parents. This makes sense. Older kids may be experiencing harassment that could "out" things to their parents that they would prefer to keep hidden. Older kids are also more likely to be concerned about losing their phones, their access to social media or gaming, or the freedom to hang out with their friends.

Takeaways . . .

- We have to discuss with our children, honestly and openly, the dangers associated with being online. This includes really difficult conversations around sex, pornography, predators, bullying, and more. Unfortunately, we have to have these discussions at a relatively early age, before we may feel our kids are ready for them. Most victims are targeted at around age thirteen. If your child is old enough to get a cell phone or a social media account, then your child must be mature enough to have honest conversations about the risks that they may be exposed to. If your child isn't ready to hear about it, they might not be ready to have access to the technology yet.

- Provide your kids with some recommendations for safe and accurate resources to get their questions answered. Kids are conditioned to Google everything. Tell them you understand that they may have questions (which is totally normal) and they may not feel comfortable asking you about them (also normal). But explain that going to chat rooms, Reddit threads, or anonymous forums to get those questions answered provides predators with the means to target them.

- Have conversations with your kids about how predators work: how they develop relationships to build trust, so that kids develop a loyalty to their "friend" and won't tell their parents what's going on. Make sure that they know that anyone who asks them to keep a secret from their parents is not their friend. That is the universal mode for all predators; telling their victims their relationship must be a secret. The difference between privacy and secrecy is shame.

- Make sure accounts are private and that your child knows not to post pictures that provide easy clues as to where they live or go to school, like geotagging their updates.

- Collaborate on a few checklist items that your kid can use to self-assess whether their online connections are safe or not. Red flags include:
  - This person says I shouldn't tell anyone that we're talking.
  - If I have to lie about a friendship or relationship, is it a healthy one?
  - I've never met this person before, and yet I'm communicating with them a lot.
  - This person is interested in me romantically or sexually, and they've asked me to keep that a secret.
  - Am I 100 percent sure that this person with whom I'm chatting/playing a game/texting is who they say they are? How can I be sure? Is it because I have mutual friends or contacts? Have those friends met this person before, and are they 100 percent sure that the person is who they say they are?

- Kids are more likely to engage in risk behavior when they're around their friends. Talk to your kids about this and create some awareness that perhaps they behave slightly differently when they're with their buddies. Ask for examples of people who seem to act one way when they're with their friends and another way when adults are around. Use this information to make choices about how to enforce tech rules when kids are hanging out at your house.

- Only about 5 percent of young people talk about sex online with people they don't know.[13] Kids who do this, or who post overtly sexual images of themselves, are at greater risk of being sexually solicited. This is a huge red flag and risk factor.

- Another risk factor is accepting strangers into contacts, followers, or friends lists. Make sure that kids understand that they shouldn't do this. It's also a risk factor when kids frequently communicate with strangers or on anonymous forums. This includes gaming, on consoles, mobile devices, and computers.

- Don't let your knee-jerk reaction be taking away your kid's phone. If you have an agreement about drinking and driving or being in a social situation that feels unsafe, create a similar understanding about things that occur online and feel dangerous or risky. This agreement has to include the understanding that if your child comes to you for help, they will not lose their phone, device, or social media accounts (as this fear is a primary factor that keeps kids from telling adults in the first place).

- While most kids understand that they shouldn't share information with strangers, many will absolutely share things like their address, phone number, school, age, and email on a website or online form that looks legitimate or is on a site they trust. If there's a contest or giveaway online, or an app they want that asks for that information, even smart kids may be fooled into sharing their personal information.

- How kids choose to deal with bullying (their coping choices) has the potential to make things better or worse for them. We need to teach our kids to appraise difficult situations and then choose some kind of action to take. Taking action, even with limited effect, tends to help kids rebound faster. The most useful active coping strategy for kids is telling an adult.

- Collaborate with your kids to create an online incident emergency plan. Getting adults, school officials, or law enforcement quickly involved can prevent the escalation of bullying. It doesn't have to be you, but work with kids to identify a trusted adult that everyone can agree on.

- A strong argument can be made for all pediatricians to screen kids with general questions about their online lives. Ask your pediatrician to have this discussion with your kids.

- There is a lot of evidence about what works in terms of reducing more traditional forms of bullying, and one of the most effective methods of reducing both victimization and perpetration is parental involvement.

- There are many options for private messaging and video chatting within the functionality of apps and games, and it's critical that parents know about them before approving downloads and new accounts.

- Talk to your kids about basic cybersecurity like passwords, two-factor authentication for social media accounts, and lockdown of devices when not in use. One in five kids have shared a password with a friend. The more social media accounts a child has, the more likely that child is to share passwords with their friends [14] If your child already has multiple social media accounts (and most teens do), you need to address this with them pronto.

10 | Hoping for the Best and Avoiding the Worst

MY STORY (AGE FORTY-FIVE)

I had a conversation with my son recently that led not to a fight but to a long grumble, and contributed to what feels like a growing distance between us. I think it's becoming a rite of passage for families with kids in elementary school and middle school. My son asked me again why I wouldn't let him have a Snapchat or an Instagram account.

"I know we've already talked about this, but . . . I'm literally the only kid I know who doesn't have one."

I felt the frustration coming off him and it felt just like my own. I tried to answer, but before I could finish he shrugged and walked away, knowing it was the wrong time to fight this particular battle. The terms of use for most of the apps he wants say that users must be thirteen, and he's only twelve. It was a rule I'd enforced with his sister, and he knew I wasn't changing my mind about it.

He struggled with the unfairness of how some people's parents understand and let their kids get their accounts early, while other parents like me don't. He thought I was being ridiculous and unyielding. What he didn't know is how much I struggled with all of this. When it comes to social media and kids, nothing is simple.

I know that he's not the only kid in seventh grade without Snapchat. In fact, it may be only a minority in his class who actually have it. But it doesn't seem that way to him. The kids who do have social media are so visible that everyone else just gets lost. He feels like he's being left behind, and wherever he looks, he sees the evidence of it. The other kids speak a language that he doesn't know. They connect and communicate in ways he is excluded from. And it's taking place all the time. Like every minute, they're texting and Snapping and liking and following. And if you're not a part of it, then you're just . . . not.

I mean, I know my kid and I know that what's best for him is to wait another year. But with that choice comes very real social consequences. And he has to pay them, not me. This is a trade-off I'm making for him, and frankly it feels like a no-win situation. If I let him get on social media early, I run the risk of his encountering a situation that he may not be able to handle. If I don't allow him on social media early, he runs the risk of being excluded from a big group of kids. As if middle school weren't hard enough.

And I know of so many other families for whom this just doesn't seem to be an issue. Their kids have had these accounts since fifth grade or younger, and it seems like it's no big deal. I wonder if by holding off, I'm making it a bigger thing than it needs to be. I wonder if those parents felt pressure from their kids and from other parents, but just went in a different direction.

Among parents, these decisions get super weird. Sometimes we talk to each other about it. "When did you let your kid get Snapchat?" is as loaded a question for me right now as "Are you breastfeeding?" was fifteen years ago. When I hear these questions from other parents, I'm always thinking: What's the answer you want to hear? What is it you're looking for from this conversation? Validation? An argument?

It's playing out in the dark in some ways. No one really knows what everyone else is doing, and no one is advertising their decisions because it always comes with some kind of judgment. And, of course, it's also playing out right there in public, because once a kid has a phone or an Instagram account, it becomes common knowledge. At my house, every kid we know who is allowed to have social media or have two gaming systems or sleep with their iPhone next to their bed becomes part of the argument for why I should be more like that kid's parents.

Every couple of weeks, it seems, I get a reminder of why I'm making the choices I am. I'll hear about kids getting bullied or sexting or doing something stupid online. I'll see an article or everyone I know will share the same story on Facebook. It's weird, because those days are hard and affirming at the same time. It's awful to hear about these things happening, and it breaks my heart when it's a kid I know. But it also strengthens my resolve and reminds me why I believe my son needs to wait.

We went through all this a couple of years ago with my older daughter. She probably could've handled social media much earlier than she got it. She's very different from her brother. And her friends are different too. I didn't realize it as much then, but those friend groups are almost as big an issue as the kid's personality. It's not just about what your kid is going to post online but also what they're going to be seeing. It's about how they talk to one another and how they treat one another. And all that stuff? That's totally out of my control. I have no control over what other kids post, what they say or do.

While she probably disagrees, I think that making my daughter wait to get on social media saved her a lot of drama. By the time she was allowed to jump in the pool, most of the kids had already learned to swim, and a lot of the splashing and flailing around had stopped.

I've had to ask myself a lot of hard questions about what my kids could handle and to seriously consider if we were ready. What is this kid showing me they can handle? Can I trust them to make good choices, at least most of the time? Am I prepared for their social lives to go from our living room and our backyard to the comparative privacy of their phones? Am I ready to not be in the loop on a lot of things going on with them? Are we ready to handle all the what-ifs and know what to do?

And is there a point at which maybe they're ready and I'm not? All I can do is make the best choices for my kids that I can, coming from a place of being informed. And then just hope for the best.

_____

How Do You Know the Right Thing to Do?

As my kids will very happily tell you, I don't have all the answers when it comes to parenting or technology. That's the reason I wrote this book, because I needed to figure out what I was doing. I was less interested in the technology itself, because that's always changing. I wanted to understand the underlying adolescent development and behavioral issues that drive the technology's use, because who kids are and how they grow—that hasn't changed.

So many of the answers I found reaffirmed what I already knew. The things that are most important in terms of preparing our kids for a positive digital experience in adolescence are essentially the same things we've always known teenagers needed. The annoying part about all this is how none of these truths involve easy answers:

- Every kid is different, even within the same family.

- Kids change so much year to year, and rules need to change with them.

- Parents need to model the behavior they expect from their children.

- Open communication is critical, which means we need to listen more and talk less.

- Everyone makes mistakes, sometimes bad ones.

- Trust starts with giving kids the chance to prove they're ready.

- You must love the kid you've got.

- Your job is to make sure that someday your kids won't need you.

I have a real problem with some of these truths. First of all, I'm not good at listening, especially when it comes to video games. Second, I know that I'm raising my kids to be adults—but letting go is really hard. I don't want to. Third, trusting them to be safe? Out there in the big world, both real and digital? That's terrifying.

In this chapter, we're going to focus on the protective factors, best practices, and expert recommendations identified throughout the book. I hope that by focusing on the good, we can navigate this journey with our kids.

Don't Worry About What Other Parents Are Doing

Another truth that became glaringly obvious to me while writing this book is that our social environments drive so much of how we think and what we do. We can do everything right, but we're still competing with the media, friends, quickly evolving social norms, and brains that believe that "Well, it seemed like a good idea at the time" is a reasonable justification for doing something stupid. Social media and the constant connectivity of smartphones magnify and enhance those social influences—for everyone. So it's time we all learned to look at them with a more critical eye.

We're all subject to the influence of what we think is normal. Especially in our roles as parents, we're drawn to socially normative and safe behaviors as a way of providing security for our children. We seek to avoid judgment, particularly when it's directed at our kids or our parenting. In fact, there is no faster way to make someone defensive or angry than to be critical of their children or their parenting, especially on the Internet. But if we're going to tell our children to tune out the bullshit, then we need to be prepared to do the same thing.

How we arrived at this moment in parenting culture was the result of a million factors. It should be clear, though, that where we are now is not where we'll always be. We don't have to hold ourselves up to whatever gold standard currently exists. It's a ridiculous contest where the rules always change and no one wins. And yet we live in a world where social comparison drives much of what we do and how we define our own success. It doesn't matter what the issue is—when it comes to raising kids, someone is going to think what you're doing is wrong, and they will have a blog post to prove it.

The best thing you can do to raise responsible and happy digital citizens is to tune out what everyone else is doing and focus on being a resource and mentor for your kid. That may not look like "normal." Sometimes what works for everyone else doesn't—and shouldn't—work for you. Maybe it's because your kids are wired differently, or because of your family's values system or economic situation. In any case, it really doesn't matter what everyone else is doing. All that matters is that you are there for your kids. If others want to judge you for that, please imagine me rolling my eyes at them and then handing you a cup of coffee.

Atypical Kids Need Atypical Rules

If your child has ADHD, autism, anxiety, or depression, you may need a whole different set of rules around technology. Depending on the kid and the condition, this could take many different forms, and none of them might be considered normal. We do not care what uninformed people think of our unique and specific situations. It could be that your child with anxiety isn't allowed to have Instagram or is allowed to have only limited access. For a kid on the spectrum, it could mean a lot more video games than some people are comfortable with. If video games (or watching other people play video games) help that kid decompress and self-soothe, and their team (doctors, therapists, teachers, etc.) are on board with it, then I repeat: It does not matter what anyone else is doing. What matters is making informed choices with your child and for your child's best interests.

Be a Mentor

In her 2015 article for *The Atlantic*, "Parents: Reject Technology Shame," Alexandra Samuel writes that it is misguided for parents to vilify one another for their tech choices. Her findings imply that there's really only one thing that matters—helping your kids navigate this new environment. She surveyed ten thousand families in North America and found that the group of parents she called digital mentors tended to have the best outcomes. These are the parents who take an active role in their kids' online lives. They represent about a third of all parents in her study and are parents of kids of all ages, from babies to college students.

Digital mentors talk to their kids about how to responsibly use the Internet, social media, and technology, and they do it about once a week—meaning these conversations are ongoing and fluid. They also use technology to connect with their kids, playing games with them, watching YouTube videos, using apps together, and messaging each other. These parents research devices, games, apps, and accounts for their kids and with their kids.

Moreover, Samuel's study found that children of parents who simply limit technology, without providing guidance and support on how to use it, "are the most likely to engage in problematic behavior: They're twice as likely as children of mentors to access porn, or to post rude or hostile comments online; they're also three times as likely to go online and impersonate a classmate, peer, or adult. Shielding kids from the Internet may work for a time, but once they do get online, limiters' kids often lack the skills and habits that make for consistent, safe, and successful online interactions."

Mentor First, Monitor Second, Trust Always

In her excellent book *Screenwise*, author Devorah Heitner talks about the relationship between mentoring and monitoring. Both are important and both need to be built on trust. She describes the mentor role in this way: "Mentors recognize the need to observe kids in their habitat in order to get a better understanding of their lived experience. Mentors don't want to *catch* their kids doing the wrong thing; they want to *teach* their kids to do the right thing! Mentors understand that tech limits alone are no substitute for engagement."

If you're going to monitor your kids' online lives, you have to do so with transparency. It should be clear to your child what you're doing and why you're doing it. The intention behind monitoring is not to have a "gotcha" moment. If you're sure a "gotcha" moment is inevitable and you're planning a stakeout to bust your kids, then maybe your kid isn't ready to have a phone, or maybe the problem is bigger than tech use.

Parents who are overly reliant on monitoring instead of mentoring may get a false sense that everything is fine as long as no issues pop up when they look at their kids' tech use or social media. This is especially true if they depend on an app or program to do it for them. Monitoring should be about accountability, and it works both ways. My kids hate that I periodically check their phones, but they know that the more responsible they are, the more hands-off I become. They also know my phone's password, and they are on it all the time—playing games, picking the playlists we listen to, and texting their dad for me when I'm driving. We understand that privacy isn't something that really exists online or on our phones—and that things we never imagined could get seen by an audience we didn't intend.

Remember What Is Age-Appropriate

Kids will act their age, whether they're online or in the cafeteria at school. It's important to meet your kids where they are and to keep your expectations for them aligned with what's reasonable for their stage of development. Are teenagers going to be sexually curious? Yes. Are they going to guard their privacy and resent your interference? They will. Will these things be easy to deal with? Probably not.

Deborah Gilboa, a family practitioner, a parenting expert, and the founder of AskDoctorG.com, told me that parents are often dealing with teenagers who may think they can handle more freedom and autonomy than they're actually ready for: "When a kid says, 'You don't trust me,' I say, 'I do trust you. I trust that you're a good kid. I also trust you to be fourteen. So I trust you sometimes to be impulsive or to grab the cheap joke instead of remembering to be kind. That's all I'm saying. I trust your brother to be a responsible kid for his age, but I also trust him to be six, so I'm not leaving him home alone.'"

All my research shows younger kids consistently experience problems on social media that they're less cognitively and emotionally prepared to handle. Not only are younger kids less mature and more impulsive, but so is their peer network. Plenty of good kids make bad choices online every day. And you know what? They're acting their age. Many of the blunders younger kids make online are developmentally and age-appropriate; they're just taking place in a group chat instead of on the playground. I'm not saying you have to make your kids wait until they're older to get social media, though that is the choice I'm making. If you decide to get those accounts early, mentoring and monitoring become even more important, especially when it comes to setting limits on how and when it can be used and who they're allowed to interact with.

Use the Imaginary Audience as a Framework

The Imaginary Audience describes a psychological phase of development that most kids experience in their early teens. Looking at how the Imaginary Audience works can really help parents understand why kids use this technology and respond to it the way they do. Social media is meeting a core need for kids during this phase. They star in, curate, and create their social media feeds, becoming the protagonist of that story. Social media makes the Imaginary Audience real for them and, as a result, may make them feel even more self-conscious.

Help kids manage this phase and their social media use in their early teens by reframing messages around the Internet and social media toward active decision-making and anticipating consequences, instead of being focused on the feedback and affirmation cycle. Ask them to think objectively about who might see the things they post or text and how those things might be interpreted. Challenge them to consider their social media and online presence from the perspectives of different people who might see it and how it might make them feel. Avoid making the Imaginary Audience more salient to them by stressing things like "Someone is always watching" or "You never who is paying attention to what you post."

The chart on the next page is an example in the context of talking to your kids about staying safe online.

TALKING TO KIDS ABOUT STRANGERS ON THE INTERNET
(two slightly different approaches)

Everyone you don't know is a potential predator. Actually, predators are everywhere. You probably know a couple. Trust no one.	You're in control of what you click on, what you share, who you follow, and knowing when you need help. Use common sense and good judgment.
⬇	⬇
THREATS EVERYWHERE. CONSTANT VIGILANCE.	THINK FIRST, THEN POST. HAVE A PLAN IF THINGS GET WEIRD.
⬇	⬇
No, seriously. That person who just friended you is not a kid from your school; he's probably an old man who drives a windowless van.	What are some strategies for confirming that people are who they say they are? Who can you go to if something messed up happens?
⬇	⬇
Kids learn that danger is everywhere, they have no control over it, and there's nothing they can do except feel vaguely freaked out all the time.	Kids learn that they have control over their online choices, strategies for dealing with problems, and options for what to do if things get scary.

Not All Tech Is the Same

It's easy to lump screen time together, but we shouldn't conflate all types of tech use. Being on social media is not the same thing as creating content or researching something you want to learn. Watching TV is not the same thing as doing homework on a computer.

Jessica Lahey, author of *The Gift of Failure*, told me, "We may need to broaden our understanding of what limits are placed on different kinds of screen time. For example, if my kid is holed up in his room watching YouTube videos, that's one kind of screen time and that deserves one set of limits. But if my two children, who are five years apart and have very little in common, are playing a video game together? That is not the same thing at all. That is brother time, and that's them talking to each other, and laughing, and being cooperative."

Try to encourage the good and limit the stuff that brings less value to your kids' lives. Work with your kids to establish rules around screen time that make sense to them and encourage them to use technology for growth and communication.

TALK ABOUT WHY MULTITASKING IS A PROBLEM

Parents multitask every day and, generally, it's seen as being positive. It helps us get a lot of things done and be more productive. We field emails from work while helping with algebra homework, cooking dinner, and listening to music. Wireless mobile devices and the Internet take multitasking to a whole new level. When it comes to technology, multitasking is more accurately described as "rapid task switching." This is an important distinction because the consequences of rapid task switching are almost uniformly negative.

In fact, research shows that people who digitally multitask have "less brain density in areas dealing with cognitive and emotional control" and that "multitasking is correlated with lower emotional intelligence," which implies that it could have a detrimental impact on our relationships. This is supported by multiple research studies, which have found that digital multitasking results in decreased reported well-being, poor academic achievement, decreased ability to sustain attention, and higher levels of depression and anxiety. Students who rapidly switch tasks during class are less likely to remember the content being taught. In fact, some research has shown that multitasking during a cognitive exercise can lower IQ by up to fifteen points.[1]

Despite overwhelming evidence regarding its negative effects, digital multitasking feels good. It triggers the reward centers in our brains, giving us those lovely dopamine hits we all enjoy so much. Those good feelings create a positive feedback loop, encouraging us to do it more. The more we do it, the shorter our attention span becomes and the less tolerance our brains have for being bored.

The key to cutting back on media multitasking is to set limits and use tools and strategies to help with focus. Yes, there is an app for that. You can also set timers, leave your phone in another room (it probably needs to charge anyway), or choose to work off-line by disabling your Internet connection. The most useful way to enforce these rules is for adults to model the behavior they want to see in their kids (*ugh, this again*) and to implement family-wide tech-free time every day, specifically set up for everyone to get things done.

Set Reasonable Limits

Part of teaching kids how to self-regulate their tech use and create healthy habits is to set reasonable limits and enforce them consistently. This is important for several reasons. The data overwhelmingly supports moderate use for good outcomes, as well as for reasons related to safety. The more teens are on their phones, the more likely they are to encounter inappropriate content, develop problematic use, and experience decreased mental health and well-being.

Use apps to help with setting limits, but be careful not to become reliant on them to do the heavy lifting for you. Setting up an app to turn your kids' devices on or off or to block adult content is a really useful tool, but it can't take the place of teaching kids what they should do if porn finds its way onto their phones. An app should never be a substitute for parenting. Here are some guidelines you might find useful:

- Charge phones overnight in a common area or in a parent's bedroom.

- Carve out mandatory screen-free time and encourage tech breaks: at the table, during religious services or education, at bedtime, with their grandparents (unless they're co-viewing something), etc.

- Create rules for different types of screen time—gaming, TV, social media, and so forth.

- Work with kids to set limits, as they will be more likely to abide by them if they have a say in what the rules are.

- Put phones away during homework time to help with focus and cut down on digital multitasking.

- Communicate about consequences before you attempt to enforce them. Make sure kids understand what will happen if they don't follow the established rules and limits.

- Be consistent and calm in enforcing the rules.

- Walk the walk and model the behavior you want to see.

No One Should Sleep with a Phone in the Room

This might be the single most important suggestion in this entire book. I know you've heard it before, but it's true. First of all, this practice prioritizes sleep, which is the mother of all protective factors. For teens, a lack of sleep is associated with impulsivity, risk-taking, attention problems, depression, anxiety, obesity, heart disease, and decreased academic performance—just to name a few. Technology is stimulating, which makes sleep harder, and the blue light from screens can disrupt circadian rhythms. This is not just a problem for kids. Do yourself a favor and leave your phone in another room at night; you will get more sleep and feel better for it.

The other reason why I strongly discourage having a phone in your teen's bedroom late at night is because it's what I call a modifiable risk factor. Kids just do not need access to their phones in the middle of the night. When they're up late and tired, they are more prone to the disinhibition effect. There have also been many, many regrettable incidents that were shared with me over the course of my research for this book that could have been entirely prevented by charging the kid's phone in the kitchen.

I have taken those hard-earned lessons to heart. By enforcing this rule, I have also created an ongoing source of conflict between the teenagers in my household—who believe it to be totally unfair and unreasonable—and me. I have tried explaining the evidence-based logic behind this rule, which is truly based on my concern for the welfare of our family. These children do not care. I am the bad guy (a role I do not like), but I can live with that. Sadly, being the parent of teens sometimes means being the brick wall against which they bang their heads.

Being a Good Friend Online

The social lives of kids are so entwined with technology that it's impossible to tease the real and digital lives apart. What we can do is establish expectations for being a good friend that are the same for both spheres:

- Be considerate of other people's feelings in what you say and post.

- Don't deliberately leave someone out by not including them in something you post or by not tagging them in photos.

- Every type of social media has its own unspoken rules about what is polite and what is rude, as does texting. Try to be mindful of these rules and considerate of others.

- Rise above the groupthink or hive mind mentality. In fact, if you see a group of people ganging up on or targeting someone, you should say something, tell an adult, or report it.

- Never share a friend's secret or private information without permission.

- Do not take or share images or videos without consent.

- Arguments and conflicts should be kept private and respectful.

- Always try to resolve conflicts in person, not online or via text.

- Don't subtweet or make passive-aggressive comments about people without actually naming or tagging them. They will find out and there will be drama.

- In gaming situations, keep trash talk funny. Don't say things that are really personal or cruel.

- Stick up for your friends if you see someone being abusive or targeting them.

- Never trash-talk or mess with people because of their race, gender, identity, or appearance.

- If you make a mistake or do something wrong, take responsibility and apologize.

Encouraging Healthy Relationships and Digital Dating

The social lives of teenagers involve constant contact, which can accelerate and inflate a sense of closeness within relationships, resulting in issues with appropriate boundaries. It's important to discuss what level of contact feels comfortable to both people in a relationship. Should it be every day or every couple of hours? What feels caring to one person may feel intrusive to another.

Healthy relationships are defined by open communication. Discussions about respect, boundaries, and consent need to take place at the beginning of the relationship to make sure that everyone is on the same page. As parents, we have to talk about body autonomy and consent with our teenagers, both boys and girls, over and over again. Consent doesn't just apply to physical or sexual contact within a relationship; it also applies to language, boundaries, and communication. Consent is also relevant to images—specifically any image that could be considered sexting.

Be a Resource

There is overwhelming research that tells us that when kids have a question about drugs, alcohol, or sex, the first place they go is the Internet. This very natural tendency can expose kids to risk. For example, kids will often Google questions when it comes to drugs and alcohol, including the potential side effects for prescription drugs. When they do this, what do they find? Message boards moderated by volunteers with no expertise or ability to verify the accuracy of the information provided— other than to Google it themselves. This can lead to some very dangerous outcomes.

For kids in the LGBTQ community, looking to the Internet to answer questions about emerging identity and sexual health makes a lot of sense. There are also much-needed opportunities to connect with friends and role models and find community. Unfortunately, these kids are much more likely to be harassed, bullied, and sexually solicited online. Kids who chat online about sex, especially in a chat room, open themselves up to being sexually solicited. This behavior is consistently identified as a risk factor.

What this should tell us is that parents need to provide safe and accurate resources for kids, which respect their natural inclinations toward privacy. Many strategies are safer than Google. You can buy books and store them somewhere they can be discreetly accessed if needed. You can identify another trusted adult, one who is much cooler and possibly younger than you, as the go-to person for your kids to talk to. You can also create a folder of bookmarked websites (ones you've looked over) and tell your kids they're free to peruse anything on those sites privately. See Appendix 2 on page 251 for a list of websites to get you started.

Find the Lessons in Video Gaming

Video games are a great opportunity to encourage analytic thinking. There can be many positive benefits of gameplay, and all of them are enhanced when you take the time to articulate what the games are teaching. That's the thing about games—there are rewards and feedback for certain skills and behavior. What are they? How are those skills applied in real life?

Encourage Critical Thinking and Metacognition

Metacognition essentially means thinking about your thinking. Technology offers so many opportunities to look more deeply at the world around us and to better understand and analyze how things work. These are skills that young teens are only just developing because the parts of their brains that allow for this type of thought are just waking up. Having conversations that encourage analytic thinking strengthens that function, enhances their overall cognitive functioning, and encourages intellectual curiosity.

Here are some examples of questions to have your teens consider:

- *On buying video games:* One game is more expensive, but is it more enjoyable? How many hours do you estimate you'll end up spending on one game versus another? Which is the better value when you consider it that way?

- *On Instagram:* Which kids in your class consistently get the most likes and comments? What kinds of pictures are they sharing? Is it because they have the most followers and therefore the largest audience? Do they know all the people who are following them? Are they asking for people to like or comment on their photos? Is that an effective strategy to get likes?

- *On trade-offs and time:* How much time are you spending on your phone or device every day? What kind of trade-offs are you making to be online? What are you giving up to browse, to be on social media, or to play a game?

- *On social norms:* Based on what you're seeing right now, it looks like everyone is partying on the weekend. Is that true, or is it just a subgroup of people who are really visible on Snapchat? Are any of the images something that could get someone in trouble? If it's making you feel weird, should you stop looking at their stories on Friday night?

Social Comparison and Social Media

Social media is like a funhouse mirror—it reflects and distorts reality. Social comparison is an important variable in many of the bad outcomes associated with social media, like depression and a decreased sense of well-being. The best way to counteract social comparison is to be aware of it. Kids know that what they see is both real and a very distorted reflection of reality. Help them to process this and place the things they see in that context.

Break down how social comparison works. Explain how it feels good when you compare favorably with someone and how it feels bad when they come out ahead of you. Have kids reality-check what they see on Instagram and on Snapchat with what they know in real life. Use analogies comparing social media to a highlight reel. Focus on people who use social media not for affirmation or comparison but to share things that matter to them, such as humor, art, movies, music, memes, or ideas. Look at people who do a good job being their authentic selves online.

DUCK SYNDROME

After a spate of college suicides, researchers at Stanford University coined the phrase *duck syndrome*. Ducks appear to glide smoothly across the surface of the water, leaving ripples in their wake, moving forward with seemingly little effort. Underneath the water and hidden from view, however, the duck is paddling furiously. Similarly, as students enter college, they may look at their peers and see them all gliding around, while they themselves struggle to adapt and keep up.

Duck syndrome is in many ways the perfect analogy for why so many people react to social media as they do. Social media is the pretty, well-tended pond that hides the imperfections and, more important, the effort required to move forward through life. It reinforces the notion that everything is better and easier for everyone else, that you're the only one who is struggling as everyone else glides ahead.

This negatively impacts the mental health and well-being of young adults in several ways. Those who present an idealized image of themselves on social media struggle with the disparity between their real lives and the expectations created by their near-perfect image online.

Others suffer from a sense that they're not measuring up. In an article from the Child Mind Institute, Dr. Jill Emanuele states, "Kids view social media through the lens of their own lives. If they're struggling to stay on top of things or suffering from low self-esteem, they're more likely to interpret images of peers having fun as confirmation that they're doing badly compared to their friends."[2]

The best way to counteract the effects of duck syndrome is to talk about it with your kids and put it on their radar. Give them a framework to put the things they see into perspective, to remind them that someone's Instagram feed is merely showing the surface (that person gliding across the water), while leaving out the important stuff (those stubby webbed feet frantically swishing back and forth, working really hard to stay afloat).

Be Realistic About Predators and Bad Guys Online

We have to teach our children to recognize how predators function online, how they gain trust and develop connections, and where they are most likely to reach out to victims. But we also have to teach them that most of the danger posed to them online will come from other kids and people they know in real life. Teaching negotiation skills and providing scripts to help them say no to peers who would coerce them into doing things that are dangerous or could hurt them is critical. Working with kids to have a plan for what to do when things get scary is also important; we must let them know that telling a trusted adult is always better than suffering through bullying, harassment, or abuse alone.

Laura Parrott-Perry, cofounder and CEO of Say It Survivor, told me, "When we speak to parents about risk, they want to have the stranger-danger conversation. The fact is that when it comes to child sexual abuse, 93 percent of it comes from someone who is already in your child's life. Yes, the risk of your child encountering a predator is real, but it's small. The overwhelming risk to your child comes from other places that are much less comfortable and easy to talk about. The amount of time you spend talking about risk and teaching about safe choices should be commensurate with where the danger is actually coming from."

Make Privacy and Safety a Priority

There are a lot of things that families and kids can do to keep themselves safe. The goal should be to empower your children to be their own first line of defense. Here are some key safety and privacy precautions that parents need to think about:

- Make sure that you have all your child's usernames and passwords for every account.

- If your kids take their phones to school, they should be password-protected.

- Make sure your kids know that they should not share passwords with their friends under any circumstances.

- Tell them not to provide personal information online (their real name, birthdate, phone number, or address, for example) to people, games, apps, or websites—even those claiming to be giving away cool stuff. They should always ask parents to take a look first.

- Tell them not to geocode their location on social media posts. If an app has a mapping feature, turn it off.

- Encourage them to be aware of the story that their social media tells. It may tell someone what school they go to, what town they live in, what sports teams they're on, and so forth.

- Warn them not to post pictures that identify their family's home or vehicle (especially house numbers or license plates).

- Tell them not to live-link to other accounts in their social media profiles. Most profile information is public, even if the account itself is locked down.

- Tell them not to allow people to follow or friend them unless they know them in real life.

- Tell them that under no circumstances should they direct message (DM) or chat with people they don't know in real life.

HAVE AN AGREEMENT AND A PLAN

If something bad or scary happens online, kids who are angry, scared, or ashamed may not make the best choices or exhibit the soundest judgment. All families should think and talk through some of the mistakes that kids could make and figure out how they would handle them. Parents should also think about a general plan for how they would handle hard situations ahead of time, since these experiences can be incredibly stressful.

A plan for parents around bullying or inappropriate peer-to-peer behavior online could look something like this:

1. Make sure your kid is okay and has the necessary help and support.
2. Document everything (repeat as needed).
3. Contact the service provider or social media platform to report the incident.
4. Contact the other family. If the issue still isn't resolved or if you do not want to contact them, move on to step 5.
5. Contact the school, if appropriate.
6. If not resolved, contact the police.

Obviously if a crime has taken place or you fear that one will take place, go directly to the police.

As far as an agreement with your teen goes, it can mirror other agreements you might have with your teen to prevent drunk driving:

- If kids agree to prioritize their safety by telling you about something that has happened, even if it means admitting that they've broken rules or done something illegal, then you promise to help them as best as you can and there will be no discussion of discipline or consequences on day one.
- Parents should acknowledge that while there may be limits placed on the phone later, based on the individual situation, teens will not lose their phone entirely.
  - This is done not to condone anything, but because the data shows that many kids will not seek help, even in very dangerous situations, because they're worried about getting in trouble and losing their phones.
- NOTHING IS MORE IMPORTANT THAN THE SAFETY OF YOUR CHILD. And no mistake or situation is so serious that they can't come to you with it.

> • If kids are too scared or the subject matter is too sensitive to discuss with a parent, then kids and parents can mutually agree upon a trusted adult who the child can go to.

In conclusion, let's focus more on our kids and less on their phones and social media accounts. In almost every survey in which young people are asked about the impact of technology on their lives, they tell us the same thing. It isn't good or bad, it's both. As parents, we have to be aware of that. If we think of social media as a seesaw that tips between being positive and negative, perhaps the most important thing we can do for our kids is to help them become aware of (and responsible for) their own tipping points.

Technology certainly doesn't make that easy. It's designed to be distracting, engaging, and immersive. It's engineered to keep us compulsively using it, even when we're not really deriving any enjoyment or value from it. But we're smarter than our smartphones, especially when we're motivated by a desire to keep our families happy and healthy.

Being mindful and aware of the choices we make online and the habits we cultivate can go a long way toward limiting the negative effects of technology on our well-being. When does browsing make you feel happy, or jealous, or annoyed at yourself for wasting time? What are some ways we can identify when the scales start to tip toward the negative, and what actions can we take to protect ourselves from those feelings? In her excellent book *Social Media Wellness*, author Ana Homayoun asks kids she works with to keep track of their daily digital media habits, including those things that make them feel energized and positive, or exhausted and overwhelmed.

Having our children take responsibility for these things is critical. This technology isn't going anywhere; in fact there are clear social and professional benefits to using it well. Our kids will mature and change over time, and technology will certainly evolve. What will remain valuable throughout their lives, both online and off, is the ability to advocate for themselves. When gaming or social media makes them feel bad, when texts or emails become aggressive, or when tech use starts to feel out of control, kids should feel empowered to trust their feelings and take a step back. We need to teach them to identify and manage these situations, giving them the tools and encouragement they need to do so.

They're going to grow up, become adults, and leave us. Our job is to teach them as best we can to handle anything life—or their cell phones—can throw at them. The struggle and story of parenting is managing the tension between protecting and caring for our children and teaching them to protect and care for themselves.

APPENDIX 1:
CELL PHONE CONTRACT OR AGREEMENT

Many families find that when they give their child a cell phone, particularly their first cell phone, having a contract or a written agreement is helpful. Here is a list of things you may want to consider when creating your own.

I suggest you think carefully about how you define the terms, avoiding those that are subjective or vague. For example, requiring a twelve-year-old to "make good choices online" is unfair. What does "good" mean anyway? And who gets to decide that?

Here are three reasons why contracts or agreements can be great:

1. You can create it with your kids, so they feel more invested in its terms.
2. Everyone is on the same page and expectations are totally clear.
3. When rules get broken, parents can remain neutral while enforcing consequences, minimizing arguing or drama.

Here are three reasons why contracts or agreements can be meaningless or ineffective:

1. Parents don't enforce consequences or don't do so consistently.
2. The rules or terms don't change as needed or as the child gets older.

3. The rules or terms are impossible for kids to live up to or are too vague/subjective.

The following is a list of things to consider including in a cell phone contract. These are merely suggestions and hypotheticals to think about. Your specific contract should reflect your child's age and maturity and your family's situation.

- Who pays for the phone?
  - Who pays for services, data, games, in-app purchases, music, etc.?
  - If the phone is broken or lost, who pays to fix or replace it?
  - If a new screen protector or case is required, who pays for that?

- When is access to the phone allowed?
  - Not during school
  - Not in a bedroom at night
  - Charges in the kitchen at nine p.m. every night
  - No texts or calls after ten p.m.
  - Only after school and on weekends

- Parents must approve all apps and downloads

- Parents must have all usernames and passwords to all accounts

- Monitoring policies (be transparent to build trust)
  - Parents can have access at any time, to anything
  - Parents will periodically "spot check" to make sure all is well
  - Parents will check phones daily
  - Parents will check phones but allow kids certain degrees of privacy (will not read texts, DMs, etc.)

- Requirements to keep phone:
  - Grades/homework
  - No phone during homework time
  - Behavior
    - No issues/trouble at school (emails from teachers, detentions, etc.)
    - Follow all classroom or school rules with regard to using/having a phone
    - No fighting with parents
    - Follow house rules
    - Do all chores
    - When in public or as a guest in someone's home, follow rules of basic etiquette and use phone respectfully (specifics should be discussed)

- Online behavior
  - Will not seek out adult or explicit materials
  - Will not use bad or abusive language
  - Will never ask for or create explicit images of self or others
  - Will immediately tell parent or trusted adult if someone sends them such an image
  - Never share personal information (address, phone number, birth date, etc.)

- Social media behavior
  - Parents must approve all social media accounts
  - No new, spam, fake, group, or private accounts can be created without parents' permission
  - Parents must have all usernames and passwords
  - Parents must be friends or followers on all accounts
  - No rude, aggressive, or bullying behavior on social media is allowed

- No posting explicit or inappropriate materials
- Parents may ask that a post be taken down, and the kid must comply
- Don't geocode posts or share their location
- Don't share photos that reveal their address, license plate, phone number, etc.

- Safety
  - If anyone threatens, harasses, or bullies the child, they will tell parents immediately
  - They will not communicate with people they don't know in real life
  - They will not add strangers as contacts, friends, or followers
  - They will not have public social media accounts
  - No texting and driving (when they're old enough)

Consequences should be part of the agreement and should be clearly stated. The following are merely suggestions. Consequences should be cumulative.

When a rule is broken, the following consequences will be enforced:

- First offense, kid loses or has limited access to phone for one day

- Second offense, kid loses phone for one week

- Third offense, kid loses phone for two weeks

(Limiting access to the phone is also an option. Being grounded from their phone can also include a five-minute morning check-in and a five-minute evening check-in so that kids can respond to anything that has come up and not feel completely socially isolated. I heard from so many kids that the fear of losing their phone completely was a big factor in lying to their parents and being sneaky about rule breaking.)

If a social media rule is broken, the following consequences will be enforced:

- First offense, kid loses access to social media account for one day

- Second offense, kid loses access for one week

- Third offense, kid loses access to their account or has to share the account with their parents, who have full access

Lastly, these rules should change over time. The goal is to give kids the chance to become more responsible. As they prove themselves and as they get older, it's a good idea to revisit your agreement and adjust it to provide more freedom and flexibility.

If you'd like to cut and paste this language (or a more recent version of it), you can find it online at www.RantsfromMommyland.com; look for the "Kid's First Cell Phone Contract or Written Agreement Ideas" page at the top.

SEXUALITY AND SEX ED
ONLINE RESOURCES FOR TEENS

In providing this list, I need to make a couple of things clear.

First, I'm a public health professional who believes that clinically accurate, science-based, and age-appropriate information should be provided to young people so they can make well-informed decisions about their bodies and health.

Second, I'm a mom, and fielding questions like "Hey, so what's masturbation?" or "Why do people laugh every time the number sixty-nine comes up?" make me profoundly uncomfortable and I get super awkward, really fast.

Third, the sites on the next page may not be a good fit for you. They may be wildly too progressive or ridiculously regressive, depending on your perspective and background. That's okay. Your family's values should be part of how your kids learn about sexuality, so pick what works for you.

Fourth, sometimes our kids' questions push the boundaries of our personal values or religious beliefs. Often, those questions are just about curiosity. Maybe they want to know what something means because they keep hearing about it on the bus or in the locker room. It's important that they have places to get answers that satisfy their curiosity, or they will keep looking for answers. Remember, they'll usually go to Google (where they could be directed anywhere) or to their friends (who generally don't know any more than they do).

Fifth, this list of resources is not comprehensive and may change over time. For the most current iteration of this list, please see the Rants from Mommyland website and look for the "Sexuality and Sex Ed On-line Resources for Teens" link at the top of the page.

Amaze: https://amaze.org/

Center for Young Women's Health: https://youngwomenshealth.org

Girlology: https://www.girlology.com

Go Ask Alice!: https://goaskalice.columbia.edu

It Matters (app only): http://www.itmatters.me

Love Matters (for teens with disabilities): https://lovematters.in/en

MTV's It's Your Sex Life: http://www.itsyoursexlife.com

My Sex Doctor (app only): http://mysexdoctor.org

Our Whole Lives (curriculum/in-person classes): https://www.uua
    .org/re/owl

Planned Parenthood: https://www.plannedparenthood.org/learn
    /teens

Safe Teens: https://safeteens.org

Scarleteen: http://www.scarleteen.com

Sex, Etc: https://sexetc.org

Society for Adolescent Health and Medicine: https://www
    .adolescenthealth.org/Resources/Clinical-Care-Resources/Sexual
    -Reproductive-Health/Sexual-Reproductive-Health-Resources
    -For-Adolesc.aspx#Friendly

Stay Teen: https://stayteen.org

Teen Health Source: http://teenhealthsource.com

Young Men's Health: https://youngmenshealthsite.org

ACKNOWLEDGMENTS

The most important people I need to thank are those who make up my online family, the community that has supported me and Rants from Mommyland since 2009. You will never know how much your friendship and encouragement have changed my life, made me a better person, and pushed me to be brave. There are simply no words sufficient to express my gratitude to all of you. For those of you who reached out to share your stories with me for this book, I'm so grateful. *Thank you forever.*

Without my friend Kristin Wilson Keppler, none of this would have happened. She told me that we had to write a blog, though I was convinced I had nothing to say that anyone wanted to read. She believed in me when I didn't believe in myself, and she will forever be the Kate to my Lydia. To Claire Goss, my ongoing love and thanks; Mommyland might not have made it without you.

Thank you to my friends and family. To my mom, Jane Wesby, whose steadfast love and support have never wavered. To my sister, Sophy, who is my favorite. To my mom squad, who sat with me while I freaked out, wondering if this book would ever happen; who love my kids like they were their own; who show me how to be a better mom every day; and who promised me they would still be my friends even if I turned out to be a horrible failure as a writer.

Kara Kinney Cartwright encouraged me to take an idea and turn it into a pitch, then an article, then a book proposal. She was positive and supportive at every step and nudged me to keep going when I wanted to quit. You're the best accountability buddy in the entire world.

Many, many thanks to Megan Sullivan, Sammy Nickalls, and all the other young people I interviewed for this book, most of whom wish to remain anonymous.

To all the experts who were especially generous with their time and knowledge, thank you so much: Jessica Lahey, Dr. Clifford Sussman, Julie Lythcott-Haims, Jessica McCabe, Dr. Jean Twenge, Dr. Larry Rosen, Ana Homayoun, Glennon Doyle, Eliza Harrell, and Laura Parrott Perry, among many others.

Thank you to Sara Bliss, who encouraged me to get in touch with her literary agent at Stonesong, which led me to work with the wonderful Leila Campoli. Thank you so much, Leila, for all your help and support. Thank you to my editor, Joanna Ng, for the opportunity to write this book and work with you. To the wonderful team at TarcherPerigee, thank you for all your help.

To my husband, Matt, nothing in my life would be possible without your love and support. Thank you for everything.

Lastly, to the law enforcement professionals, the staff at the National Center for Missing and Exploited Children, the educators and administrators, and the child safety professionals working on the front lines to keep our children safe in both their real and digital lives, my sincerest and most profound thanks.

NOTES

CHAPTER ONE: THE LAST ANALOG DINOSAURS RAISING THE FIRST TRUE DIGITAL GENERATION

1. "Risk & Protective Factors," U.S. Department of Health and Human Services, 2001, https://youth.gov/youth-topics/juvenile-justice/risk-and-protective-factors#_ftn1. (Accessed December 14, 2017.)
2. "Changes in Men's and Women's Labor Force Participation Rates," U.S. Department of Labor, Bureau of Labor Statistics, TED: The Economics Daily, January 10, 2007; https://www.bls.gov/opub/ted/2007/jan/wk2/art03.htm. (Accessed December 13, 2017.)
3. W. Bradford Wilcox, "The Evolution of Divorce," *National Affairs*; https://www.nationalaffairs.com/publications/detail/the-evolution-of-divorce.
4. Julie Lythcott-Haims, *How to Raise an Adult: Break Free of the Overparenting Trap and Prepare Your Kid for Success* (New York: Henry Holt and Company, 2015).
5. Lynne Griffin, "Lessons from the New Science of Adolescence," *Psychology Today*, September 8, 2014; https://www.psychologytoday.com/us/blog/field-guide-families/201409/lessons-the-new-science-adolescence.
6. Chatterjee, R. "Americans Are a Lonely Lot, and Young People Bear the Heaviest Burden," NPR, May 2018, https://www.npr.org/sections/health-shots/2018/05/01/606588504/americans-are-a-lonely-lot-and-young-people-bear-the-heaviest-burden.
7. "Global Apple iPhone Sales from 3rd Quarter 2007 to 4th Quarter 2018," Statistica; https://www.statista.com/statistics/263401/global-apple-iphone-sales-since-3rd-quarter-2007/. (Accessed December 13, 2017.)
8. "Smartphone Penetration Rate as Share of the Population in the United States from 2010 to 2021," Statistica; https://www.statista.com/statistics/201183/forecast-of-smartphone-penetration-in-the-us/. (Accessed December 13, 2017.)
9. Horace Dediu, "When Will the US Reach Smartphone Saturation?" ASYMCO, October 7, 2013; http://www.asymco.com/2013/10/07/when-will-the-us-reach-smartphone-saturation/. (Accessed December 13, 2017.)

10. Brian X. Chen, "What's the Right Age for a Child to Get a Smartphone?" *New York Times*, July 20, 2016; https://www.nytimes.com/2016/07/21/technology/personal tech/whats-the-right-age-to-give-a-child-a-smartphone.html. (Accessed December 13, 2017.)

11. Jingjing Jiang, "How Teens and Parents Navigate Screen Time and Device Distractions," Pew Research Center, August 22, 2018; http://www.pewinternet .org/2018/08/22/how-teens-and-parents-navigate-screen-time-and-device -distractions.

12. Susan Davis, "Addicted to Your Smartphone? Here's What to Do," WebMD; https:// www.webmd.com/balance/guide/addicted-your-smartphone-what-to-do#1.

13. Casey Schwartz, "Finding It Hard to Focus? Maybe It's Not Your Fault," *New York Times*, August 14, 2018; https://www.nytimes.com/2018/08/14/style/how-can-i -focus-better.html.

14. Adolescent Brain Cognitive Development Study (website); https://abcdstudy.org /index.html

15. Drew P. Cingel and Marina Krcmar, "Understanding the Experience of Imaginary Audience in a Social Media Environment: Implications for Adolescent Development," *Journal of Media Psychology: Theories, Methods, and Applications* 26.4 (January 2014): 155–60.

CHAPTER TWO: SOCIAL MEDIA AND THE IMAGINARY AUDIENCE

1. Amy Alberts, David Elkind, and Stephen Ginsberg, "The Personal Fable and Risk-Taking in Early Adolescence," *Journal of Youth and Adolescence* 36.1 (January 2007): 71–76.

2. Mariam Arain, Maliha Haque, Lina Johal, et al., "Maturation of the Adolescent Brain," *Neuropsychiatric Disease and Treatment* 9 (April 3, 2013): 449–61; https:// www.ncbi.nlm.nih.gov/pmc/articles/PMC3621648/.

3. David Elkind, "Egocentrism in Adolescence," *Child Development* 38.4 (December 1967): 1025–34.

4. Michael Bernstein, Eytan Bakshy, Moira Burke, and Brian Karrer, "Quantifying the Invisible Audience in Social Networks," Facebook Research, April 27, 2013; https://research.fb.com/publications/quantifying-the-invisible-audience-in -social-networks/.

5. Cingel and Krcmar, "Understanding the Experience of Imaginary Audience," 155–60.

6. Drew P. Cingel, Marina Krcmar, Megan K. Olsen, "Exploring Predictors and Consequences of Personal Fable Ideation on Facebook," *Computers in Human Behavior* 48 (July 2015): 28–35.

7. Farhad Manjoo, "Facebook's Bias Is Built-In, and Bears Watching," *New York Times*, May 11, 2016; www.nytimes.com/2016/05/12/technology/facebooks-bias-is-built-in-and-bears-watching.html.

8. Catalina L. Toma and Jeffrey T. Hancock, "Self-Affirmation Underlies Facebook Use," *Personality & Social Psychology Bulletin* 39.3 (January 2013): 321–31.

9. Cingel, "Exploring Predictors," 28–35.

10. Monica Anderson, "Parents, Teens and Digital Monitoring," Pew Research Center, January 7, 2016; http://www.pewinternet.org/2016/01/07/parents-teens-and-digital-monitoring/. (Accessed August 21, 2017.)

CHAPTER THREE: WELL-BEING, SELF-ESTEEM, AND SOCIAL COMPARISON IN THE SELFIE GENERATION

1. Jane E. Brody, "Hard Lesson in Sleep for Teenagers," *New York Times*, October 20, 2014; https://well.blogs.nytimes.com/2014/10/20/sleep-for-teenagers/. (Accessed December 14, 2017.)

2. Emily Weinstein, "The Social Media See-Saw: Positive and Negative Influences on Adolescents' Affective Well-Being," *New Media & Society* 20.10 (February 2018): 3597–623; https://doi.org/10.1177/1461444818755634.

3. Andrew K. Przybylski, Kou Muruyama, Cody R. DeHaan, and Valerie Gladwell, "Motivational, Emotional, and Behavioral Correlates of Fear of Missing Out," *Computers in Human Behavior* 29.4 (2013): 1841–48.

4. Melissa G. Hunt, Rachel Marx, Courtney Lipson, and Jordyn Young, "No More FOMO: Limiting Social Media Decreases Loneliness and Depression," *Journal of Social and Clinical Psychology* 37.10 (2018): 751–768.

5. Dong Liu and Roy F. Baumeister, "Social Networking Online and Personality of Self-Worth: A Meta-Analysis," *Journal of Research in Personality* 64 (October 2016): 79–89.

6. Ibid.

7. Ibid.

8. Roy F. Baumeister, Jennifer D. Campbell, Joachim I. Krueger, and Kathleen D. Vohs, "Does High Self-Esteem Cause Better Performance, Interpersonal Success, Happiness, or Healthier Lifestyles?" *Psychological Science in the Public Interest* 4.1 (May 1, 2003): 1–44.

9. Will Storr, "The Man Who Destroyed America's Ego," *Matter* (blog), Medium.com, https://medium.com/matter/the-man-who-destroyed-americas-ego-94d214257b5. (Accessed December 14, 2017.)

10. Charles M. Blow, "The Self(ie) Generation," *New York Times*, March 7, 2014; https://www.nytimes.com/2014/03/08/opinion/blow-the-self-ie-generation.html.

11. Jean M. Twenge and W. Keith Campbell, *The Narcissism Epidemic: Living in the Age of Entitlement* (New York: Atria Books, 2013), 31.

12. G. Kedia, T. Mussweiler, and D. E. Linden, "Brain Mechanisms of Social Comparison and Their Influence on the Reward System," *Neuroreport* 25.16 (November 12, 2014): 1255–65.

13. Ibid.

14. Gemma L. Tatangelo and Lina A. Ricciardelli, "Children's Body Image and Social Comparisons with Peers and the Media," *Journal of Health Psychology* 22.6 (2017): 776–87; https://doi.org/10.1177/1359105315615409.

15. Ibid.

16. "Selfie Trend Increases Demand of Facial Plastic Surgery," American Academy of Facial Plastic and Reconstructive Surgery, March 11, 2014; https://www.aafprs.org/media/press_release/20140311.html. (Accessed December 14, 2017.)

17. L. M. Hopper, S. P. Lambeth, S. J. Schapiro, and S. F. Brosnan, "Social Comparison Mediates Chimpanzees' Responses to Loss, Not Frustration," *Animal Cognition* 17.6 (November 2014): 1303–11.

18. Emma Young, "Are You Turning Your Child into a Self-Loving Narcissist?" *New Scientist*, July 6, 2016; https://www.newscientist.com/article/2096103-are-you-turning-your-child-into-a-self-loving-narcissist/. (Accessed December 14, 2017.)

CHAPTER FOUR: TEEN FRIENDSHIPS IN THE AGE OF THE INTERNET

1. Amanda Lenhart, "Teens, Technology and Friendships," Pew Research Center, August 6, 2015; http://www.pewinternet.org/2015/08/06/teens-technology-and-friendships/. (Accessed September 16, 2017.)

2. Jean M. Twenge, *iGen: Why Today's Super-Connected Kids Are Growing Up Less Rebellious, More Tolerant, Less Happy—and Completely Unprepared for Adulthood—and What That Means for the Rest of Us* (New York: Atria Books, 2017), 75.

3. Monica Anderson and Jingjing Jiang, "Teens' Social Media Habits and Experiences," Pew Research Center, November 28, 2018.

4. Cecilie Schou Andreassen, Ståle Pallesen, and Mark D. Griffiths, "The Relationship Between Addictive Use of Social Media, Narcissism, and Self-Esteem: Findings from a Large National Survey," *Addictive Behaviors* 64 (January 2017): 287–93.

5. Elias Aboujaoude, M. W. Savage, V. Starcevic, and W. O. Salame, "Cyberbullying: Review of an Old Problem Gone Viral," *Journal of Adolescent Health* 57.1 (July 2015): 10–18.

6. Melikşah Demır and Lesley A. Weitekamp, "I Am So Happy 'Cause Today I Found My Friend: Friendship and Personality as Predictors of Happiness," *Journal of Happiness Studies* 8.2 (June 2007): 181–211.

7. Sherry Turkle, *Reclaiming Conversation: The Power of Talk in a Digital Age* (New York: Penguin, 2015), 13.

8. Anderson, "Teens' Social Media Habits and Experiences."

9. "Social Media, Social Life: How Teens View Their Digital Lives," Common Sense Media Research Study, June 26, 2012; https://www.commonsensemedia.org /research/social-media-social-life-how-teens-view-their-digital-lives. (Accessed September 16, 2017.)

CHAPTER FIVE: DIGITAL DATING AND TEEN RELATIONSHIPS ONLINE

1. Monica Anderson, "Teen Voices: Dating in the Digital Age," Pew Research Center, October 1, 2015; http://www.pewinternet.org/online-romance/. (Accessed December 10, 2017.)

2. Ibid.

3. Ibid.

4. J. M. van Oosten, J. Peter, and I. Boot, "Exploring Associations Between Exposure to Sexy Online Self-Presentations and Adolescents' Sexual Attitudes and Behavior," *Journal of Youth and Adolescence* 44.5 (May 2015). 1078–91.

5. Kimberly J. Mitchell, David Finkelhor, Lisa M. Jones, and Janis Wolak, "Prevalence and Characteristics of Youth Sexting: A National Study," *Pediatrics* 129.1 (January 2012): 13–20.

6. Janis Wolak, Kimberly J. Mitchell, and David Finkelhor, "Internet Sex Crimes Against Minors: The Response of Law Enforcement," Crimes Against Children Research Center, University of New Hampshire, November 2003.

7. L. F. O'Sullivan, "Linking Online Sexual Activities to Health Outcomes Among Teens," *New Directions for Child and Adolescent Development* 144 (Summer 2014): 37–51.

8. Suzan M. Doornwaard, Regina J. M. van den Eijnden, Geertjan Overbeek, and Tom F.M. ter Bogt, "Differential Developmental Profiles of Adolescents Using Sexually Explicit Internet Material," *Journal of Sex Research* 52.3 (2015): 269–81.

9. Suzan M. Doornwaard, Tom F. M. ter Bogt, Ellen Reitz, and Regina J. M. van den Eijnden, "Sex-Related Online Behaviors, Perceived Peer Norms and Adolescents'

Experience with Sexual Behavior: Testing an Integrative Model," *PLOS One* 10.6 (June 18, 2015), https://doi.org/10.1371/journal.pone.0127787.

10. Kathleen A. Hare, Jacqueline Gahagan, Lois Jackson, and Audrey Steenbeek, "Revisualising 'Porn': How Young Adults' Consumption of Sexually Explicit Internet Movies Can Inform Approaches to Canadian Sexual Health Promotion," *Culture, Health & Sexuality* 17.3 (2015): 269–83.

CHAPTER SIX: THE SOCIAL CULTURE OF VIDEO GAMES

1. "Essential Facts About the Computer and Video Game Industry: 2017 Sales, Demographic, and Usage Data," Entertainment Software Association, 2017.

2. Maeve Duggan, "Gaming and Gamers," Pew Research Center, December 15, 2015; http://www.pewinternet.org/2015/12/15/gaming-and-gamers/.

3. "Essential Facts About the Computer and Video Game Industry," ESA.

4. Bruce D. Homer, Elizabeth O. Hayward, Jonathan Frye, and Jan L. Plass, "Gender and Player Characteristics in Video Game Play of Preadolescents," *Computers in Human Behavior* 28.5 (September 2012): 1782–89.

5. S. M. Coyne, L. M. Padilla-Walker, L. Stockdale, and R. D. Day, "Game On . . . Girls: Associations Between Co-Playing Video Games and Adolescent Behavioral and Family Outcomes," *Journal of Adolescent Health* 49.2 (August 2011), 160–65.

6. Patrick M. Markey and Christopher J. Ferguson, *Moral Combat: Why the War on Violent Video Games Is Wrong* (Dallas: BenBella Books, 2017).

7. C. J. Ferguson, "Do Angry Birds Make for Angry Children? A Meta-Analysis of Video Game Influences on Children's and Adolescents' Aggression, Mental Health, Prosocial Behavior, and Academic Performance," *Perspectives on Psychological Science* 10.5 (September 2015): 646–66.

8. C. J. Ferguson, B. Trigani, S. Pilato, S. Miller, K. Foley, and H. Barr, "Violent Video Games Don't Increase Hostility in Teens, but They Do Stress Girls Out," *Psychiatric Quarterly* 87.1 (March 2016): 49–56.

9. M. M. Spada, "An Overview of Problematic Internet Use," *Addictive Behaviors* 39.1 (January 2014): 3–6.

10. P. J. Adachi and T. Willoughby, "Does Playing Sports Video Games Predict Increased Involvement in Real-Life Sports over Several Years Among Older Adolescents and Emerging Adults?" *Journal of Youth and Adolescence* 45.2 (February 2016): 391–401.

11. L. J. Smith, M. Gradisar, D. L. King, and M. Short, "Intrinsic and Extrinsic Predictors of Video-Gaming Behaviour and Adolescent Bedtimes: The Relation-

ship Between Flow States, Self-Perceived Risk-Taking, Device Accessibility, Parental Regulation of Media and Bedtime," *Sleep Medicine* 30 (February 2017): 64–70.

12. L. J. Smith, M. Gradisar, and D. L. King, "Parental Influences on Adolescent Video Game Play: A Study of Accessibility, Rules, Limit Setting, Monitoring, and Cybersafety," *Cyberpsychology, Behavior, and Social Networking* 18.5 (May 2015): 273–79.

CHAPTER SEVEN: DIGITAL ADDICTION AND RISKY BEHAVIOR ONLINE

1. Alberts, "The Personal Fable and Risk-Taking in Early Adolescence."

2. Laurence Steinberg, *Age of Opportunity: Lessons from the New Science of Adolescence* (New York: Mariner Books, 2015).

3. D. Wang, L. Zhu, P. Maguire, Y. Liu, K. Pang, Z. Li, and Y. Hu, "The Influence of Social Comparison and Peer Group Size on Risky Decision-Making," *Frontiers in Psychology* 7, August 17, 2016.

4. Ibid.

5. "The Consequences of Underage Drinking," Substance Abuse and Mental Health Services Administration, https://www.samhsa.gov/underage-drinking/parent-resources/consequences-underage-drinking.

6. C. Cheng and A. Y. Li, "Internet Addiction Prevalence and Quality of (Real) Life: A Meta-Analysis of 31 Nations Across Seven World Regions," *Cyberpsychology, Behavior, and Social Networking* 17.12 (December 2014): 755–60.

7. "Alcohol Facts and Statistics," National Institute on Alcohol Abuse and Alcoholism (website); https://www.niaaa.nih.gov/alcohol-health/overview-alcohol-consumption/alcohol-facts-and-statistics. (Accessed December 14, 2017.)

8. Shea Bennett, "Social Media Addiction: Statistics & Trends [infographic]," *Adweek*, December 30, 2014; http://www.adweek.com/digital/social-media-addiction-stats/. (Accessed December 14, 2017.)

9. "Delayed Gratification: Learning to Pass the Marshmallow Test," Positive Psychology Program, November 29, 2016, https://positivepsychologyprogram.com/delayed-gratification/. (Accessed December 10, 2017.)

CHAPTER EIGHT: GROWING UP ONLINE WITH
ANXIETY, DEPRESSION, ADHD, OR AUTISM

1. "Study: Students More Stressed Now Than During the Depression?" *USA Today*, January 12, 2010; https://usatoday30.usatoday.com/news/education/2010-01-12-students-depression-anxiety_N.htm. (Accessed December 14, 2017.)

2. Catharine Morgan, Roger T. Webb, Matthew J. Carr, et al., "Incidence, Clinical Management, and Mortality Risk Following Self Harm Among Children and Adolescents: Cohort Study in Primary Care," *BMJ* (October 18, 2017): 359, https://doi.org/10.1136/bmj.j4351.

3. Julianna W. Miner, "Why 70 Percent of Kids Quit Sports by Age 13," *Washington Post,* June 1, 2016; https://www.washingtonpost.com/news/parenting/wp/2016/06/01/why-70-percent-of-kids-quit-sports-by-age-13.

4. "Anxiety and Depression Facts & Statistics," Anxiety and Depression Association of America (website); https://adaa.org/about-adaa/press-room/facts-statistics. (Accessed December 14, 2017.)

5. Nancy A. Cheever, Larry D. Rosen, L. Mark Carrier, and Amber Chavez, "Out of Sight Is Not Out of Mind: The Impact of Restricting Wireless Mobile Device Use on Anxiety Levels Among Low, Moderate and High Users," *Computers in Human Behavior* 37 (August 2014): 290–97.

6. Deborah Richards, Patricia H. Y. Caldwell, and Henry Go, "Impact of Social Media on the Health of Children and Young People," *Journal of Paediatrics and Child Health* 51.12 (December 2015): 1152–57.

7. In this study, being popular was determined by having all the kids in a given grade rank one another's names. So this was an external measure of social connectedness, not one based on a person's perception of their own connectedness to friends and classmates. J. Nesi and M. J. Prinstein, "Using Social Media for Social Comparison and Feedback-Seeking: Gender and Popularity Moderate Associations with Depressive Symptoms," *Journal of Abnormal Child Psychology* 43.8 (November 2015): 1427–38.

8. Liu Yi Lin, Jaime E. Sidani, Ariel Shensa, et al., "Association Between Social Media Use and Depression Among U.S. Young Adults," *Depression and Anxiety* 33.4 (April 2016): 323–31.

9. Hunt, "No More FOMO: Limiting Social Media Decreases Loneliness and Depression."

10. Patrick W. O'Carroll and Lloyd B. Potter, "Suicide Contagion and the Reporting of Suicide: Recommendations from a National Workshop," Morbidity and Mortality Weekly Report: Recommendations and Reports, Centers for Disease Control and Prevention, April 22, 1994, 9–18.

11. Josh Constine, "Facebook Acquires Anonymous Teen Compliment App tbh, Will Let It Run," *TechCrunch*, October 16, 2017; https://techcrunch.com/2017/10/16/facebook-acquires-anonymous-teen-compliment-app-tbh-will-let-it-run/. (Accessed December 14, 2017.)

12. "Attention-Deficit/Hyperactivity Disorder (ADHD)," Centers for Disease Control and Prevention, November 13, 2017; https://www.cdc.gov/ncbddd/adhd /data.html. (Accessed December 14, 2017.)

13. Chaelin K. Ra, Junhan Cho, Matthew D. Stone, et al., "Association of Digital Media Use with Subsequent Symptoms of Attention-Deficit/Hyperactivity Disorder Among Adolescents," *JAMA* 320.3 (January 17, 2018): 255–63.

14. M. O. Mazurek and C. Wenstrup, "Television, Video Game and Social Media Use Among Children with ASD and Typically Developing Siblings," *Journal of Autism and Developmental Disorders* 43.6 (June 2013): 1258–71.

CHAPTER NINE: SAFETY, PREDATORS, HARASSMENT, AND
BULLYING ONLINE

1. Trevor Tompson, Jennifer Benz, and Jennifer Agiesta, "The Digital Abuse Study: Experiences of Teens and Young Adults," Associated Press–NORC Center for Public Affairs Research, 2013.

2. Lisa M. Jones, Kimberly J. Mitchell, and David Finkelhor, "Online Harassment in Context: Trends from Three Youth Internet Safety Surveys (2000, 2005, 2010)," *Psychology of Violence* 3.1 (2013): 53–69.

3. Wheaton's Law is an axiom created by actor, writer, and Internet/nerd culture hero Wil Wheaton. It states simply the following, as a rule by which to conduct oneself online and in person: "Don't be a dick."

4. Janis Wolak, et al., "Online Predators—Myth Versus Reality," 2012 Massachusetts Family Impact Seminar, Purdue; https://www.purdue.edu/hhs/hdfs/fii/wp -content/uploads/2015/06/s_mafis03c03.pdf.

5. Janis Wolak, David Finkelhor, and Kimberly J. Mitchell, "Internet-Initiated Sex Crimes Against Minors: Implications for Prevention Based on Findings from a National Study," *Journal of Adolescent Health* 35 (November 2004). 424.e11–e20.

6. Benjamin Wittes, Cody Poplin, Quinta Jurecic, and Clara Spera, "Sextortion: Cybersecurity, Teenagers, and Remote Sexual Assault," Brookings Institution Report, May 11, 2016.

7. Kimberly J. Mitchell, Lisa Jones, David Finkelhor, and Janis Wolak, "Trends in Unwanted Sexual Solicitations: Findings from the Youth Internet Safety Studies," Crimes Against Children Research Center (February 2014).

8. Tompson, "The Digital Abuse Study: Experiences of Teens and Young Adults."

9. M. P. Hamm, A. S. Newton, A. Chisholm, et al., "Prevalence and Effect of Cyberbullying on Children and Young People: A Scoping Review of Social Media Studies," *JAMA Pediatrics* 169.8 (August 2015): 770–77.

10. Tracy Evian Waasdorp, Elise T. Pas, Benjamin Zablotsky, and Catherine P. Bradshaw, "Ten-Year Trends in Bullying and Related Attitudes Among 4th- to 12th-Graders," *Pediatrics* 139.6 (June 2017), http://pediatrics.aappublications .org/content/139/6/e20162615.

11. Aboujaoude, et al., "Cyberbullying," 10–18.

12. P. M. Valkenburg and J. Peter, "Online Communication Among Adolescents: An Integrated Model of Its Attraction, Opportunities, and Risks," *Journal of Adolescent Health* 48.2 (February 2011): 121–27.

13. M. L. Ybarra, K. J. Mitchell, D. Finkelhor, and J. Wolak, "Internet Prevention Messages: Targeting the Right Online Behaviors," *Archives of Pediatrics & Adolescent Medicine* 161.2 (February 2007): 138–45.

14. Lenhart, "Teens, Technology and Friendships."

CHAPTER TEN: HOPING FOR THE BEST AND AVOIDING THE WORST

1. "How Are Multitasking Millennials Impacting Today's Workplace?" Bryan College, July 16, 2016, https://www.bryan.edu/multitasking-at-work/.

2. Rae Jacobson, "Social Media and Self-Doubt," Child Mind Institute (website); https://childmind.org/article/social-media-and-self-doubt/.

INDEX

Page numbers in **bold** indicate charts or tables; those in *italics* indicate figures.

abduction, 196
abortion (teen) statistics, **10**
abuse history risk factor, 199, 201
acquaintances vs. friends, 95
acting differently online, 88
action steps, cyberbullying, **206**, 216–17
active sexting, 116
addiction. *See* digital addiction
ADHD, 1, 139, 173, **174**, 186–88, 189, 191, 192, 223
Adweek, 162
affirmation, seeking with a hashtag, 185–86
age-appropriate, remembering, 45–46, 226
Age of Opportunity (Steinberg), 13
age risk factor, 198, 202, 214, 226
aggression, video games, 126, 137–38, **138**, 139
aggressive kids risk factor, 198, **200**, 224
agreement and a plan, having an, 24, 207, 216, 240–42, 245–49
AIDS/HIV, 29–30, 100
"always on" mentality, 100
Amazon, 131
American Academy of Facial Plastic and Reconstructive Surgery (AAFPRS), 66
American Academy of Pediatrics, 115, 118
American Medical Association, 186–87, 210
American Psychological Association (APA), 137, 138
America's growing smartphone addiction, 19, **19**
Andre's story (age twenty-five), 123–25
Android smartphones, 15
Angry Birds, 15, 127
anxiety disorders, 178–81
  cell phones as cause, 180–81
  digital addiction, risky behavior, 161, 162

friendships, 89, 90, 94
growing up online with, 170–72, 173, **174**, 175, 176, 177, 178–81, 182, 191, 192
hoping for best, avoiding worst, 223, 229, 231
raising a screen-smart kid, 10
safety, predators, harassment, bullying, 212
social anxiety on social media, 178–79
well-being, self-esteem, social comparison in the Selfie Generation, 52, 56
See also growing up online with anxiety, depression, ADHD, or autism
Apple, 19
Aristotle, 100
AskDoctorG.com, 44, 68, 226
ASKfm, 26–28
asynchronous interactions, 88–89
The Atlantic, 175, 224
atypical kids need atypical rules, 223
autism spectrum disorders (ASD), 139, 173, **174**, 188–90, 192, 223
awkward eighth grader is a mother, 4–5

behavioral rehearsal, 32–33, *33*, 37–38, *39*, 76–77
binge drinking, **10**, **54**, 155, 156
birth (teen) statistics, **10**
body dysmorphic disorder, 66
boundaries, issues around, 106, 108, 119–20
boys
  digital dating, 102, 108, 111, **112**, 115, 116, 118
  friendships, **85**, 85–86, 91–92
  growing up online with anxiety, depression, ADHD, or autism, *174*, 175
  safety, predators, harassment, bullying, 198–99, **200**, 212

boys (*Cont.*)
  video games, 127, 129, 130, 132–33, 139
  well-being, self-esteem, social comparison
    in the Selfie Generation, 66–67
brain
  cell phones and, 19–20, 158–59
  digital addiction, risky behavior, 150,
    156, 163–65, 167, 168
  executive function, 31, 150, 187, 188–89
  friendships, 88, 90
  growing up online with anxiety,
    depression, ADHD, or autism, 172,
    186–87, 187–88, 188–89
  hoping for best, avoiding worst, 222,
    229–30, 235–36
  prefrontal cortex, 31, 93, 150, 187, 188
  puberty and, 17, 30, 31–32, 93, 150
  resetting, 140, 163–65, 167
  safety, predators, harassment, bullying,
    196, 205
  social media and Imaginary Audience, 44
  video games, 140
  well-being, self-esteem, social comparison
    in the Selfie Generation, 64, 65–66
  See also raising a screen-smart kid
breakups, 106–7, 120
Breen, Galit, 82
Brookings Institution, 204
*Brown v. Entertainment Merchants
  Association*, 137
bullying, 210, 211, 212, 217
  See also cyberbullying

Call of Duty, 139
Campbell, W. Keith, 61, 62, 63
Candy Crush, 19, 127, 140, 159, 164
cannabis industry, 157
canoe, paddling to nowhere, 150, 154
Casey, James, 131
caterpillars and chrysalis stage, 38
Caulfield, Holden (Salinger character), 36, 41
causative vs. correlative findings, 90, 176
celebrities, following, 39, 66, 157, 168, 184–85
cell phones
  anxiety symptoms from, 180–81
  brains and, 19–20, 158–59
  contract or agreement, 245–49
  developmental overdrive and, 17, 20
  first phones, 17, 30–31, 44–48, 64, 79,
    82, 150

greatest risk behavior may just be using
    the phone itself, 158–59
  penetration rate, 14
  See also raising a screen-smart kid
Center for Internet and Technology
  Addiction, 159
Centers for Disease Control and
  Prevention (CDC), 103, 175
charging phones in common area, 48, 53,
    75, 76, 230, 231, 232, 246
chat rooms, 101, 200, 201, 214, 235
chatting with strangers risk, 129–30
child abuse, 196–97
Child Mind Institute, 238
chrysalis stage, Imaginary Audience, 37–38
Cingel, Drew, 42, 43
Clash of Clans, 130
cockpit effect, 89
Common Sense Media, 55, 93, 144, 159, 160
communication/contact expectations, 105,
    105–6, 108–10, 109
communication overload, 191
community of gamers, 123, 124–25,
    127–28, 129, 131, 138
compassion, passion, responsibility (CPR), 63
competitive sports vs. gaming, 141
consent, healthy relationships, 234
consequences of actions, 17, 21, 25, 31, 44,
    45, 46, 63
convenience, safety, logistics, friendships, 83
cool/popular, 2
coping strategies, cyberbullying, 213–14
Coppins, Parker, 132
Cornell Research Program on Self-Injury
  and Recovery, 177
correlative vs. causative findings, 90, 176
Cosmopolitan, 171
courtship, new normal of, 100–101, 120
"covering things up," 209
critical thinking and metacognition, 235–36
cyberbullying, 207–14
  action steps for, 206, 216–17
  commonality of, 210
  coping strategies, 213–14
  digital dating, 113, 117
  effects of, 211–12
  friendships, 90, 94
  growing up online with anxiety,
    depression, ADHD, or autism, 178,
    185–86

hoping for best, avoiding worst, 220,
235, 239, 240–42, 247, 248
raising a screen-smart kid, 8, 16
risk factors for, 212–13, 216
safety, predators, harassment, bullying,
196, 197, 198, 203, 207
schools and, 208–10
social media and Imaginary Audience,
26–28
social support for, 213–14
suicidal thoughts and, 211–12
video games, 135, 136
what to do if your child is a victim, 207–8
See also bullying; safety, predators,
harassment, and bullying
Cyberbullying Research Center, 211
cybersecurity, 217

danger risk, collective awareness of, 12–13
dating and relationships. *See* digital dating
and teen relationships
daydreaming and blurting, 1, 32
depression
digital dating, 98
friendships, 88, 90
growing up online with anxiety,
depression, ADHD, or autism, 170,
172, 173, **174**, 175, 176, 178, 179, 182,
183, 190, 191
hoping for best, avoiding worst, 223,
229, 231
raising a screen-smart kid, 10
safety, predators, harassment, bullying,
194, 199, 212
social comparison and, 50, 51, 56, 64–68,
69, 70, 184–86, 192, 236–38
video games, 139
well-being, self-esteem, social
comparison in the Selfie Generation,
52, 53, 57, 67, 69
See also growing up online with anxiety,
depression, ADHD, or autism
Destiny, 128
developmental overdrive and cell phones,
17, 20
*Diagnostic and Statistical Manual of
Mental Disorders*, fifth edition
(*DSM-5*), 160, 161, 162
digital addiction and risky behavior, 147–69
anxiety disorders, 161, 162

brain and, 150, 156, 163–65, 167, 168
friends and risky choices, 150–51, 201,
215–16
greatest risk behavior may just be using
the phone itself, 158–59
growing up online with anxiety,
depression, ADHD, or autism, 173,
180–81, 186, 192
Hope's story (age eighteen), 147–49
problematic tech use, 162–65
risk behavior, kid's perspective, 151–52,
168
socially normal risky behavior, 154–55,
168
social marketing and influencers,
156–58, 168
social media, 147, 148, 149, 150, 153–54,
155, 156, 157, 158, 159, 160, 162, 164,
165, 168, 173
social reference points (SRPs), 152–53,
154, 168
"symptoms" of tech addiction, 161
takeaways, 166–69
tech addiction, 19, **19**, 20, 159–61
tech breaks, taking, 163–65, 231
understanding adolescent risk behavior,
149–50
video games addiction, 8, 139, 141, 146,
159, 160, 161, 162, 165, 186
willpower, delayed gratification, and
marshmallows, 165–66, 167
See also raising a screen-smart kid
digital dating abuse (DDA), 108
digital dating and teen relationships, 97–122
boys and, 102, 108, 111, **112**, 115, 116, 118
communication/contact expectations,
105, 105–6, 108–10, **109**
cyberbullying, 113, 117
dating and relationships, 103–7, **105**,
120, 122
depression, 98
girls and, 102, 108, 111, **112**, 115, 116, 118
hookup culture, 101, 102–3, 110, 148
hoping for best, avoiding worst, 234
John's story (age sixteen), 97–99, 105
LGBTQ teens, 119, 121, 199, 201, 234–35
new normal of teen courtship, 100–101,
120
pornography, 101, 102, **112**, 113, 117–19,
122, 160, 224

digital dating (*Cont.*)
sexting, 23, 102, 112, 113–17, 121, 122, 204, 207, 209, 220, 234
sexual norms, and hooking up, 101–3, **103**
sexual risk behavior, **112**, 112–13, 120, 121
sexy selfies, posting, 110–11, 116, 120
social media, 101–3, **103**, 104, 105, **105**, 106–7, 108, 109, **109**, 120, 121
takeaways, 119–22
"the Talk" or leaving it to Google, 101
unhealthy aspects of, 107–10, **109**
See also raising a screen-smart kid
direct messaging (DM), 129–30, 240
dirty needles, 29–30
discussions with kids about safety, 207, 213, 214, 215
Disney Interactive Media Group, 130
Disney XD, 132
Ditch the Label, 136
divorce rate increase, 11, 13
documenting abuse, importance, 208, 241
dopamine, 20, 36, 187, 188, 230
Dopamine Labs, 159
drama and fighting online, 91–92, **92**
drinking, **10**, 155–56, 157, 168
driving simulation with friends study, 151, 201
drug use statistics, **10**, 114
duck syndrome, 237–38

early termination, 166
economic recession of early 1980s, 11, 13
educational system changes, 12, 13
"Egocentrism in Adolescence" (Elkind), 33
eighth grade choices, 28–29
eighth grader's pimple, *34–35*
Electronic Arts, 130
Elkind, David, 33, 36, 43, 44
Emanuele, Jill, 238
emojis and dating, 83, 104, 105
emotional contagion theory, 183–84
emotional intelligence and multitasking, 229
empathy, 62, 89, 90–91
Entertainment Software Rating Board, 144
esports, 131–32
Everdeen, Katniss (character), 36
evolutionary psychology, 142–43
executive function, 31, 150, 187, 188–89
expert, cautionary tale, or both? 6–7
extroverts and social media, 57–58

Facebook, 15, **18**, 39, 41, 52, 57–58, 67, 68, 127, 147, 156, 159, 160, 162, 164, 171, 178, 183, 184, 186, 220
FaceTime, 46, 83, 97, 100, 210
failure, learning from, 124, 143
See also mistakes
falling in love outbreak, 2–3
family agreement, 24, 207, 216, 240–42, 245–49
"family" phone, 47
family relationships risk factor, 200, 201
FarmVille, 127
The Fear, 195–96
fear of missing out (FOMO), 56–57, 70, 154, 181
feeling the pressure, friendships, 92–93
Ferguson, Christopher, 134–35
fight or flight, 196
"finsta" Instagram account, 86
first smartphones, 17, 30–31, 44–48, 64, 79, 82, 150
fMRI research, 64
"followers," social media, 38–39
free-range/feral kids, 2, 9–10
friend online, being a good, 232–33
"friends," social media, 38–39
friendships in the Age of the Internet, 72–96
acting differently online, 88
anxiety disorders, 89, 90, 94
bad news, 89
boys and, **85**, 85–86, 91–92
brain and, 88, 90
building strong friendships, 83–84
convenience, safety, logistics, 83
cyberbullying, 90, 94
depression, 88, 90
digital addiction, risky behavior, 150–51, 201, 215–16
drama and fighting online, 91–92, **92**
empathy, 62, 89, 90–91
feeling the pressure, 92–93
girls and, **85**, 85–86, 91–92
good news, 89–90
hoping for best, avoiding worst, 232–33
independence, tech for, 79–80, 82–83
"I pretty much lost everyone," 73, 74–78
Maria's story (age fifteen), 72–74
monitoring social media, 80–82, 96
oversharing, 77–78
real life vs. online friends, 86–88, 94, 95, 96

rich get richer, 93–94, 182
risky choices and, 150–51, 201, 215–16
rules (your), but *not* your kids, 75–76
socializing online, how kids, 84–86, **85**
social life and digital social life rules, 48, 96
social lives today vs. yesterday, 78–79
social media, 73, 75, 77, 80, 82–83, 84,
  85, **85**, 86, 87–88, 90–92, **92**, 93, 95, 96
strong-tie friendships, 86–88, 94
takeaways, 94–96
tech and culture, 79–82
video games, 82, 84, **85**, 85–86, 87, 91, 95
weak-tie friendships, 86–88, 94
See also Internet impact; raising a
  screen-smart kid
funhouse mirror, social media, 153–54, 236

gambling and Internet use, 159, 160
Gamergate, 133
Gamer Motivation Profile, 132
gaming. *See* video games
Gauntlet Legends, 124
gender and video games, 127, 129, 130,
  132–34, 139
generalized anxiety disorder (GAD), 180
generational differences, 9–15, **10**, 52, 64–65,
  78–79, 82, 100, 103, **103**, 151, 155, 176
Gen Z or iGen or Selfie Generation, 56
Gen Z @ Work (Stillman and Stillman), 56
geocode, 240, 248
*The Gift of Failure: How the Best Parents
  Learn to Let Go So Their Children Can
  Succeed* (Lahey), 59–60, 71, 228–29
Gilboa, Deborah, 44, 68, 226
girls
  digital dating, 102, 108, 111, **112**, 115,
    116, 118
  friendships, **85**, 85–86, 91–92
  growing up online with anxiety,
    depression, ADHD, or autism, *174*, 175
  safety, predators, harassment, bullying,
    198, 200, 212
  video games, 127, 130, 132–33, 133–34
  well-being, self-esteem, social comparison
    in the Selfie Generation, 65–66, 69
good, the bad, and the outcomes, 52–54, **54**
Google, 214, 234, 235
"gotcha moment" and monitoring, 225
grade inflation, 59
Grand Theft Auto, 139

Green, John, 36
Greenfield, David, 159
grooming process, predators, 202–3, 215, 238
groupthink, rising above, 233
growing up online with anxiety,
  depression, ADHD, or autism, 170–92
  ADHD, 1, 139, 173, **174**, 186–88, 189,
    191, 192, 223
  autism spectrum disorders (ASD), 139,
    173, **174**, 188–90, 192, 223
  boys and, *174*, 175
  brain, 172, 186–87, 187–88, 188–89
  cyberbullying, 178, 185–86
  digital addiction, 173, 180–81, 186, 192
  emotional contagion theory, 183–84
  finding friends and community when
    you're a different kind of kid, 177–78
  girls and, *174*, 175
  mental health of U.S. teens, *174*, 174–75
  Sammy's story (age twenty-four), 170–72
  seeking affirmation with a hashtag, 185–86
  smartphones, destroyed a generation?
    175–77
  social media, 172, 173, 175–76, 177,
    178–79, 181, 182, 190, 191, 192
  social media, a healthy place to be?
    173–74, **174**
  takeaways, 190–92
  video games, 176, 186, 187, 192
  See also anxiety disorders; depression;
    raising a screen-smart kid

Hallowell, Edward, 187
harassment. *See* safety, predators,
  harassment, and bullying
Harrell, Eliza, 76
hashtag, seeking affirmation with, 185–86
heart disease, 7, 53, 231
Heitner, Devorah, 21, 225
helicopter parents, 13, 82
historical overview to figure out how we
  got here, 11–13
HIV/AIDS, 29–30, 100
hive mind mentality, rising above, 233
Homayoun, Ana, 75, 242
hookup culture, 101, 102–3, 110, 148
Hope's story (age eighteen), 147–49
hoping for the best and avoiding the worst,
  218–43
  age-appropriate, remembering, 45–46, 226

hoping for the best (*Cont.*)
  agreement and a plan, having an, 24, 207, 216, 240–42, 245–49
  anxiety disorders, 223, 229, 231
  atypical kids need atypical rules, 223
  brain, 222, 229–30, 235–36
  critical thinking and metacognition, 235–36
  cyberbullying, 220, 235, 239, 240–42, 247, 248
  depression, 223, 229, 231
  digital dating, 234
  don't worry about what other parents are doing, 222–23
  duck syndrome, 237–38
  friend online, being a good, 232–33
  friendships, 232–33
  how do you know the right thing to do? 221–43
  Imaginary Audience framework, 227, 228
  Julianna Miner's story (age forty-five), 218–20
  mentor, being a, 224–25, 226
  monitoring and mentoring, 21, 225, 226
  multitasking is a problem ("rapid task switching"), 229–30, 231
  predators and bad guys, being realistic about, 238–39
  privacy and safety a priority, 239–42
  resource, being a, 234–35
  setting reasonable limits, 230–31
  sleep and mental health, 24, 46, 53–54, **54**, 121, 142, 146, 190–91, 231–32, 246
  social comparison and social media, 50, 51, 56, 64–68, 69, 70, 184–86, 192, 236–38
  social media, 218, 219, 220, 222, 224, 225, 226, 227, 228, *228*, 231, 233, 236–38, 240, 241, 242, 243, 247–48, 249
  tech is not all the same, 228–29
  video games, 124, 131, 143, 145–46, 219, 231, 233, 235, 243
  See also raising a screen-smart kid
how do kids react when abuse happens? 205–7, **206**
how do you know the right thing to do? 221–43
How to ADHD (YouTube), 187, 188
How to Raise an Adult (Lythcott-Haims), 12

iGen, 56
iGen: Why Today's Super-Connected Kids Are Growing Up Less Rebellious, More Tolerant, Less Happy—and Completely Unprepared for Adulthood—and What That Means for the Rest of Us (Twenge), 78–79, 175, 176
Imaginary Audience, 32–34, *33*, 227, *228*
  See also social media and the Imaginary Audience
independence, tech to gain, 79–80, 82–83
individuation process, 32, 37
Indonesia, 29–30
influencers and social marketing, 156–58, 168
Instagram, 4, 7, 9, 16, **18**, 21, 30, 46, 49–50, 51–52, 55, 56, 61, 72, 74, 85, 86, 105, 129, 147, 150, 157, 178, 179, 185, 192, 210, 218, 219, 236
intention, predicting behavior, 110
Internet impact, 13–15, 16, 22
  See also friendships in the Age of the Internet
introverts and social media, 58
invincibility and Personal Fable, 36, 113, 150
iPhones, 7, 8, 9, 15–16, 19, 30, 46, 61, 64, 150, 162, 176, 210, 219
iPods, 14, 147
"I pretty much lost everyone," 73, 74–78
IQ and multitasking, 229–30
Is Everyone Hanging Out Without Me? (And Other Concerns) (Kaling), 56

Jackson, Percy (character), 36
Jacquelin's story (age nineteen), 26–28
JAMA, 66, 186
Jill's story (age twelve), 49–51
John's story (age sixteen), 97–99, 105

Kaling, Mindy, 56
Kardashians, the, 192
Katherine's story (age twenty-one), 130, 193–95, 196, 201–3
Kelly, Margo, 193, 194
kids are individuals, 23, 221, 223
kids targeting kids, 197
Kindness Wins (Breen), 82

Lahey, Jessica, 59–60, 71, 228–29
last analog dinosaurs raising the first true digital generation. *See* raising a screen-smart kid
League of Legends, 133
LGBTQ risk factor, 119, 121, 199, 201, 234–35
life skills, 21–22, 44
likeforfollow, 185
limiters' kids, 224
listening, importance of, 221
live-linking to other accounts, 240
Looking for Alaska (Green), 36
lurkers/lurking, 4, 58, 93, 96, 182
Lythcott-Haims, Julie, 12, 67

Maria's story (age fifteen), 72–74
marshmallow study by Stanford, 165
Match 3, 132
McCabe, Jessica, 187–88, 191
Me, MySpace, and I: Parenting the Net Generation (Rosen), 14
mental health of U.S. teens, *174*, 174–75
mental health problems risk factor, 199, 201
mentor, being a, 224–25, 226
metacognition, 235–36
Metro, 171
Microsoft, 130
middle school, 2, 4, 15, 16, 28, 30, 31–45, 33, 34–35, 48, 104, 135, 147, 194, 207, 210, 218, 219
millennials, 61
mindfulness and meditation, 166
Minecraft, 140, 177, 189, 192
Miner, Julianna
  Julianna Miner's story (age forty-five), 218–20
  Julianna Miner's story (age thirteen), 1–4
  mommy blogging and parenting norms, 5, 5–6, 7, 125
  note and social rejection, 2–4, 17, 74–75
  public health perspective, 6, 7, 8, 22, 23, 29, 53, 151–52, 155–56, 251
  See also raising a screen-smart kid
misogynist subculture, 133
mistakes, 4, 10, 17–18, 21–22, 31, 42, 44, 82, 151, 221, 226, 233, 240
  See also failure, learning from
modeling behavior by parents, 24, 57, 67, 68–69, 84, 96, 166, 221, 230, 231

mommy blogging, parenting norms, 5, 5–6, 7, 125
monitoring and mentoring, 21, 225, 226
monitoring social media, 80–82, 96
Moral Combat: Why the War on Violent Video Games Is Wrong (Ferguson), 134
MTV, 43, 171
multiplayer online role-playing games (MMORPGs), 127, 129, 130, 139, 145
multitasking, 229–30, 231
MySpace, 14

narcissism, 37, 61–63, 64, 71, 90–91
The Narcissism Epidemic (Twenge and Campbell), 61, 71
National Center for Missing and Exploited Children (NCMEC), 13, 76
National Institute of Mental Health, 180
National Institutes of Health, 20
A Nation at Risk, 12
The New Republic, 171
The New York Times, 12
Nintendo 64, 123, 125
Nokia, 19

obesity, 53, 54, 61, 88, 231
obsessive-compulsive disorder (OCD), 66, 180
online bullying. *See* cyberbullying
online incident emergency plan, 217
Operation Game Over, 130
oversharing, 77–78
Overwatch, 133

parents
  don't worry about other parents, 222–23
  guilt, 11–12
  modeling behavior, 24, 57, 67, 68–69, 84, 96, 166, 221, 230, 231
  mommy blogging, parenting norms, 5, 5–6, 7, 125
  monitoring kids online/parenting kids, 21
  social comparison and, 67–68
  social media and, 18–22, *19*, *20*
  video games, 126–27, 134–35, 143–46
  See also raising a screen-smart kid
"Parents: Reject Technology Shame" (Samuel), 224

Parrott-Perry, Laura, 202–3, 239
participation trophies, 59
passive sexting, 116
passwords, 46, 107, **109**, **206**, 213, 217, 225, 239, 246, 247
Patz, Etan, 12
pediatricians screening kids, 217
pedophiles, 196
peer appearance culture, 65
peers as social reference point, 152, 168
perfect people, 50, 51–52, 55, 65–66
Personal Fable, 33, 34–35, *34–35*, 36, 37, 41, 43, 113, 150
personal information, protecting, 112, 195, **200**, 211, 216, 239, 247
perspective and gaming, 125–26, **126**
Pew Research Center, 18, 55, 79, 86, 91, 92, 104, 105, 106, 107, 129
Pinterest, 67, 183
Pisani, Elizabeth, 29–30
PlayStation, 85, 130, 143
Pokémon Go, 15
popularity of online platforms, **18**
pornography, 101, 102, **112**, 113, 117–19, 122, 160, 224
post-traumatic stress disorder (PTSD), 180
potential outcomes of online activity, considering and predicting, 43–44
Potter, Harry (character), 36
praise vs. satisfaction of mastery, 60–61, 70
predators, 196–97, 238–39
    See also safety, predators, harassment, and bullying
prefrontal cortex, 31, 93, 150, 187, 188
pregnancy (teen) statistics, **10**
presidential election (2016), 55
Prior, Tris (character), 36
privacy and safety a priority, 239–42
private messaging, 169, 217
ProAna, 183
problematic gaming vs. engagement, 139–40, 146
problematic tech use, 162–65
protective factors, 7, 22, 53, 59, 70, 88, 94–95, 231
Psychology Today, 13
puberty (adolescence), 31–44
puberty and brain, 17, 30, 31–32, 93, 150
public health perspective, 6, 7, 8, 22, 23, 29, 53, 151–52, 155–56, 251

raising a screen-smart kid, 1–25
    adopting new technology, 14–15
    anxiety disorders, 10
    awkward eighth grader is a mother, 4–5
    brains and cell phones, 19–20, 158–59
    cyberbullying, 8, 16
    depression, 10
    developmental overdrive and cell phones, 17, 20
    expert, cautionary tale, or both? 6–7
    generational differences, 9–15, **10**, 52, 64–65, 78–79, 82, 100, 103, **103**, 151, 155, 176
    historical overview, 11–13
    Internet impact, 13–15, 16, 22
    Julianna Miner's story (age thirteen), 1–4
    mommy blogging and parenting norms, 5, 5–6, 7, 125
    parents on social media, 18–22, **19**, *20*
    protective factors, 7, 22, 53, 59, 70, 88, 94–95, 231
    responsible digital behavior, 23–25
    risk factors, 7, 22, 53
    social media, 6, 7, 9, 16, 17, **18**, 23
    so what does this mean for all the kids getting phones? 16–18, **18**
    super peers, 21, 154, 192
    takeaways, 23–25
    video games, 8, 20
    we're all figuring this out as we go along, 8
    what happened to me when my kid got an iPhone, 15–16
    what this book is, and what it isn't, 22–23
    See also brain; cell phones; digital addiction and risky behavior; digital dating and teen relationships; friendships in the Age of the Internet; growing up online with anxiety, depression, ADHD, or autism; hoping for the best and avoiding the worst; Miner, Julianna; parents; safety, predators, harassment, and bullying; social media; video games; well-being, self-esteem, and social comparison in the Selfie Generation
RantsfromMommyland.com, 249
"rapid task switching," 229–30, 231
rational behavior on social media, 29–31
real life vs. online friends, 86–88, 94, 95, 96

Reclaiming Conversation: The Power of Talk in a Digital Age (Turkle), 89
Reddit, **18**, 134, 214
red flags to self-assess safety of online connections, 207, 213, 214, 215
refusal skills, 168–69
reminiscence bump, 37
resiliency, learning from video games, 143
resource, being a, 234–35
responsible digital behavior, 23–25
"revenge porn," 204
rich get richer, 93–94, 182
risk behavior, kid's perspective, 151–52, 168
risk factors, 7, 22, 53, 150–51, 197–201, **200**, 201, 212–13, 215–16, 216
risks and impacts of video games, 138–39
Roblox, 130
Rosen, Larry, 14–15, 84, 181
rules
    atypical kids need atypical rules, 223
    changing as kids change, 221
    different types of screen time, 231
    social life and digital social life rules, 48, 96
    your rules, but *not* your kids, 75–76

safety, predators, harassment, and hullying, 193–217
    agreement with kids as safety net, 24, 207, 216, 240–42, 245–49
    anxiety disorders, 212
    boys and, 198–99, 200, 212
    brain, 196, 205
    coping strategies that work, 213–14
    cyberbullying, 196, 197, 198, 203, 207
    depression, 194, 199, 212
    discussions with kids, 207, 213, 214, 215
    documenting abuse, importance, 208, 241
    The Fear, 195–96
    girls and, 198, 200, 212
    grooming process of predators, 202–3, 215, 238
    how do kids react when abuse happens? 205–7, **206**
    Katherine's story (age twenty-one), 130, 193–95, 196, 201–3
    predators, 196–97, 238–39
    privacy and safety a priority, 239–42
    risk factors, victimization, 197–201, **200**, 216
    school, contacting, 208–9

sextortion, 204–5
social media, 196, 197, 198, 199, 200, 203, 204, 214, 216, 217
    takeaways, 214–17
    video games, 129–30, 144–45, 214, 216
    See also cyberbullying; raising a screen-smart kid
Sammy's story (age twenty-four), 170–72
Samuel, Alexandra, 224
Say It Survivor, 202, 239
Schneiderman, Eric, 130
school, contacting, 208–9
schools and cyberbullying, 208–10
Schrobsdorff, Susanna, 176–77
screen-free time, mandatory, 231
screen-smart kid. *See* raising a screen-smart kid
Screenwise: Helping Kids Thrive (and Survive) in Their Digital World (Heitner), 21, 225
Secret, 186
seeking affirmation with a hashtag, 185–86
self-affirmation, 60–61
self-disclosure, 77
self-esteem, 12, 13, 55–61, 62, 70–71, 94
self-focus, 62, 63, 66
self-harm, 155, 175, 183, 184, 211
Selfie Generation, 36
    See also well-being, self-esteem, and social comparison
self-regulation, 140, 165–66, 167, 187, 188–89, 230
separation anxiety, 181
setting limits and consistent enforcement, video games, 141–42, 144, 145, 167–68
setting reasonable limits, 230–31
Seventeen, 65
sexting, 23, 102, 112, 113–17, 121, 122, 204, 207, 209, 220, 234
sextortion, 204–5
sexuality, adolescent, 100–101, 102, 103, **103**, 120, 121
sexuality, sex ed online resources, 251–52
sexually explicit Internet material (SEIM), 118–19, 121, 122
sexual risk behavior, **112**, 112–13, 120, 121
sexual solicitation, 196, 197, 207
sexy selfies, posting, 110–11, 116, 120
Shakespeare, William, 149–50
Sims, 132
single-parent households, 11, 13

Skype, 46, 188

Skywalker, Luke (character), 36

sleep and mental health, 24, 46, 53–54, **54**, 121, 142, 146, 190–91, 231–32, 246

sleepovers, 47, 72, 75, 76

smartphones, **19**, 175–77

Snapchat, 4, 17, **18**, 21, 29, 42, 84, 85, 86, 87, 102, 106, 129, 152, 159, 192, 218, 219, 236, 237

"Snapchat dysmorphia," 66

social anxiety disorder (SAD), 180

social anxiety on social media, 178–79

social capital, 52, 57, 88, 129, 185, 190

social comparison, 50, 51, 56, 64–68, 69, 70, 184–86, 192, 222–23, 236–38

social culture of video games. *See* video games

socializing online, how kids, 84–86, **85**

social life and digital social life rules, 48, 96

social lives today vs. yesterday, 78–79

socially normal risky behavior, 154–55, 168

social marketing and influencers, 156–58, 168

social media

digital addiction, risky behavior, 147, 148, 149, 150, 153–54, 155, 156, 157, 158, 159, 160, 162, 164, 165, 168, 173

digital dating, 101–3, **103**, 104, 105, **105**, 106–7, 108, 109, **109**, 120, 121

friendships, 73, 75, 77, 80, 82–83, 84, 85, **85**, 86, 87–88, 90–92, **92**, 93, 95, 96

funhouse mirror and, 153–54, 236

growing up online with anxiety, depression, ADHD, or autism, 172, 173, 175–76, 177, 178–79, 181, 182, 190, 191, 192

healthy place to be? 173–74, **174**

hoping for best, avoiding worst, 218, 219, 220, 222, 224, 225, 226, 227, 228, *228*, 231, 233, 236–38, 240, 241, 242, 243, 247–48, 249

parents on social media, 18–22, **19**, *20*

raising a screen-smart kid, 6, 7, 9, 16, 17, **18**, 23

rational behavior on, 29–31

safety, predators, harassment, bullying, 196, 197, 198, 199, 200, 203, 204, 214, 216, 217

self-esteem and, 55–61, 70–71, 94

sexual norms, and hooking up, 101–3, **103**

social comparison and, 50, 51, 56, 64–68, 69, 70, 184–86, 192, 236–38

social media seesaw, 54–55, 57

"super peer," 21, 154, 192

video games, 47, 129, 136, 139

well-being, self-esteem, social comparison in the Selfie Generation, 51, 52, 53, 54–55, 55–61, 57, 62, 64–65, 66, 67, 68, 69, 70–71, 94

social media and the Imaginary Audience, 26–48

behavioral rehearsal, 32–33, *33*, 37–38, 39, 76–77

brain, 44

chrysalis stage, Imaginary Audience as, 37–38

cyberbullying, 26–28

eighth grade choices, 28–29

eighth grader's pimple, *34–35*

first smartphones, 17, 30–31, 44–48, 64, 79, 82, 150

hoping for best, avoiding worst, 227, *228*

Imaginary Audience, 32–34, *33*, 38–39, 227, *228*

Jacquelin's story (age nineteen), 26–28

middle school, 31–44, *33*, *34–35*, 44–45

Personal Fable, 33, 34–35, *34–35*, 36, 37, 41, 43, 113, 150

potential outcomes, considering and predicting, 43–44

rational behavior for social media, 29–31

stereotypes and Imaginary Audience, 35–37

takeaways, 45–48

video games, 47

well-being, self-esteem, social comparison in the Selfie Generation, 62

See also raising a screen-smart kid

Social Media Wellness: Helping Tweens and Teens Thrive in an Unbalanced Digital World (Homayoun), 75, 242

social norms, 236

Social Norms Theory, 155

social reference points (SRPs), 152–53, 154, 168

social support for cyberbullying, 213–14

solitary gamers (myth), 126, 127–28

Sony, 130

so what does this mean for all the kids getting phones? 16–18, **18**

"spam" Instagram account, 86
sponsored content, 157, 168
Spring Break (MTV), 43
Stanford University, 165, 237
Steinberg, Laurence, 13
stereotypes and Imaginary Audience, 35–37
Stillman, David and Jonah, 56
Storr, Will, 61
"stranger danger," 197, 239
strategy, video games, 124, 131, 145
strong tic friendships, 86–88, 94
structured play (play dates), 12, 13
substance (drug) use, **10**, 155–56, 157, 168
suicide, **54**, 113, 174, 175, 194, 211–12, 237
super peers, 21, 154, 192
Supreme Court, 137, 138
Sussman, Clifford, 160, 163, 167, 187, 190

takeaways
    digital addiction, risky behavior, 166–69
    digital dating, 119–22
    friendships, 94–96
    growing up online with anxiety, depression, ADHD, or autism, 190–92
    raising a screen-smart kid, 23–25
    safety, predators, harassment, bullying, 214–17
    social media and Imaginary Audience, 45–48
    video games, 143–46
    well-being, self-esteem, social comparison in the Selfie Generation, 68–71
"the Talk" or leaving it to Google, 101
TalkingAboutIt, 170, 171, 172
"talking back" to social comparisons, 70
talking on phone, **85**
TBH hashtag, 185–86
tech
    addiction, 19, **19**, 20, 159–61
    adopting new technology, 14–15
    culture and, 79–82
    not all the same, 228–29
    tech breaks, taking, 163–65, 231
    use and outcomes, 187, 190, 191
TED Talks, 29, 158–59
"Teen Depression and Anxiety: Why the Kids Are Not Alright" (Schrobsdorff), 176–77

teen friendships in the Age of the Internet. *See* friendships in the Age of the Internet
Temple University, 13, 151
text-back culture, 97, 98, 99, 104, 105, 106
texting, 4, 9, 16, 52, **54**, 72, 73, **85**, 93, 96, 97, 98, 99, 104, 193, 215, 219, 225, 233, 248
These Little Waves (blog), 82
Thinspiration, 183
tilting, 136
Time, 176
time online risk factor, 198, 200, 201, 217, 230
To Write Love on Her Arms, 171
traditional media vs. social media, 40–41
trash-talking and cyberbullying, video games, 135–36, 139, 145, 233
trust, 27–28, 221, 222, 226
trusted adults to talk to, 122, 238–39, 242
Tumblr, **18**, 177
Turkle, Sherry, 89
Twenge, Jean, 61, 62, 71, 78–79, 175, 176
Twitch, 131, 132
Twitter, **18**, 42, 127, 147, 148, 162, 170

"Ugliest Person" on Instagram, 49–50
understanding adolescent risk, 149–50
unhealthy digital dating, 107–10, **109**
University of Pennsylvania, 57
"unseen other," 42, 43, 44, 47–48
U.S. Department of Justice, 137
USA Today, 175
usernames, 46, 85–86, 239, 246, 247

vape pens, 148
video games, 123–46
    addiction, 8, 139, 141, 146, 159, 160, 161, 162, 165, 186
    aggression and, 126, 137–38, **138**, 139
    Andre's story (age twenty-five), 123–25
    being twelve and, 128
    boys and, 127, 129, 130, 132–33, 139
    brain, 140
    community of gamers, 123, 124–25, 127–28, 129, 131, 138
    cyberbullying, 135, 136
    depression, 139
    friendships, 82, 84, **85**, 85–86, 87, 91, 95
    gender and, 127, 129, 130, 132–34, 139
    girls and, 127, 130, 132–33, 133–34

video games (*Cont.*)
  growing up online with anxiety, depression, ADHD, or autism, 176, 186, 187, 192
  hoping for best, avoiding worst, 124, 131, 143, 145–46, 219, 231, 233, 235, 243
  learning from, 124, 131, 143, 145–46, 235
  lessons, 124, 131, 143, 145–46, 235
  needs being met? 128, 142–43, 145
  parents and, 126–27, 134–35, 143–46
  perspective and gaming, 125–26, **126**
  problematic gaming vs. engagement, 139–40, 146
  raising a screen-smart kid, 8, 20
  risks and impacts of, 138–39
  safety, predators, harassment, bullying, 129–30, 144–45, 214, 216
  safety in video games, 129–30, 144–45
  setting limits, 141–42, 144, 145, 167–68
  social lives of teens and, 129
  social media, 47, 129, 136, 139
  takeaways, 143–46
  trash-talking and cyberbullying, 135–36, 139, 145, 233
  watching other kids playing, 131–32, 144
  who really plays video games? 127–28
  See also raising a screen-smart kid

Walsh, Adam, 12
watching other kids playing video games, 131–32, 144
weak-tie friendships, 86–88, 94
weed, smoking, 148, 152, 154
Weinstein, Emily, 55
well-being, self-esteem, and social comparison in the Selfie Generation, 49–71
  anxiety disorders, 52, 56
  boys and, 66–67
  brain, 64, 65–66
  compassion, passion, responsibility (CPR), 63
  depression, 52, 53, 57, 67, 69
  fear of missing out (FOMO), 56–57, 70, 154, 181
  girls and, 65–66, 69
  good, the bad, and outcomes, 52–54, **54**
  Jill's story (age twelve), 49–51
  modeling behavior by parents, 24, 57, 67, 68–69, 84, 96, 166, 221, 230, 231
  narcissism, 37, 61–63, 64, 71, 90–91
  parenting and social comparison, 67–68
  perfect people, 50, 51–52, 55, 65–66
  self-esteem, 55–61, 70–71, 94
  self-focus, 62–63, 66
  sleep and mental health, 24, 46, 53–54, **54**, 121, 142, 146, 190–91, 231–32, 246
  social comparison, 50, 51, 56, 64–68, 69, 70, 184–86, 192, 236–38
  social media, 51, 52, 53, 54–55, 55–61, 62, 64–65, 66, 67, 68, 69, 70–71, 94
  social media and Imaginary Audience, 62
  social media seesaw, 54–55, 57
  takeaways, 68–71
  well-being, 52–55, **54**, 57
  See also raising a screen-smart kid
we're all figuring this out as we go along, 8
Werther (Goethe character), 36
what happened to me when my kid got an iPhone, 15–16
what to do if your child is a victim, cyberbullying, 207–8
Wheaton's Law, 198
Whitlock, Janis, 177
Who R U Really? (Kelly), 193, 194
willpower, delayed gratification, and marshmallows, 165–66, 167
The Winter's Tale (Shakespeare), 149–50
women's labor force increase, 11, 13
Words with Friends, 127
World of Warcraft, 130

Xbox, 83, 85, 128, 130, 143

Yik Yak, 186
Youth Internet Safety Survey (YISS-3), 114, 197
YouTube, 15, **18**, 96, 131, 132, 177, 187, 188, 189, 224, 229

Zomorodi, Manoush, 159
Zuckerberg, Mark, 156

ABOUT THE AUTHOR

Julianna Miner is an adjunct professor of global and community health at George Mason University. With twenty years' experience in the field of public health, she has served as the director of social marketing for the Alabama Department of Public Health and the strategic planning director of the Fairfax County Health Department. Miner is also the creator of the popular parenting blog Rants from Mommyland, *Parents* magazine's funniest blog of 2013; and was named one of Disney Babble's "10 Best Humor Bloggers." Her articles on parenting, public health, and technology have been featured in *The Washington Post*. She lives with her husband, three kids, and two ridiculous dogs in the Washington, DC, suburbs.